Rescuing Religion

Rescuing Religion

HOW FAITH CAN SURVIVE ITS
ENCOUNTER WITH SCIENCE

John Van Hagen

Foreword by Thomas Sheehan

POLEBRIDGE PRESS
Salem, Oregon

The art work on the front cover depicts a salt molecule as the center-piece of a stained glass window. While science describes this important substance and its properties in technical terms, religion speaks of it meta-phorically. For example, Jesus describes his followers as the "salt of the earth." Yet the gospel writers are insistent that should the followers lose this dynamic quality of enhancing the world and each other, they are worthless. (Mark 9:50; Matthew 5:13; Luke 14:34)

Cover art and interior design by Robaire Ream

Library of Congress Cataloging-in-Publication Data
Van Hagen, John, 1940-
  Rescuing religion : how faith can survive its encounter with science
    / John Van Hagen.
    p. cm.
  Includes bibliographical references and index.
  ISBN 978-1-59815-037-7 (alk. paper)
1. Apologetics. 2. Religion and science. 3. Church history. I. Title.
  BT1103.V35 2012
  239--dc23

                                                    2012000856

Table of Contents

Foreword

In this eminently readable and deeply informed book, psychologist Dr. John Van Hagen invites the reader to face the crisis that threatens the survival of contemporary Western religion, especially Christianity, and to creatively forge an authentic life beyond traditional religious dogma and practice.

Underlying the text is the conflict between science and religion that has been brought on by recent advances in Near Eastern archaeology, biblical studies, and historical research. Van Hagen refers throughout to "the new information" about both Tanakh (the Jewish bible) and the Christian scriptures, information that often clashes with long-standing religious beliefs. The danger, as he sees it, is that most people will hold rigidly to only one side of the conflict, be it religion or science, to the exclusion of the other. Van Hagen's book argues for an alternative by showing how religious communities of the past, both Jewish and Christian, and eminent figures of our own times—Viktor Frankel, Barack Obama, Mikhail Gorbachev—struggled with analogous conflicts and forged new contexts and concepts to resolve them.

To begin with, there is some bad news about the Good Book. Traditional biblical archaeology as carried out by, for example, William F. Albright, Roland de Vaux, and Kathleen Kenyon typically used Tanakh as a handbook to guide the search for historical biblical sites. Today, however, archeologists of ancient Palestine, whether Israeli or American, whether religious or not, have reached a scientific consensus that there is no good evidence in the material record to support the historicity of the traditional biblical stories

about the patriarchs Abraham, Isaac, and Jacob (traditionally ca. 2000 to 1500 BCE), including the call of Abraham
and the covenant God made with him; or about the story
of Joseph and the famine that brought the Israelites to
Egypt (traditionally during the Hyksos period, 1720–1550
BCE); or about Moses confounding the pharaoh and leading
the twelve tribes out of Egypt (after 1300 BCE); or about
Joshua's conquest of Canaan ca. 1100 BCE. On the contrary, these archeologists find that much of the material record argues against the historicity of these biblical tales.

Likewise, the best contemporary scholarship on the
Christian scriptures argues that Jesus (in Aramaic, *Yeshua,*
i.e., Joshua) was understood by his contemporaries as a
charismatic and very human prophet dedicated to a more
user-friendly reform of the Judaism of his day. Jesus had no
intentions of founding a new religion that would have himself as its center, would be open to Gentiles, and would su-
percede Judaism. Least of all did he intend the apostolic succession of bishops, so dear to the Roman Catholic Church
and the Anglican Communion. His preaching was focused
on Jews, not Gentiles, and on a benign reinterpretation of
Halakha (Jewish law and traditions), in part along the lines
of his quasi-contemporary, Rabbi Hillel (110 BCE?–10 CE),
and in part along more radical trajectories.

These scholars—Christian and non-Christian alike—argue on the basis of scientific-historical investigations of the
New Testament that Jesus did not present himself as the
Messiah ("Christ"). In fact, he likely rebuked those who
claimed he was such a figure. Least of all did he think he was
God, the equal of his "Father" in heaven, the way the relatively late gospel of John (ca. 100 CE) presents him. Jesus
preached not himself but what he called "the kingdom of
God," God's gracious empowerment of the least fortunate:
the impoverished, the unclean, the social and religious
outcasts. He called for *metanoia*, not "repentance" as it is

usually translated but radical conversion to a life of justice and mercy. Jesus presented himself as a Jewish holy man, of which there were many in the Palestine of his day, and like them he was known for his wondrous deeds, usually called "miracles." In that regard, Catholic scholar Father John P. Meier, after an exhaustive analysis of the four gospels, argues that out of the thirty-two miracles attributed to Jesus by the evangelists, only twelve (that is, 38%) have a chance of having *any* historical event underlying them, and even then not necessarily a miraculous event.

Some Christian scholars, like Dr. Van Hagen, argue that Jesus looked forward to an apocalyptic cosmic in-break by God to establish a kingdom on earth. Others make the case for a prophetic Jesus who was eschatological ("the time for conversion is *now*") but not apocalyptic (i.e., not expecting an imminent crash-and-burn end to the world). In either case, whether apocalyptic or not, the portrait of the historical Jesus limed by these scholars arguably cannot be brought into line with orthodox Christian doctrines about Jesus as the Second Person of the Trinity who took on human flesh to redeem humankind from sin. And worst cut of all, contemporary Christian scholars—except for some hold-outs like Anglican Bishop N.T. Wright—find no evidence that Jesus' "resurrection" (in Greek, his being metaphorically "awakened" or "stood back up") was a historical event that took place at a certain enclosed tomb three days after his execution.

Dr. Van Hagen's book, which is aimed at "skeptical believers," probes that sore point of apparent conflict between science and religion and the possibility that believers will be caught between traditional doctrine and the historical information that clashes with it. In the first two parts of his book Van Hagen ferrets out what he calls the "story behind the story," that is, the facts on the ground as they have been construed by contemporary historians, facts that he shows not only conflict with but also can destroy the elaborate, often fanciful "alternative histories" created by the biblical writers.

He finds it to be more often the case that myth creates its own "history" rather than being a record of "what really happened" (von Ranke). In other words, the bible forges a parallel, God-driven "alternative history" as an antidote and corrective to factual history. Following the best scholarship on Tanakh, he argues that most of what we know as the Jewish bible was written and/or edited only during the Persian Period (538–333 BCE), even though many of the books purport to recount events that took place as far back as the Middle and Late Bronze Ages and the early Iron Age (roughly 2000 to 900 BCE). Among these constructions of an alternative history is the story of the covenant that YHWH/Adonai made with Abraham, along with the promise that, among other territories, the land of Canaan, including the modern West Bank and Gaza, would be the possession of his descendants.

These writings and redactions, Van Hagen shows, were ways that the Jews of the Persian period—still reeling from the destruction of the Jerusalem temple in 586 BCE but now the protected occupants of Yehud, the small area around Mizpah and Jerusalem—attempted to create a grandiose master-narrative of their monotheistic covenant with the High God. They wrote themselves and their ancestors into a centuries-long story, in fact an alternative universe of "salvation history," which included Joshua's triumphant conquest of Canaan and David's and Solomon's rule over an expansive Israelite kingdom. In this way they were able to explain to themselves their current suborned situation. They imagined that their god would remain faithful to what they construed as the covenant with Abraham, and therefore they could look forward to the restoration of a large Jewish kingdom theocratically ruled by a Davidic warrior-prince sent by God. This is a classic example of a counterfactual: history being written by the losers rather than the winners.

And the early Christians did much the same thing when, as in Paul's letters or the four gospels, they produced religious narratives that tied their martyred prophet into what they interpreted as the Jewish expectation of a messianic savior. In early Christian hermeneutics, Jesus became, first, a martyr who witnessed to God's kingdom right up to death; then God's deputy, the "Son of Man," who would soon return to usher in God's kingdom on earth; then later the currently reigning salvific prime minister of this kingdom— until finally the gospel of John interpreted him as God's equal and as eternally existent before all time. It would be hard to think up a grander narrative than this—the redemptive incarnation of God that forever binds together heaven and earth, time and eternity, the divine and the human.

In Van Hagen's account, there is an analogy between how both the Jewish and the Christian communities forged new identities in and through the various crises that beset their journeys of faith when history failed to fulfill their hopes. It is a story about how the peoples of the book, through a process of creative hermeneutical imagination, found new and healing meanings for themselves and their communities by forging narratives that reinterpreted the present and re-imagined the future.

The author urges upon us such a historical-hermeneutical reconfiguration of both our religious and non-religious lives in an age when science seems on the verge of explaining life itself without any need for supernatural intervention and when secular analyses can adequately account for economic, social, political, and ideological processes. "If we are to evolve," he writes, "we need more than reason; we need a mythical view that inspires us to face the crises of our time." Some myths, of course, can be deleterious. For example, the warrior myth of Joshua subduing the cities of Canaan has the God of the Israelites direct, or at least approve of, mass murder—virtual genocide—against the ethnically and religiously "other." Likewise, the mythical salvation history called *Against Heretics*, which was written by Irenaeus, the Christian bishop of Lyon, ca. 180 CE (and which survived as a story well into the twentieth century), excludes from salvation those who claimed to believe in Jesus but who were adjudged to be heretics by Irenaeus for not subscribing to his cosmic master-narrative. Myths, in short, can be dehumanizing and even murderous—as we can see from the Christian myth of the Jews as murderers of Jesus (cf. 1 Thess 2:14–15 and Matt 27:25).

Van Hagen calls not so much for a new religious myth as for a humanizing story that includes everyone, and nature as well, in a community dedicated to life, more life, and the best possible life for all. He sees this "new creation" as a process of self-discipline and individual responsibility for the sake of the common good, a process that, like life, is often ambiguous and awkward, but a process that values one's own tradition while valorizing others as well.

What does all this have to do with religion today, especially Christian religion? There is a strong evolutionary motif running through this book, often conjugated with the theme of therapeutic resolutions to personal and social crises. Van Hagen's vision is broad and ameliorative, but decidedly realistic. He sees the challenge for the churches today as not simply to accept evolution [in all senses] but to see it as part of the process of faith, for individuals and also communities. Rather than privileging its own survival needs, the church can embrace those of others; rather than focusing entirely on maintaining its own traditions, it can support the preservation of all traditions that contribute to the common good. We can once again strive to create a new kind of community, one in which serious differences are tolerated for the sake of that larger good. In such a revitalized version of Christianity, both members and the larger society would be challenged to develop moral behavior that might enable us to survive as a species. We are all, Christians and non-Christians, part of a unique cosmic process in which change is the only constant and extinction is always a possible outcome.

Notice that the book is entitled *Rescuing Religion*, not *Rescuing God*. Van Hagen carefully walks on this side of a possible natural-supernatural divide. The therapeutic rituals he recommends we develop and the narratives he suggests we shape are not necessarily focused on a supernatural, self-revealing god; they can be secular as well. The criterion is simply: Do they advance the common good and one's own life and health? The value systems he argues for in this book embrace the atheistic and the agnostic, the secular and the sacred, without any commitment to a supernatural god. He counsels not religious spirituality alone but non-religious as well. The last part of the book is dedicated to sketching a set of moral virtues that he would have non-believers as well as religionists sign on to. In these pages one hears the seasoned therapist, never imposing on his interlocutor, never judging, but always helping the patient to gradually break through the false stories that impede full human flourishing and to find his or her way to a healthy, productive life.

God, as we know, is a bit on the ropes these days, at least in some public squares, battered by the often simplistic arguments raised by scientists and journalists alike. One of the virtues of Van Hagen's book is that he gives God a break, and allows the (endless?) sabbatical rest that God chose for himself on the seventh day according to the creation story. The core of that story is the empowering of human beings for a rich and satisfying life in nature and in community—without any deep back-up that one could invoke in times of crisis or need. While on sabbatical God doesn't read email or answer the phone. In fact, the God of Judaism and Christianity is the first and best secular humanist: God creates the *saeculum*, the secular order (and declares it "very good," in effect sacred) and then turns over the whole show to humankind, to develop and direct for better or worse and without appeal to the supernatural. The God of Judaism and Christianity is no longer at home, at least not where one might expect a respectable God to be found. In one story, God is poured out, without remainder, into the world and its peoples. In another, God has left us entirely alone and, like Samuel Beckett's Godot, will never come back. Bereft of all gods, we are left with the supreme task that makes religion look like child's play: the challenge of humanizing ourselves and others.

John Van Hagen has taken the usual markers of religion—creed (or story), code (or ethics), cultic practices (prayer and liturgy) and dissolved them into what he calls *communitas*, a community of flexibility, cooperation, imagination, story-telling, and yes, even love. In *Rescuing Religion* he has shown one possible way of rescuing ourselves.

—Thomas Sheehan

Preface

When I told a friend of mine, who happens to be a Catholic nun, that the title of my book is *Rescuing Religion*, she quickly shot back, "It needs it." I think the rescue requires more than simply introducing reforms. I believe religion can only be rescued if it confronts the scientific world that challenges its own stories of origin, as well as offers another way of seeing the world. By the same token, our more scientific side is challenged to make room for a religious view of life that is captured in the strivings of humans everywhere.

This book is meant for skeptical believers: those who feel caught between the poles of both the religious and scientific worldviews. About half of us claim to have had significant religious experiences. Yet we are also people of science. We are accustomed to medical breakthroughs that cure illness and dramatically improve the quality of life. Yet religion also contributes to both our individual and collective well-being. Sociologists have documented how participation in a religious community is positively correlated with better physical and psychological health, as well as being a force for contributing to the common good. Many of us who participate in religious communities have personally experienced the power of religion.

When I first heard the story of Adam and Eve, I was young. The message I picked up from the story was "be obedient," so I was an obedient child. When I read it as a teenager, I heard a cautionary warning about sexual behavior, so I became more than a little uptight about sex. In my twenties I understood that the story of Adam and Eve being driven out of the garden was all about becoming independent and breaking away from the comforts of one's family.

As I struggled to evolve in this world, I felt supported and guided by an alternative universe with the powerful capacity to assist me. In my experiences, I followed what might be called the Supreme Court version of religion: religious teachings must be adapted to different circumstances, just as the Supreme Court interprets the U.S. Constitution differently over time.

To push that analogy a bit, what would the Supreme Court do if the justices discovered that the Constitution was written in the nineteenth century and individuals such as Jefferson and Madison were creatures of fiction and never really existed? One response would be to appreciate the power of whoever created the document and peopled the story of its creation with characters of such intelligence and foresight. I propose this kind of response to the new information from biblical studies. Rather than destroy our faith, these discoveries can open up another view of revelation. We can not only focus on the writings but learn to appreciate the writers and the spiritual crises that prompted them to write what they did. We look to the stories behind the stories.

I wrote this book because I believe new information about religion offers us an opportunity to rethink the values and significance of our deeply held religious beliefs. Additionally, such rethinking can open up a way of appreciating the religious spirit that is within us, within all people, and that comes alive especially in times of crisis.

We have a crisis in religion right now. Scholarship has activated it by arguing that Moses never existed and that Jesus never started a church. Additionally, more scientific explanations of religious phenomena—that they come from deep within us—challenge our understanding that such experiences are engendered from on high. Such a crisis invites us to reconsider what religions have always taught: to look within ourselves and develop awareness and consciousness of who we are and what we are about.

Although such a journey within will always be difficult, we can be comforted by people who survived their own crises by unleashing a spiritual power that enabled them to defy empires. Jews maintained and even refined their identity despite being conquered and reconquered. Early Christians resisted a materialistic culture enforced by a militaristic state. Additionally, I offer examples of others who found strength not necessarily in a religious context but in one that we can consider to be spiritual. Finally, I argue that such a crisis does not mean abandoning our particular belief systems or practices, but encourages us to accept that they are, like ourselves, fragile and fallible. I also believe that acceptance and integration of this new information might increase the tolerance and openness needed to address the more global problems we face in this particular stage in human evolution.

My journey, like everyone else's, was not made alone. I thank the many friends and family members who helped me by their questions and aided me by their interest. I appreciate the editorial staff at Polebridge Press, including Larry Alexander and Cassandra Farrin, and Bob Miller, editor of *The Fourth R*, for their help along the way. I especially want to thank Professor Tom Sheehan of Stanford University, who has been my partner in dialogue for some ten years as we hashed out the implications of the new information not only for religions but for ourselves.

Finally I dedicate this book to my wife, Phyllis Van Hagen, for her long-lasting support and ever-present encouragement.

Introduction

Until recently, the Jewish Scriptures and the Christian Scriptures, or New Testament, were presumed to be historically based unless new evidence could prove otherwise. Starting with the Jewish Scriptures, that presumption has been reversed due to modern scholarship.[1] We are faced with writing that does not so much record the past, but *creates* it.[2] Some researchers, for instance, argue that "Islamic writings should be regarded primarily as sacred literature, not as history."[3] This paradigm shift from history to something like myth has also emerged in the work of Karen Armstrong, who reminds us that myth is not a far-fetched story but a dynamic force that guides us in our lives.[4] However, much of the present debate about religion is still rooted in the older paradigm of Scripture as history. For example, Richard Dawkins, in his popular book *The God Delusion*, takes aim at the belief that there is a god who reveals ultimate truth through the Scriptures. However, the emerging paradigm suggests something dramatically different: truth emerges from the struggles of people here below, not from a message from on high. The new journey to faith begins with identifying those early writers and appreciating their struggles and challenges. In this process we can identify more with their spiritual journeys than with the beliefs and practices they developed on the way.

In the Jewish Scriptures, the writers were members of the Jewish elite who struggled to breathe life into the nearly moribund Persian province of Yehud, later called Judea. They began writing in the sixth century BCE, after their country had been conquered and their temple destroyed. The writers often took opposing views as they constructed an imaginary past peopled with heroes like Abraham, Moses, and David. However they generally agreed that their one god would reestablish a new kingdom on Earth and give special place to those remaining faithful to that God's teachings. Still, they argued about exactly how this would happen, although some believed that a chosen one, a messiah, would arrive to help bring it about.

The writers of the New Testament were elite members of a new hybrid group, mostly Jewish Christians, who believed that a prophet named Jesus was this Messiah. Aside from Paul, they were writing after the Jewish temple had again been destroyed by a foreign enemy, this time the Romans in 70 CE. Like their spiritual ancestors who wrote 600 years before, these evangelists constructed an alternative kingdom to the one that physically conquered them. Yet a closer reading of the gospels reveals that stories about Jesus were not eyewitness accounts but reflections of a tiny group of believers who were describing their own religious experiences in a way that might convince others to join their movement. Modern scholarship continually tries to peel back those faith-driven descriptions and uncover the historical Jesus.

But the loss of Scriptures as historical documents introduces the possibility of seeing them as valuable spiritual or mythical ones. If we can empathize with the writers and the communities they represented, we can begin to appreciate faith as something necessary to be more completely human, especially in the face of adversity. With the word *faith*, I am using psychologist James Fowler's description of it as the way a person moves into the "force field of life." Initially a primitive, somewhat instinctual "guidance system," faith can develop into a way of "finding coherence in and giving meaning to the multiple forces and relations that make up our lives."[5] Though most of us will not be conquered by regressive regimes nor have the most basic symbols of our religion destroyed, we will be challenged to find a value system that offers guidance and meaning in a world that values power and tolerates oppression. Psychologists such as Fowler offer us a lens to look at this all-important faith process and appreciate the value that religion can have for individuals and the larger community.

As a clinical psychologist who practiced for thirty years, I know how harmful it can be when a person's guidance system is faulty, when the perceptions of oneself and the world are self-limiting if not self-destructive. Yet as someone who left home as a teenager to join the seminary and was ultimately ordained a Roman Catholic priest, I have experienced how helpful that guidance system was in my own life and in the lives of those I worked with, however briefly, in my few years of ministry. Also, I have been inspired by people whose faith has motivated them to join in common efforts towards peace and justice. In the past decade or so, as I have absorbed the new information about biblical studies as well as written about it and given workshops on the topic, I have realized how subjective and idiosyncratic the spiritual journey is, even if a person hears the same information or comes from the same religious tradition.

With such diversity, how can we tell if our guidance system is off course? How can one be religious when it is precisely in religion that one finds blatant examples of the abuse of power and a tolerance for oppression? How does one respond to another meaning-making system that offers a different alternative universe, especially if one really cares about and is invested in one's own? These kinds of questions can tempt one simply to throw religion aside as something inherently unworkable in today's postmodern world. However, it is precisely at this time of multiple belief systems that we are challenged to hold on to a particular faith and simultaneously to tolerate the faiths of others.[6] If we give up our faith, we run the risk of giving up a guidance system that is even more important in a postmodern age that preaches a gospel of relativism. Yet that system would be difficult to hold onto without a commitment to put into practice its values and a desire to understand its story.

Therefore in the three sections of this book, I combine new information on the Scriptures with the personal stories of modern faith journeys. Part I looks at the impact of recent discoveries on our understandings of the great stories in the Jewish Scriptures and the people who wrote them. Chapter 1 summarizes the discoveries of the past twenty years or so and suggests ways a more mythical understanding of these texts can be helpful today. Chapter 2 looks at the harmful potential in the same texts and suggests ways of distancing ourselves from their noxious effects. I close Part I by describing Viktor Frankl's journey to faith, which was informed by his own Jewish beliefs. What I see emerging is a journey to faith traveled by those whose religious vision maintained them despite overwhelming odds.

Part II looks behind the stories in the Christian Scriptures to reveal the conflict and confusion that characterized the first two centuries of the Jesus movement. Chapter 4 emphasizes the difference between the Jesus of history and the Christ of faith. Chapters 5 and 6 describe the dramatic changes to the Jesus movement in both the first and second centuries, respectively.[7] Here again we see the power to inspire and the potential for harm, this time with a special emphasis on the difficulties of forming community. I close this section by sketching out U.S. President Barack Obama's journey to a Christian faith. What I see emerging is a new journey to faith characterized by a struggle to find community.

Part III looks at a more scientific view of life, including the religious values hidden in a more humanistic description of our world. Chapter 8 looks at the therapeutic power of narrative, and chapter 9 does the same for ritual,[8] emphasizing the presence of these elements in nonreligious settings. Chapter 10 revisits the perennial science-versus-faith struggle. I see religion and science in a dialectical relation-

ship, a conflict that challenges us to wrestle with such opposing poles as part of our own psychological and spiritual
development. This section closes with the more humanistic
journey of faith taken by former Soviet Union head of state
Mikhail Gorbachev, who was able to change his own views
of reality by taking in new information that went against his
basic beliefs. What I see emerging is a new journey to faith
characterized by creatively managing the conflict between
traditional faith and new information. My concluding chapter underscores the universality of the search for meaning
while identifying a form it may take in our own time.

Part I

The Jewish Journey to Faith

The major stories of the Hebrew Bible—those of Abraham, Moses and David—are foundational not only for the Jewish religion but also for religions and religious individuals who see God at work in the world in a way that provides purpose and meaning. By embracing these stories, people find courage and hope in the midst of oppression and even forgiveness in a time of despair. These stories are so powerful that they live on, transcending their Jewish roots and entering the imaginations of those who hear them.

But how strong is the foundation if it is not built on true events? Biblical scholarship over the past thirty years has concluded that those inspiring stories of the Hebrew Bible never occurred. Instead, they came from the religious imaginations of a conquered people hundreds of years after the supposed events. Although we can be similarly inspired by their efforts, we are forewarned that elements of these stories can be destructive if taken literally.

Instead, we can appreciate that courageous people can find meaning and purpose in the midst of tremendous adversity. On the other hand, adversity can also breed suspicion of others and a powerful wish to retaliate. One individual who faced indescribable horror and yet maintained his integrity and his desire to care for others was Dr. Viktor

Frankl. He was a Jewish psychiatrist whose search for meaning helped him survive the death camps and who went on to provide hope for those oppressed by their own anxiety and depression. But first we look at the stories behind the stories of the Hebrew Bible.

Chapter 1

Beginning the Journey

Most religious history is written by sect movements. It is they who establish new faiths and it is they who renew and preserve old ones. It was an Israelite sect that gave the world Jewish monotheism, and Jewish sects have preserved this faith for more than 2000 years.
　　—Rodney Stark, Discovering God

Archaeology must take the lead in writing the history of ancient Israel; not the traditional biblical archaeology, which subjected archaeology to the text and used it mainly as a 'decoration' to the biblical stories, but the modern, bias-free, and independent archaeology.
　　—Israel Finkelstein, "Archaeology and Text"

Our journey begins with the revolutionary work of archaeologists over the past twenty to thirty years. They have turned our understanding of the Jewish Scriptures upside down. Previously, biblical archaeologists tended to accept the historicity of the stories in those writings and look for supporting evidence in their excavations and discoveries. Now the pendulum has swung the other way and archaeologists, along with other scholars, attempt to piece together a more scientific description of the peoples living in ancient Palestine. Although not without conflict, the field has gradually shifted, and several significant conclusions have even appeared in mainstream news publications. Respected archaeologists such as Israel Finkelstein and William Dever have written popular works that clearly demonstrate how new information from their field undercuts the presumed historical bases of these stories. Additionally, this new information has been screened in documentaries and published on the Internet. Yet it is difficult to integrate the sea-change that has occurred in these new understanding of biblical stories with our traditional beliefs. We seem to face an either/or choice: either stay with the traditional belief or reject it and go with factual information. The challenge is to see in these recent discoveries another revelation, another message from God that speaks to us in our times. If we pursue the story behind the Bible stories, we can begin a journey as personally relevant and inspiring as the ones written about Abraham and Moses. That journey begins with an appreciation of just how powerful those biblical stories are.

Appreciating the Emotional Investment in the Scriptures

A few times a year, I interview candidates for admission to a Roman Catholic seminary. Increasingly, many of these candidates are recent immigrants who come to the United States from other cultures. As I listen to their stories, I am touched by how hard it must have been for them to leave their homelands and try to fit into a foreign culture. In some instances, they have left their native countries in a dramatic fashion. Vietnamese families have escaped on boats, only to be threatened by pirates. Mexicans have crossed the border illegally and then learned to live with the threat of being arrested and deported.

More problems developed once they were here. They had to learn a new language, as well as adjust to a culture that was more individualistic than family-focused. They frequently had to accept menial jobs to survive, working long hours while they simultaneously learned how to adapt to this new culture. In the midst of these hardships, these men found guidance and strength in their faith. They would feel God's presence encouraging them to continue, despite the dangers and setbacks. Once they succeeded, they were immensely grateful to the god they believed had carried them through the journey.

If we can put ourselves in these latter-day exiles' mindset for a moment, we can appreciate how invested they might be in the Bible's stories about God's guidance and the Israelites' rescue. I wonder how they might react when they go to their seminary library and begin to study the scholars who tell a different story behind those tales. What might I say to them when they discover that the often quoted, inspiring story of Abraham is revealed to be just that—a story? Could I help them when they discover that God did not intervene in history to free the Israelites from Egyptian domination or that the story of Moses and the Jews crossing the Red Sea never happened? That God never gave the Ten Commandments on Mount Sinai and no one wandered in the desert for forty years? That there was no promised land to be taken from Canaanites because Joshua never conquered it? These men would be experiencing cognitive dissonance, a conflict between preexisting beliefs and disconfirming information. Must they choose one over the other?

Before discussing the new information with them, I think I would emphasize a few things. First, I would underscore that their religious experiences are valid: the loss of the Exodus to the realm of myth rather than history in no way devalues one's own efforts in modern life. They were in distress, and their faith in God was helpful to them. In fact, peeling back the stories of the Jewish Scriptures reveals a community in conflict struggling to survive in the face of nearly insurmountable obstacles. As I argue below, the story behind the stories begins in 586 BCE when Jerusalem was conquered by the Babylonians and their sacred temple destroyed. For some time, Jerusalem was a ghost town with many inhabitants scattered or taken away to exile. When the Persians conquered the Babylonians a few years later, they set up a small province, Yehud, centered geographically around the ruined city. However, they established its capital at a small city a few miles north of Jerusalem, Mizpah, which brought into prominence the cult center nearby at Bethel.[1] Despite all these setbacks, the Jewish people regrouped, their capital and its temple were restored, and their religion experienced a new birth. About a hundred years later, Mizpah was greatly reduced and Jerusalem again became the center of the province.

Although scholars continue to offer different ideas about the size of Yehud, the consensus seems to be that it was relatively small. Reconstruction from archaeologists graphically shows us just how small it could have been (see map, p. 13).

Second, I would emphasize that the word *myth* has developed a bad reputation: it's assumed to refer to something that just isn't true, like the claim that eating carrots is good for your eyesight. We might better define a myth as an inspiring story. Such a description points to the interactive element that is at the heart of a myth. We don't just read the story, we are so touched by it that it moves us to act. A myth can be both map and toolbox for a spiritual journey. The shift from history to myth brings to the fore our own responsibility to live out the truth captured by the story. *Myth* is a partial answer to the question of if the Bible is not history, what is it?

For the Jews of Yehud, the Bible stories were also the heart of a national autobiography, written by several authors in dialogue and debate with one another.[2] The common point of departure was to reconstruct a past that defined who they were and taught them how to survive as a defeated people on the fringes of the vast Persian empire. Stories were so realistic and emotionally engaging that they could inspire other oppressed peoples, perhaps including seminarians who hear God's call despite the noise and turbulence of an even larger empire.

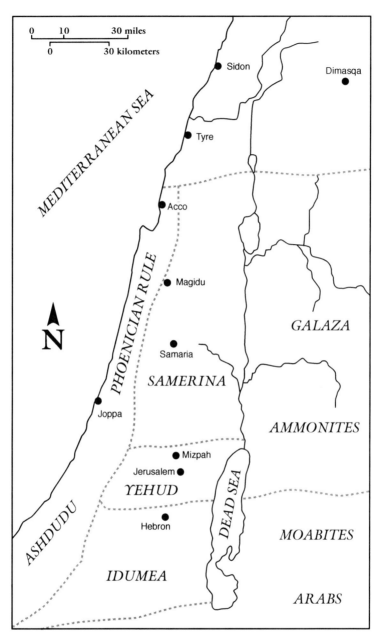

Yehud during the Persian period. Yehud was one of several provinces in the larger district or satrapy, which in turn was only one of the satrapies into which the Persian Empire was divided.

Finally, I would ask that we step back from the dramatic changes in Scripture studies in the past twenty years and appreciate that the new information has come in such a short period of time that there is still much discussion not only about the details but about the big picture as well. In 1986, for example, a textbook by J. Maxwell Miller and John H. Hayes, *A History of Ancient Israel and Judah*, was seen as a radical departure from the more traditional approach because it treated the Exodus from Egypt and the conquest of Canaan as not being historical. In a revised edition of the book prepared some twenty years later, the authors noted that these views were now widely accepted and that their present work was seen as less radical and even moderately cautious. In 1988, archaeologist Israel Finkelstein published findings that all but destroyed the traditional story of Joshua's conquest, arguing that the archaeological evidence pointed to the Israelites as being indigenous to Palestine. Fellow archaeologist William Dever, although he often clashed with Finkelstein over the dating of some archeological findings, attributes to his work the almost universal consensus that the Exodus from Egypt under Moses and the conquest of Palestine by Joshua did not happen. All biblical archaeologists and most biblical historians support such a view. Both scholars have published popular works that spell out this new, widely accepted model: Finkelstein's *The Bible Unearthed* (2001) and Dever's *What Did the Biblical Writers Know and When Did They Know It?* (2001). Such books also demonstrated that the stories of the patriarchs— Abraham, Isaac, and Jacob—were also not strictly historical, continuing the work of biblical scholar Thomas Thompson who took that position in the 1970s.

Beliefs do not change that easily, and a paradigm shift from historical to mythical will take time because faith traditionally demands that certain things really happened. For example, in his 1974 book Thompson quoted

Catholic biblical scholar Roland de Vaux as positing that if biblical history is erroneous, his faith would also be.[3] What might be helpful is to trace some of the discoveries that have radically changed our ideas about the Bible as an historical document. Easier said than done! The experts disagree, sometimes quite heatedly, in their efforts to reconstruct how the Bible was written and what is historical. For those of us wishing to explore this new information, we must appreciate that our own beliefs will influence the conclusions we accept or reject. We really cannot pretend to be neutral: we have our own agenda, just as those biblical writers had theirs.

To challenge the stories' historicity would be to contest most believers' religious education and belief systems. Even those who would not describe themselves as believers may also be influenced by Bible stories that offer a worldview in which justice will prevail, the virtuous life will be rewarded, and God will intervene in human history. Such ideas can become part of a culture, especially in the United States, which has historically seen itself as the new Israel, a country God has endowed specially to be an example to the world. What about the state of Israel? Are that country's claims to the land based on stories that are not historically accurate? Belief in the stories leads to a belief in God, who will act again in history on the side of the righteous. Christians may be especially troubled by this information because Jesus is usually seen as a culmination of God's working in history for the salvation of people. So much is at stake.

Several years ago, I was a juror for a civil case in which the plaintiff believed asbestos poisoning had compromised his health. For days, experts on both sides tried to convince us of the rightness of their positions and their opponents' flawed thinking by quoting studies and statistics. Neither side could deliver the knockout blow, so it was left to us nonexperts to determine the fairness of the plaintiff's claim.

By a close vote, we decided in favor of the plaintiff, an el-
derly African American gentleman whose health was clearly
compromised. We supported his claim for damages against
the asbestos company. We all looked at the same evidence,
but I suspect that our individual prejudices and back-
grounds greatly influenced our conclusions. I am reminded
of that experience as I try to sort through all the conflicting evidence concerning the historicity of Bible stories: our
biases and life experiences powerfully affect us. As a regular
churchgoer, I have a vested interest in traditional religion,
but as a psychologist I am committed to exploring conflict
in the hope of finding some level of resolution. These and
other factors, some of which I am not even aware, will influence my conclusions as a nonexpert in a field where the
experts are still sorting through the data and arguing about
its meaning.

Where to Start?

One place to start this discussion is by acknowledging our
own leanings when we review material, and our own investment in the belief system based on the historical events that
the Jewish Scriptures narrated. It is also helpful to keep in
mind that a review of the scholarly opinions reveals two
outlying positions, commonly called maximalist and mini-
malist. The former group holds that the Scripture stories
were basically factual and were passed down relatively intact
through oral traditions until they were written down some
time later. The latter group has argued that we can simply
disregard the past two hundred years of biblical scholarship
because the maximalist scholars tended to treat the texts as
historical.

Returning for a moment to the struggling seminarians,
I might encourage them to find some middle ground between the extremes as a place to start. While I may pursue
that approach because it is my natural inclination, the so-

called middle-of-the-road approach is often neither static nor comforting. It requires us to hold in tension the opposite pulls not only of differing experts, but also of the conflict between science and religion. Although it does not offer the certainty of some extreme positions, the middle ground can become the place to find a dynamic compromise between scientific findings and historically based religions. With the right support, this struggle with opposing positions can help us negotiate our own identity as individuals who live in both scientific and spiritual worlds. I find myself drawn into this conflict because I value both scientific discoveries and my own faith.

It will come as no surprise, then, that in reviewing theories regarding when the basic historical Jewish writings were created—Genesis through the Books of Kings—I look for some middle ground. The argument that makes most sense to me points to the 200 years of the Persian period (538–330 BCE), namely, the time after the return from Babylon in the sixth century BCE up to the point when the Greeks under Alexander the Great overran the Persian empire. This middle position acknowledges that on one hand, oral traditions and some writings may go back much further, but were rewritten during the Persian era. On the other hand, the Persian-era documents were likely revised in the later Greek era—some, such as the book of Daniel, are actually dated to that period.

However, dating these writings to the Persian era focuses our attention on the historical context in which they took shape—and we know that context is essential to meaning. When we contextualize the Jewish writings within the Persian era, the fact that such inspirational writing could have occurred during that bleak period is remarkable. It was a time of political instability—factions fought to fill the power vacuum created by the loss of the monarchy, the economy was in ruins, and major cities were destroyed.

Additionally, the tiny province could easily have been swallowed up by what was the greatest empire on earth at the time. But perhaps most significant of all, the Jews' powerful god had failed to preserve the holy city Jerusalem and its temple. How could they have survived as a people?

The New Beginnings
of an Ancient People

When the Persians conquered the Babylonians in 538 BCE, they reorganized their new empire. The Persian ruler Cyrus created the small and relatively impoverished province of Yehud in the process. Yehud was so insignificant that it was probably initially placed under the direction of a larger province in the area. Jews who had been deported were encouraged to return, although the numbers of returnees noted in the book of Nehemiah are now believed to be highly inflated, given recent archaeological evidence. Subsistence farmers who worked the land were required to pay taxes to the empire in addition to supporting their local leaders and, eventually, rebuilding Jerusalem and the temple. When they lost their monarchy, the Jews also lost the rallying point for their own sense of identity, as well as a center of power that could provide direction and organization.

In the Persian era, leadership of Yehud was divided among a few powerful families, and sharp divisions arose between those who had remained in the province and the exiles who returned from Babylon. On a more psychological level, all the various groups had to reconcile their dreams of being Yahweh's chosen people with the reality of their new circumstances. Faith and fact collided in the bleak landscape of the impoverished province of Yehud. Yet this same conflict was the backdrop for a truly remarkable religious development. Some of the Jews, especially those who were returning from Babylon, saw in their desperate circumstances the opportunity to renew their faith and, in the process, reemphasize their identity as a chosen people.

Although our knowledge of the Persian period is obscured by lack of information and contradictory writings, we do know of one historical event that some religious Jews used as a catalyst for reassessing their situation: the area's original inhabitants returned. The return of exiles was a Persian political policy that applied to many peoples at the time. The empire sustained itself by delegating some authority to the provinces and thereby tolerating a modest degree of independence and diversity. However, some Jews saw the hand of God in the decree of the Persian ruler, Cyrus. Cyrus was God's anointed, a messiah, one especially chosen to do God's will (Isa 45:1). Furthermore, his act was the key to understanding a new and alternative version of reality, in which God was in charge of everything and had allowed the Jews to be nearly destroyed so that they could be reestablished in a show of divine power. By portraying God as transcending and then determining history, these Jewish writers were constructing monotheism, the belief in one god.

Rather than identify themselves with a powerful but still human king, Jews were encouraged to swear allegiance to an all-powerful god. During this period the Jewish religion made a dramatic leap from the practices of their ancestors. We tend to think of the stories of Abraham and Moses as evidence that the early Israelites believed in one god, but that is not correct: they worshiped many gods. "Biblical passages, archaeological data and the other evidence all suggest that much or all of that period to the end of the Judean monarchy, Israel and Judah were polytheistic societies."[4] During the time they were occupied by the Persians and became a marginalized pawn in a large empire, they came to believe in a supernatural, cosmic god that was the ruler of all. They became monotheists who believed that this almighty god had destined them for greatness. They wrote themselves into the stories they created and claimed that they were the survivors and therefore the inheritors of those promises: they were the last of the Israelites.

The New Information

Scholars still disagree about the connection between the Jews of the sixth century BCE and the people who lived in Palestine hundreds of years before. At one pole are those who argue that there is no direct line between Canaanites/ Israelites of 1200 BCE—when Israel was mentioned in an Egyptian monument—and the inhabitants of Yehud some 700 years later. According to these authors, the story of Israel from Abraham to David is a foundational myth, something like what the Roman poet Virgil developed in his *Aeneid* regarding the mythical founding of Rome by Aeneas. The stories of Abraham, Moses, and David created a connection to God's past promises: they were God's chosen people and this was the land God had given them, no matter what their conquerors thought. Instead these scholars argue that biblical history begins with a small kingdom centered in northern Palestine beginning in the ninth century BCE and a smaller one centered in the south beginning in the eighth century BCE. There was not a kingdom under David and then Solomon that united north and south; there was no connection between people who came to be called Jews and those ancients known as Israelites.

Others argue that archaeological findings support the historicity in some of the biblical stories especially those from, say, 1000 BCE. While they see the stories of Moses and Joshua as mythical, these scholars conclude that the Bible starts describing historical events beginning with the book of Judges, which tells of the Israelite's struggles with the Philistines. Judges includes the stories of heroes like

Sampson. Next come the books of Samuel, which describe the transition from tribal groups to a monarchy, first led by Saul and then David. Although they do not take biblical stories literally as fact, some see in them a reflection of real continuity between the people known as Israel and their descendants who came to be known as Jews.

Although these two positions may eventually be resolved with the discovery of new evidence, I favor the first version, which sees the early biblical stories as a foundational myth primarily developed from legends and stories that that were reshaped and modified to serve the larger narrative. I take this position because the real protagonist of the Bible, as I see it, is the Jewish people. If an Israel existed, it is not the Israel described in the Bible. The same can be true of Sampson, Moses, and David: they exist in the Scriptures as artificial links that connect one part of the story to another, sometimes awkwardly, as when the last judge Samuel anoints the first king Saul. In fact, even God is a kind of a stage prop, changing names in the story to give continuity with the past and hope for the future. My middle ground here is that although some of the stories may have traces of history, that history is not operative because myth has taken over. To do otherwise is to depend on a description of an ancient world "which was invented in the form that we have it after that world had disappeared."[5]

Additionally, I am inclined to see the story as a myth of origin because origin myths were so significant for people to aggrandize their past by connecting it with a hero, as the Romans did with Aeneas, or with a god, as Cyrus did with Marduk in founding the Persian empire. Of course, that tendency may not be limited to the ancients. A recent article in the *New York Times* spoke of frustrated Turks glorifying the Ottoman empire because of dissatisfaction with the way things were going in their country, even though they had emancipated themselves from that empire less than a century before.[6] Second, I see these Bible stories as reflecting the struggles and questions of the leaders in the province of Yehud: Who can lead us if we have no king? How do we organize ourselves into a people with an identity that sets us off from others? How to motivate the majority of the people to buy into our vision? However, on a more personal level, I like the origin myth because it shifts our understanding of the Bible from the work of God to the work of people. I believe the power of the new information lies not so much in its destruction of traditional beliefs but in its construction of an inspiring story about just how those beliefs came to be.

Who Were the Writers?

Their novel interpretation of some historical events and their invention of others brought new meaning to the Jews' life circumstances, and the emerging Jewish elite of the Persian period created a religious history that fuels religious imaginations to this day. According to their new narrative, God allowed Jerusalem to be destroyed by the Babylonians, punished the destroyers, and then inspired Cyrus to set them free to rebuild the holy city. A past was developed that put God in charge of history. God had chosen and cared for them in the past and would exalt them in the future. The outlines of this story were spelled out in writings attributed to the Persian-era leaders Ezra and Nehemiah; in the works attributed to the prophets of that time, Haggai and Zachariah; and especially in the latter portions of the book of Isaiah, commonly called Deutero (Second) and Trito (Third) Isaiah (chapters 40–55 and 56–66). However, over the years, myths and legends continued to embellish the story, eventually creating an epic that went back to the beginning of time. Just to show that God could create a kingdom, the writers claimed that it had happened once before—in the mythical united kingdom of David and

Solomon, which, according to some stories, stretched from the Nile to the Euphrates.

Legends of a sojourn and escape from Egypt have similarly become examples of God's great power, with that Exodus and subsequent establishment of Israel as God's chosen people encompassing the same promises that were replayed when the exiles returned from Babylon to Jerusalem. The biblical story claimed that a new people was formed in the desert around Sinai and equipped with the religious tools that would maintain their identity. The more likely story is that exiles in Babylon developed the narratives and practices they introduced on their return to their nearly deserted homeland. If we trace the development of the primary historical books to this Persian era, we can see that a powerful past was created to give meaning to a problematic present—much like some Turks are doing today. At the same time, we can appreciate that what we call facts might have been adapted, embellished, or even created to emphasize the story's meaningfulness.

Power to the Priests

The narrative would not be powerful unless it had influential storytellers to relay it. Historian and biblical scholar Lester Grabbe underscores the importance of a successful transition from the king to the high priest as the chief religious figure.[7] With the monarchy destroyed, the priesthood became the new executive branch and offered the Jewish people literature and corresponding ritual practices that could address their primary need: learning to interpret and find meaning in a new situation in which they had no king, God's representative on Earth, to set the ground rules. However, the transition to priesthood as authority took decades, if not centuries. In the meantime, various factions developed the literature that challenged their competitors while it avoided antagonizing their Persian overlords.

Writing became critical in the process, not only to make sense of the situation but also to justify the actions of the members of the ruling elite who were doing the writing.

Although usually anonymous, the skillful scribe became "both thinker and religious visionary."[8] In a burst of creativity, this period saw the writing of history, prophecy, poetry, wisdom literature (Job), and short stories (Ruth and Esther), often with conflicting or at least differing viewpoints. For example, Trito-Isaiah had to cope with the promises of imminent prosperity outlined in Deutero-Isaiah that had not occurred.[9] As the Isaiah writings exemplified, the Jewish Scriptures represented an ongoing dialogue as different writers articulated their positions, often in response to other writings. There could be substantial disagreement. The book of Proverbs uses the same theme and vocabulary as Song of Songs but comes up with a different conclusion: beware of sexy women because you will lose your faith (see Proverbs 7).

It would be incorrect to imagine these writings as examples of some ongoing debate limited to the elite class. The writings of the Persian era were a major force in defining Jewish identity as a people of the book because the audiences who heard the stories would both influence and be influenced by them. "The text exists, in the final analysis, thanks to the community, for the use of the community, with a view to giving shape to the community."[10] One scholar imagines the Jewish Scriptures as being formed in a "dynamic process that reflects competition between different communities within Israel and their struggles for power."[11] Although we may never know how large these communities were, we can imagine something of the marvelous creative energy they generated. Again, much was at stake. Disparate writings continued the conversation about their privileges and responsibilities as God's chosen people.

Yet at another level these writings address the powerful emotional conflict that occurred when their alternative universe necessarily came into conflict with the real world of vast empires and near-subsistence living. Although writers such as the author of Jonah opted for a more global solution that included Gentiles, the faith/fact conflict pulled others into a violent and exclusive belief system in which their cosmic god would establish a kingdom at the expense of others. Also, as their god's promises were not fulfilled, the priestly leaders who were the main catalyst in creating the Jewish religion would become increasingly desperate. They became so focused on maintaining this alternative world through ritual and purity laws that rival factions would at times attack each other with deadly force.

The Struggle to Keep
the Promise Alive

In constructing the narrative of their fall and redemption, the writers of the Persian period had to invest in a problematic future solution to their desperate circumstances. Although it was described in a variety of ways, that future would involve God's kingdom on Earth, a kingdom centered in Jerusalem, the holy city. Initially, the reality seemed a far cry from this marvelous promise. The believers struggled with the gap between God's promises and their continuing modest role in the world. Their intense anxiety about the future provided us with beliefs and behaviors that will plague us for some time. In the Jews' search for meaning to temper the pain of their sacrifices, they imagined a future that would be divisive, exclusive, and often violent.

Impatient for the distant future, Persian-era prophet Zechariah began to describe what this future might look like in what is now defined as apocalyptic literature. Strange signs and baffling occurrences would precede the coming of Yahweh, who would finally come down from Heaven to do battle against other nations and protect Jerusalem. With God present as the king of the whole world, the world itself would be transformed. All who remained would be holy and just. Third Isaiah would add to the confusion by claiming a special role for a pious minority among the Jews themselves—namely, that they alone would be vindicated on Judgment Day.[12] Apocalyptic literature, in its own confused and esoteric way, attempted to keep alive a hope that God would intervene. However, that literature was burdened by the writers' need to protect the reputation of their just and merciful god, who they believed had made special promises to them.

The longer they waited, the more grandiose the promises became. Not only would the kingdom of Judah be restored, but so would that of Israel. The covenant of Sinai would be followed more rigorously. Eventually it would all go back to creation: their god would restore the world and place Jerusalem as its new center. Questions remained. How were the people to cooperate with this restoration? That question had many answers, which included following both the rituals and the practices of a reestablished covenant.[13] Questions piled up about how this could happen. One thought was that the people would suffer before God's kingdom could be enshrined in this world. Zechariah imagined that David's dynasty would be restored, although the new leader would be killed, perhaps by his own people. Thus, it is no wonder that Zechariah is cited more than any other prophet in the Passion narratives of Jesus.[14]

When taken literally, the apocalyptic scenarios created by the Persian-era writers can become quite problematic. For example, the belief in a powerful and avenging god can be seen as granting permission to destroy others, even waging war in a misbegotten attempt to bring God's kingdom into play. The reality of the present is ignored in favor of the imagined reality developed long ago by a threatened people. In another case, the exclusivity of the Jewish people, tempered as it was by writings that were more inclusive, failed to appreciate the contributions of other peoples. If we look at the story behind the story, we can see that the Jews lived in a rich Near Eastern culture that had developed myths, legal systems, the priesthood, and prophetic and wisdom writings, all of which were available to and adaptable by the Jewish writers. In fact, precisely during this time the peoples of the Near East were becoming more aware of common interests, including spirituality. Even the victorious Persians were imagining a cosmic struggle between good and evil that would lead to the restoration of this world.[15] The Jewish religion owes much to Canaanites and Egyptians, Sumerians and Babylonians, Persians and Greeks.

However, the Jewish writers, more than their Near Eastern neighbors, tied their ethnic identity onto the promises of their god. And as the promises laid down in the Persian period were not fulfilled, the writers imagined even more ambitious ones. In the book of Daniel written around 165 BCE, for example, God has moved beyond the promise of entering history to establish a new Jewish nation. In this next stage, God will end human history and establish God's own kingdom. This later promise brings increasing anxiety to religious Jews who argued among themselves as to who would be worthy to enter this kingdom. "Both 'Jewish' and 'kingdom' have required drastic redefinition, and the issue is now a deliverance of the true, wise 'Israel' from the oppression of the historical process."[16] The question of who is to be saved continues today, sometimes with tragic consequences.

The Story Behind the Stories

In its own way, a more realistic story of a religious renaissance that begins with the Persian occupation in the sixth century BCE may be at least as inspiring as that more fantastical one about miracles in the desert or a god ending history. In the Bible, the Israelites' god taught them a new religion. In reality, the exiles in Babylon refined their religion and, in the process, dedicated themselves to studying the law, following the prescribed diet, and celebrating the feasts. They used information from Babylonian astronomers "to fix these feasts to a calendar and thus come to think of them as regular annual holidays."[17] The exiles from Babylon did not conquer the land but created a spiritual world that influences us even to modern times.

Inspiring, but such a messy process! Writers, and presumably their communities, argued with others. The attempts to create a new nation were fumbling at best. Different leaders made a dramatic start only to disappear, never to be heard from again: Joshua, Zerubbabel, and Shesbazzar all made entrances and exits. Various governors and high priests came and went depending on the politics of the empire, the power struggles of various factions and the strength of the peasant-based economy. Even the priesthood was not that much help. It is likely that a single family of priests did not establish dynastic control during the Persian era.[18] Messiness isn't much of an ideal state to strive for, but it is closer to the trial-and-error way we live our lives. One lesson from appreciating the story behind the stories is that we have to figure it out on our own. Although we may receive support from communities or inspiration from leaders, we are ultimately the experts in deciding who we are and how we are called to live.

Placing the stories in the Persian era reminds us that intense faith often comes in times of conflict and confusion, of doubt and even despair. Although a religious epiphany might also be so meaningful, the chaos from which it sprang may temper our enthusiasm. The various writers could not have *all* been correct. Likewise, appreciating the milieu in which these writers struggled to articulate their mission can be understood as a natural condition for religion. The search for certainty and the drive to proselytize can risk being unbiblical once we appreciate the story behind the Bible stories. It can also cut us off from other voices that quite naturally see the same data through a different lens. That doesn't mean relativism but *tolerance*. It also means appreciating that something of value comes from the struggle.

Despite the political confusion and economic uncertainty of living in an occupied country, the Jewish religion developed an ideal of justice that insisted that all Jews follow the laws and practices developed during these turbulent times. We can only imagine how difficult it would be to motivate people to embrace such self-discipline. The sharp division between aristocratic and peasant classes would make this sense of fairness for all quite problematic. Prophets railed about injustice, and at least once the Persians apparently intervened because the peasant class had become so destitute they could not deliver their promised tribute. The priests and other leaders who courageously and single-mindedly created a community in the aftermath of a devastating war would lose their way when hoped-for promises did not materialize. Messiness was never an excuse to give up, but a call to be vigilant. The danger was the loss of tolerance as the struggle became more intense and factions developed. We can see signs of that conflict almost bursting through the narrative.

The moving stories of Abraham and Isaac, Moses and Joshua, and even David and Solomon can inspire us with their pageantry and rough beauty. We take less notice of the seemingly minor dramas involving priests like Aaron or the priestly tribe known as the Levites. Yet inserted into the Pentateuch are reflections of the struggles of various priestly groups in the Persian period to claim legitimacy for themselves and their laws by creating linkages with the stories of their supposedly ancient origins. While they were at it, they besmirched the stories of their rivals. For an example, priests who traced their lineage to Aaron, the brother of Moses, had to live with the Levites' story of their ancestor's supposed betrayal—his creation of the idol of the golden calf (Exodus 32). Aaronites would retaliate by inserting a story in which a grandson of Levi is annihilated by an act of God (Numbers 16). Yet through all the mud-slinging and differing rules, the Pentateuch evolved into a compromise document that reflected a weaving together of the various priestly factions and differing religious perspectives that were a part of the times.[19]

Behind those cool compromises was the fiery furnace of the Persian era. We would do well to remember that the religion formed in the crucible of these two centuries set the model for what it means to be religious, at least in the Western world. A closer appreciation of their struggle can normalize the struggle religious individuals can have at all times. The cry for justice was compromised by the drive to power. Religious positions were intimately tied into the politics and economics of the times. The future was uncertain, and disagreement was the norm. If there was a desperate need to worship a transcendent god, there was an equally powerful motive to find meaning and identity in their lives. It might not have happened but for those returning exiles, a small group of elitists who challenged a defeated people to see themselves as destined for greatness.

Religious Leadership: A Mixed Bag

The band of refugees that straggled back to Jerusalem in the last third of the sixth century BCE would have likely been the children and grandchildren of those who were exiled to Babylon some 50 to 60 years earlier. Many may never have seen their homeland before, but they came with the vision of how they would dramatically change it. They would take the practices that had sustained their identity in a foreign land and impose them upon those that now inhabited the small province. They planned to help a defeated people reinvent themselves as belonging to an all powerful god who was beyond nation, king, or even history itself. Their radical agenda would be the foundation for an imaginary world that would eventually give meaning and purpose not only to the inhabitants of Yehud, but to their fellow Jews who had migrated to other lands.

The religious leaders of the Persian era faced their own spiritual crisis and, in working through it, created a religion that moved beyond its own borders to embrace like-minded people in other lands. The system of justice they advocated pushed for fairness and equality as everyone's responsibility, not just the rulers. Yet these priests and scribes competed with fellow religionists who are just as learned and passionate but differed, sometimes dramatically, about the meaning and implications of their hard-won beliefs. Though they would be catalysts for change, they would also be powerful critics who determined who was in and who was out, who was acceptable and who was not. They would demonize not only non-Jews but also those Jews who did not follow the strict guidelines they established. They worked to exclude their rivals not only from the worship services, but also from the country.

The religious leaders of today—and tomorrow, like the seminarians—face a similar kind of crisis. How does one interpret the Bible given this new information? The pull may be either to move beyond the borders of one's faith or to intensify those boundaries by claiming the superiority of one's beliefs. The new information makes it both untenable and unhistorical to maintain the latter position. More important, the story behind the Bible stories reveals faith as a conflicted process in which articulate and well-meaning individuals and communities have differing views. The challenge is to hold on to one's own views while respectfully engaging those of others.

The challenge is also to belong to a religious community whose leaders must of necessity be limited and at least partially incorrect. When we appreciate the competitive atmosphere of Yehud, the demand was to take a position, knowing that doing so meant being in opposition to other positions. It also meant living one's life according to the particular belief system one espoused. Though such an atmosphere could engender hostility, it just as well could have led to independence. The traditional idea of a passive follower did not make much sense in Yehud.

In this more scientific reconstruction of the biblical story, we can be inspired by the resilience of the people who, despite conflicted leadership and economic hardship, were able not only to survive but also to bring out the best in themselves. The journey to faith would lead them to discover an inner strength, a noble purpose that even today can be "decidedly moral, positive, and transformative."[20] More than the physical miracles of Sinai, we can learn to appreciate the moral miracle of Yehud. Facing incredible odds, a vanquished people was indoctrinated into an alternative reality, bolstered by narrative and ritual that formed them into a community that survived into our own times.

Those of us who are not Jews are challenged to reevaluate our relationship to the Jewish Scriptures. We can be inspired by their story, but it is after all their spiritual autobiography and not ours. Given that the stories are not to be taken literally because they are not historical, we are challenged to rethink our own religion: if there was no divine promise of a messiah, who was Jesus? If there was no covenant with Abraham, what of Paul's insistence on a new covenant brought about by Jesus? If the story of salvation is not historical, how does one legitimately connect both the Jewish and Christian Scriptures? If the stories are not historical, the religious authorities who still claim that they are can rightfully be accused of trying to maintain a privileged position as primary interpreters of false foundations. On the other hand, the new information can legitimate our position as skeptical believers. We may feel the need, the value, and even the passion associated with religious beliefs, but at the same time appreciate that we are living in a time of conflicting religious claims. We are challenged to see belief as a discernment process of continued learning and practice.

Before we turn to the Christian Scriptures (part II), there is another serious difficulty posed by the Jewish Scriptures. Although we can be inspired by the story behind the story and motivated to engage in our own spiritual journey, the intensity and divisiveness now exposed also reveals what can be a powerful force for harm. The historical foundation of Western religion has been destroyed, and the edifice built on it is now shaken and severely damaged. If we choose to sort through the ruins for inspiration and guidance, we would do well to be alert to the danger lying there. More specifically, positions that demand either total obedience or the demonization of others are at least suspect. On the other hand, by knowing that this sacred material need not be taken literally, we can begin to recognize what is harmful in it. In the next chapter, the book of Joshua is used as a case study in how to recognize and avoid what can be harmful, as well to consider the potentially noxious elements in any religion that is mistakenly based on the Scriptures as historical.

Chapter 2

The Story of Joshua and His Warrior God

Joshua fit the battle of Jericho and the walls came a tumblin' down.

    —Traditional hymn

Lincoln, and those buried at Gettysburg, remind us that we should pursue our own absolute truths only if we acknowledge that there may be a terrible price to pay.

    —Barack Obama, *The Audacity of Hope*

We might remember the story of Joshua for the famous battle of Jericho, when the walls came tumbling down, an incident memorialized in the iconic African American spiritual quoted in the epigraph. Then there's the famous battle in the Valley of Gibeon, in which Joshua made the sun stop in its tracks, an incident which, much later, the church would interpret literally and use as evidence that the Earth revolved around the sun, causing a lot of grief for Galileo. The book of Joshua from which these stories come is somewhat repetitive, as the Israelites slash and burn their way through Palestine, annihilating most of its inhabitants. Just when you think the story might be basis for a video game, you start the mind-numbing chapters that describe the division of the conquered land among the various Israelite tribes. Still, Joshua is the dutiful successor to Moses. Imitating his mentor, Joshua sees that all the men are circumcised, parts the waters of the Jordan River to cross over to the Promised Land, and ends his life with a farewell address. The book comes across as a stodgy sequel that suffers in comparison with the drama and special effects of the Exodus story.

But recently the book of Joshua has moved into the spotlight to become one of the most studied and commented upon books in the Hebrew Bible. First of all, the basic story confronts us with a moral challenge because we are implicitly asked about our own position regarding justifiable behavior. Joshua and his men are convinced that they are doing God's will, which frees their consciences, allowing them to do what it takes, even slaughtering men, women and children. The book reminds us that powerful ideas can introduce a one-dimensional, simplistic view of good and evil, with disastrous consequences. We can even mistake power for virtue and then rewrite history to justify our behavior.

Biblical scholar Michael Pryor offers a moral reading of Joshua and the conquest of Palestine. Pryor points out that biblical narratives contain actions that we would today consider war crimes and crimes against humanity, and he invites us to consider the stories from the Canaanites' viewpoint. His concern is not simply that such biblical literature justifies racist and oppressive behavior but that other peoples at other times would use it as justification for their own oppressive behavior against other indigenous people. He argues that the biblical narratives would be used "for the Iberian devastation of Latin America in the late medieval period, for the Afrikaner exploitation of nonwhites in southern Africa right up to the 1990s, and...the ongoing Zionist exploitation of the Arabs of Palestine."[1]

Biblical scholars have not been immune to the seduction of this tale. Pryor quotes prominent American biblical scholars, such as William Albright and George Wright, who justify the "genocide contained in the narrative of Joshua" by arguing that the conquerors' cultural and moral superiority is a significant advance over the indigenous popula-

tion's inferiority.[2] It may be that people in the United States
are especially vulnerable to this temptation because they
have seen a similar theme used in the treatment of Native
Americans as well as African American slaves. Likewise the
tremendous accomplishments of the United States as a superior power in the world may lull us into thinking that we
are truly God's people, called to do God's work here on
Earth. However, we can counter such thinking with an appeal to the moral dimension now that we have a better idea
of just how the story of Joshua came to be.

Deconstructing Joshua

If we place the book as having being written, or at least revised, in the Persian era, the author is addressing a demoral-
ized and marginalized people in the tiny province of Yehud.
Although the exploits of Joshua may be intended to motivate people by telling an inspiring story, the message also
contains a promise. Just as Joshua established a new people
in the land, the present inhabitants were about to become a
new people chosen by God. The blueprint for becoming a
new people was to emphasize that the land belongs to God
and that people were to honor it by living justly. But Joshua
contains a warning for anyone who wants to be on God's
side: you have to work hard so that this god will not turn on
you. Joshua warns the people, "You cannot serve the Lord,
for he is a holy God. He is a jealous God; he will not forgive
your transgressions or your sin" (Josh 24:19).

In Joshua's farewell speech, he warns the people not
to transgress God's laws or terrible things will happen. On
one level that theme is part of the message of the Persian
era writers who claimed that the destruction of Jerusalem in
586 BCE was God's justifiable response to their grievous sinning. However, the Bible teaches us that we are all sinners.
So we have to be on guard not to sin too much or too griev-
ously. When we do sin, how do we find forgiveness? The

Persian era writers solved these problems by establishing the priests as the arbiters of what was bad, as well as the ones to provide the means by which transgressions and sins would be resolved. The book of Joshua gives power to priesthood as the main vehicle for identifying our transgressions and then showing us how to get right with God.

However, the moral issues and challenges sparked by a closer reading of Joshua are not the only reasons this book has become significant in the recent biblical studies. A more scientific study of the book of Joshua undermines the historical bases of familiar and foundational stories in the Bible.

New Information about Joshua

A good thing about the book of Joshua is that it gives a lot of information. Those numbing details in the book of cities captured and lands distributed have become the data base for a total revision of the history of the Israelites in Palestine. This detailed information presented scholars with the opportunity to test out hypotheses concerning that history by bringing in information from archaeology and Near Eastern studies. Scholars have had difficulty reconciling some of those details in Joshua because other books of the Jewish Scriptures—notably Judges—told a different story. Yet some earlier biblical archaeologists claimed to find evidence in their excavations of cities mentioned in the text that supported the conquest story. An uneasy peace remained until the works of recent scholars, namely, Israel Finkelstein, destroyed any historical basis for a conquest by Joshua or anyone else.[3] These scholars demonstrated that incidents recorded in the book of Joshua could not have happened. Jericho—along with many of the other cities named in the book—was uninhabited at the time of the supposed defeat, and other allegedly conquered cities didn't exist yet. "Nothing is said about pockets of Canaanites being too strong for Joshua, or cities escaping the Israelite juggernaut."[4]

Also a campaign of the size and extent of Joshua's would be expected to leave substantial archaeological evidence, but none exists. Instead, the ruins of cities attributed to Joshua's destructive forces are seen as belonging to other periods of history. For example, archaeological records prove that the destruction of cities reportedly defeated by the Israelites under Joshua—Hazor, Aphek, Lachish, and Megiddo—"took place over a span of more than a century. The possible causes include invasion, social breakdown, and civil strife. No single military force did it, and certainly not in one military campaign."[5]

The book of Joshua is like a loose thread sticking out of the Jewish Scriptures. You pull at it, and gradually some of the other stories start to unravel. Archaeology argues for an entirely different version as to how the Jewish people came to be. That evidence demonstrates that the Israelites were actually indigenous to the area we now call Palestine—the Jews did not conquer the Canaanites: they *were* Canaanites.[6] And if there was no conquest, there was no wandering in the desert to precede that conquest, nor an Exodus to precede the wandering, and so forth. The deconstruction of the book of Joshua initiates a backward-moving domino effect that challenges the most treasured stories in the Jewish Scriptures. But there is at least one more layer to the Joshua story.

The Earlier Version

According to several authors, including archaeologists Israel Finkelstein and Neil Silberman, an earlier version of the book of Joshua was developed during the reign of the Judaic king Josiah, who ruled in the seventh century BCE; at least 600 years *after* Joshua supposedly invaded the country. These authors point out that the actual campaigns of Josiah closely paralleled the fictional conquests of Joshua. For example, Josiah begins his quest by conquering Jericho and Ai, the two cities where Joshua's supposed takeover originates. More important, the theology of Joshua—that is, the insistence on absolute loyalty to Yahweh—was a hallmark of the reforming king Josiah. This earlier version is simply propaganda: the book rewrites history in an attempt to inflate Josiah's royal importance, promote his military and religious plans, and endorse the priestly bureaucracy that supported him. In the process, Yahweh becomes a fierce warrior god who annihilates Israel's enemies but threatens to turn divine wrath on the chosen people if they do not follow God's commandments. In return, God will enable the Jews to create a great country. "From the wilderness and the Lebanon as far as the great river, the river Euphrates, all the land of the Hittites, to the Great Sea in the west shall be your territories" (1:4).

For a brief moment in history, it looked like this two-part prophecy might be fulfilled on Josiah's watch. Jerusalem and its surrounding areas began to prosper after the Assyrians destroyed the so-called Northern Kingdom in 701 BCE, and refugees from there fled south. Meanwhile, the superpowers of the day, Assyria and Egypt, faced their own challenges: Assyria withdrew from areas in Palestine, and Egypt was unable to fill the vacuum. With its new wealth, Jerusalem was able to develop the army it needed to overpower other territories, as well as the propaganda to support the effort. With the superpowers in disarray, Jerusalem's forces were able to advance with impunity. Given their new power and riches, it was easy to imagine that God was making all this happen. However, that moment of blessed triumph could not last. The real universe trumped the alternative one, and Josiah was killed under somewhat mysterious circumstances at the hands of Egyptian Pharaoh Neco II. However, that alternative universe struck back with the book of Joshua.

When the reality is troublesome (Josiah failed), one can always substitute myth (Joshua succeeded).

For all its bloodshed, this earlier version has a soft side. It tries to turn sadness and tragedy into triumphant hope, a basic mainstay of most religions. In this particular version, that hope primarily rested in the king. However, as the book was revived in the Persian era, the likelihood of a king grew less and less. The new editors aimed at establishing the authority of the priests as ones who speak for God and, most important, God's promise to establish a kingdom on Earth. Joshua became a political document, reflecting the political reality of Yehud in the Persian period, when priests became God's official spokespeople and the new leaders of a hoped-for theocratic state. Biblical scholar Giovanni Garbini argues that the revised book of Joshua presents the hero as a uniquely subservient figure who focuses entirely on completing and following God's commands to Moses. Yet this revision did not benefit Moses so much as it did those who now articulated and propagated God's will—namely, the priests. This new arrangement is made explicit in a few instances in the book where the priest Eleazar is listed before Joshua. It may be significant that our present version of the book does not end with Joshua's death and burial. In the last verses, the one left standing is the priest Phineas, who has just buried his father, Eleazar. Joshua's subservience to Moses becomes code for the political powers' subservience to the religious power. The book of Joshua therefore is not so much a history of an imagined conquest as it is an argument for a theocratic state.[7]

At this point it serves us well to mention that although we may take away from the Bible an image of a land ruled by the high priest, such a view is not historically accurate. Recently, authors have placed Yehud within the political framework of the Persian empire, where a small province would have been under the direction of Persian-appointed governors, who reported to regional authorities, who in turn were responsible to the head of state. In something like a two-steps-forward, one-step-back process, it was originally proposed that Persian authorities were *directly* involved in reviewing the religious writings that developed during the 200-year period of the empire. More recently, a consensus has emerged that sees the empire as exerting some *indirect* force in the sense that the biblical writers indirectly acknowledged their loyalty to their rulers. For example, Abraham and his family come from important cities in the empire, Ur and Haran. Also, the demonizing description of the pharaoh in the Exodus story is the authors' way of stating that they are loyal to the Persia and antagonistic toward Egypt at a time when those two empires were at war. These new findings give the Bible stories an important context. Although not obvious when we are reading them, these stories touch on the messy political and economic struggles that were serious concerns at the time.

Some Lessons from Joshua

Before we get to a final layer in our excavation of Joshua, there are a few points that skeptical believers might keep in mind. First, be wary when the religious universe attempts to trump the material one. Although religion can offer support in the face of tragedy, there may be some benefit in confronting that tragedy without a spiritual painkiller. Second, be wary of those selling the drugs. Joshua both subtly and directly pushes the power of the priests. We have to be careful about buying into a religious communication that ties us into an inferior position with a superior religious authority: we can separate the message from those who claim to be the messengers. Finally, appreciating Joshua as propaganda helps us appreciate the limits of war. War did not help either the northern or southern kingdom. While some biblical writers may have become pacifists through their own reflection about what happened in the real world, their voices tend to be drowned out by authors living in an imaginary world and promising victory through violence in this one.

An Evolutionary View

Before leaving our excavation of Joshua, there is one other layer that can be explored. Joshua taps into the basic, evolutionary advantages that religion gave groups that survived in our primitive past. For small groups to achieve some competitive advantage, they had to combine a strong loyalty toward their fellow tribesmen with a fierce, warlike posture toward others who were not of their clan.[8] Excavating Joshua, we come to this primitive layer now coded into our DNA. We, too, have experienced the powerful pull of patriotism and are suspicious of strangers at our doors, let alone at our borders. Any religion that strengthened the group while it demonized the enemy was making a significant contribution to the survival of the group. From this perspective, the imagined world of Joshua reflects a realistic example of this two-part, evolution-driven survival strategy.

Much of Joshua has to do with group solidarity. The land is divided up among these supposedly warlike tribes, who are then admonished to live just and peaceful lives. A moral system that encourages self-restraint is established with consequences for those who disobey. The story of Achar, a member of Joshua's army who, against orders, kept some of the spoils from a battle, is a warning that even if one broke the rules in secret, such an offense could harm the whole community. However, in the event a feud broke out, cities of refuge were established that might give the aggrieved parties a chance to calm down and the accused a bit of due process. Uniting everything was the promise, claimed by the priests and scribes, that God would favor the people and restore the land—because, after all, both were God's to restore.

On the other side, there was no mercy for the enemy. In another biblical story, the first king, Saul, gets into trouble because he was compassionate toward a defeated enemy. All this proposed solidarity with kin and imagined violence toward others served to create a group identity that would separate people of Yehud from all other peoples. The real battle was the establishment of this group identity, and here the Jewish people really did win. It was powerful enough not just to survive centuries of persecution but to thrive over that same period.

Yet for all its clannish thinking and behavior, Joshua also reflects the ideology of the modern state. On one hand there is that need to form a national identity that is strengthened by both sanctions and approved behavior. On the other hand is the tendency to see one's nation as better than others. In the case of the United States, that ideology can have profound consequences because it is married to power. Joshua was talking about an imaginary world; U.S. civil religion operates in the real one. Yet what is helpful in one evolutionary period may be problematic in another. With its nearly intractable global difficulties, survival of the planet depends on moving away from more clannish ideologies and working to establish a more global one.

Harm Reduction

It is important to engage in the story of Joshua because the theme of a holy warfare against the evil other is, tragically, part of the Jewish and Christian Scriptures. Although developed in the Persian period, it was influential in the time of Jesus, as we can find in the Dead Sea Scrolls and the book that concludes the Christian Scriptures, Revelation. Biblical scholar George Nickelsberg speaks for many when he appreciates that the cry for justice is understandable in the writings of those who are oppressed. However, "they can bring on chaos and profound injustice when the impotent oppressed come to power in the certain conviction that they are the righteous and chosen."[9]

From a psychological perspective, we can appreciate that myths of the oppressed or alienated would have an edge to them. Like abused children who fantasize about getting even when they grow up, an oppressed people may begin to believe that the future will bring with it a reversal of fortunes, much to the oppressor's dismay. Both types of fantasies may provide comfort and boost morale during difficult moments. In the worst-case scenario, however, abuse overwhelms victims' resources and they can sink into destructive patterns involving bullying, battering, and other forms of victimizing others. The passive experience of being abused is translated into an active program of abuse. The myth becomes destructive. While we may have no illusions that war and violent solutions will cease, reflecting on the myth of Joshua may help us appreciate that powerful urges may no longer be adaptive: engaging the harmful parts of "the Good Book" can begin a different kind of religious journey.

Joshua and Us

From a psychological perspective, Joshua reflects our own needs for certainty and security as well as for the leadership that can meet these needs. The story appeals to our more primitive sense of good versus evil, our belief that we are the "good guys," and that God is on our side. The words also resonate with primal urges to seek security in others like us so that we can band together against a common enemy. In its use of both flattery and fear, the themes of Joshua can lull us into a false security that blinds us to larger problems. So seduced, we are vulnerable to giving our full allegiance to a leader, while at the same time neglecting our own responsibilities to participate in problem solving. So while the first step in deconstructing Joshua is to appreciate it as a powerful myth that brought identity to an occupied people and the second is to appreciate that it reveals how power can be misused, the final revelation is to appreciate how we give up individual power for group security.

Joshua offers comfortable solutions to our anxieties about who we are and how we can be safe. In that sense, it is like a drug that anesthetizes both our concern for others and our need to look inside ourselves for who we are. The more we take that kind of drug, the more we remove ourselves from solutions that involve others not like us, as well as slip into pseudo-identities that cover the hard work of self-discovery. In her memoir, *Lit*, Mary Karr writes of her struggle to face painful memories and harmful beliefs about herself without the mitigating effects of drugs and alcohol. She alludes to the many others who have faced the chaos in their lives and, with the support of a community and the discipline of a twelve-step program, have learned to live authentically and courageously.

With narratives like Joshua no longer credibly seen as historical, believers face a new kind of chaos. The security that came from following a religious leader who bases his or her authority on a literal reading of Scripture is not tenable. The biblically based belief that one belongs to a privileged group that can demonize others who are less fortunate, or even just different, can no longer be credible for one who takes the Bible seriously but not literally. Instead we are offered something like a twelve-step program. We are leery of authority, learn from the community, work our own program, and believe in a mysterious higher power that means different things to different people. Security comes not from some definitive doctrine or foolproof ritual but rather from truly living one day at a time.

In his novel *The Cellist of Sarajevo*, Steven Galloway describes ordinary people facing the chaos of war as their beloved city is besieged. Inspired in part by the heroism of others, a few find something more valuable than their own lives. One character that has been depicted as frightened if not cowardly as he tries to survive the siege has an epiphany of sorts. Although Dragan is still frightened, he refuses to allow his life to be dictated by his fears. He chooses to believe that war and violence must be confronted:

> He will behave now as he hopes everyone will someday behave. Because civilization isn't a thing that you build and then there it is, you have it for ever. It needs to be built constantly, re-created daily. It vanishes far more quickly than he ever would have thought possible. And if he wishes to live, he must do what he can to prevent the world he wants to live in from fading away. As long as there's war, life is a preventative measure.[10]

Closer to home we have the example of individuals who stood up in protest against the invasion of Iraq in 2003. Wright and Dixon, in their book *Dissent: Voices of Conscience*, chronicled the many individuals who sacrificed their careers as a protest against what they believed was an illegal act of war. These individuals reviewed the evidence for the invasion and found it wanting; they examined the process and doubted its legality. They appealed to a higher law—their own conscience. Although some may have been influenced by religious values, most seemed motivated by a deep appreciation of the horror of war, as well as by a sense of individual moral responsibility.[11]

In the face of chaos, individuals, locally and globally, have exemplified religious-like values in order to take an ethical stand—a belief in something more than themselves, a discernment process to discover what is right. In those moments we can see the power of an alternative universe that gives insight and direction for living in our material one. Scientist Stuart Kauffman would also argue that these moments are evolutionary: they represent those rare and critical moments when change occurs. What he sees as the engine of evolution in the biological realm, he transposes to the world of human activity, in particular ethics.[12]

Discerning Joshua

There is a way the story behind the story of Joshua is evolutionary. Having been conquered, the Jews dream of being conquerors. Scattered and dispersed, they imagine a just world in which the ancestral land is returned to them in an orderly fashion. Living in an almost forgotten province on the edge of a great empire, they see themselves as chosen to be an example to the world. If we take another step back and view the work of which Joshua is a part, we can see the contributions these writings have made to Western civilization. From the clash of opposing schools of thought would come an appreciation of the rights of the individual and a consequent basis for our understanding of law.[13] Likewise, the work of the scribes to find meaning in the direst circumstances would encourage others to so search. For all their internecine struggles, the writers also spoke of a world where justice and peace would prevail, though it might require great effort and sacrifice. In this there is the example of their savior, Moses: he would lead them from oppression, give them the structure that would define them as people, and yet not follow them into the Promised Land.

The new information that denies the historicity of the biblical stories does not mean that we must give up those values. In fact, by pushing through the history to get to the story behind it, one is offered an opportunity to both discover what is harmful in the Bible and simultaneously maintain what has always been helpful. To pursue such an opportunity means letting go of what has been comfortable and going forward without GPS. However, we can get some direction by appreciating the dangers of power. An escalating power struggle is often hidden behind the innocent stories of God's revelation. Joshua made a covenant with the people and taught them the commandments and the ordinances. Moses had done the same in the story about the delivery of the law at Mt. Sinai. In the Persian period, the priest and scribe Ezra read the law to the people, who accepted its commandments. If, as most scholars believe, these incidents of telling the law to the people and their universal acceptance thereof are not historical, they can be seen as a pattern that seeks to establish the priesthood as God's vehicle for communicating to the people. It's a less-than-equal arrangement in which the priests determine right behavior and the people's role is to embrace that behavior.

Of course, it really didn't happen that way. These stories of universal obedience by the people don't bear up when we look a little closer. Even in the time of Ezra and Nehemiah, certain groups opposed the reforms attributed to those two individuals. As the Persian period gave way to the Greek era and eventually the Roman, opposition groups such as the Pharisees and Essenes proposed their own versions of God's commandments. These groups also defined themselves as the true Israel, the ones who genuinely understood the behavior that would lead to God's blessing and avoid God's wrath. Yet all of these groups were working under two assumptions. The first was that a privileged few can define right behavior for the many; the second was that right behavior would lead to God's intervention, which was understood to be the establishment of God's kingdom on Earth. The historical books of the Jewish Scriptures, including Joshua, are seductive invitations to risk everything for the opportunity to be on the side of the warrior god.

The second of these assumptions is especially problematic because so much is at stake. If some, or even a few like Achar, don't follow the rules, terrible things will happen to an entire nation. This desperate need to "get it right" pitted religious Jew against religious Jew because right practice was a matter of survival. Roughly 200 years before Jesus, when the Jewish people gained some level of independence, opposing groups persecuted and killed each other. When the Romans conquered the Jews in 63 BCE, they established some order and prevented such internecine struggles—but

Roman occupation ultimately created only another varia-tion of the dissonance the Jews had been experiencing. What had happened to God's promise to establish a king-dom in the land given to them? The Jews soon took out their desperation on the Romans as they fought wars of reli-gious liberation, believing that God would be with them as with Joshua. In a period of less than seventy-five years, Jews revolted against the Roman empire on three occasions (66, 115, and 133 CE), causing massive destruction, hundreds of thousands of deaths, and enslavement for countless others.

The Joshua story may persist because it touches on our own fantasies about power, even if that power comes at the expense of others. Ironically, the book of Joshua was probably edited during the Persian period, a time when the relatively impoverished province of Yehud was struggling to survive. It constructed a past that did not exist to keep hope alive for the present. Thomas Thompson describes the Bible as "survival literature"[14] because the stories describe a people who are remnants of either the old Israel or a res-urrected one. In that survival process, the biblical authors erased the memories of their own beginnings as Canaanites and substituted stories of mythical beginnings that mostly ignored Palestine's early history. These myths created an identity for a marginalized people dominated by empires. By reifying these myths, the writers legitimated the abuse of power that was essentially a by-product of the text.

Which Joshua Do We Choose?

Artist and author Maurice Sendak claimed that his stories operated on two levels. The first level was simply a chil-dren's narrative: somewhat innocent, usually with a happy ending. However, there was another story that at times was presented more obviously than others in which his drawings suggested the horrors of the Holocaust or, less frightening, a child's fear of adults who appear in the stories disguised as monsters. Similarly, but in reverse order, the first level of Joshua is dangerous and horrific but also seductive as it taps into our more instinctual fears. On the other hand, it offers clues about another story that is more heroic, helpful, and meaningful. The new information about the Bible in the past twenty years brings to the surface that other story.

Immersing ourselves in that other story is challenging, not only because it is less familiar but also because it is more demanding. It challenges us to stand up against powerful forces and also supports our efforts as truly worthwhile, if not authentically religious. In the next chapter, I turn to someone who in our own day exemplified that kind of religious authenticity as he heroically faced powerful forces that threatened to destroy him. Victor Frankl not only survived but formulated a way to look at the challenges of life and find meaning that in itself could be therapeutic. He faced what in its own way is comparable to the destruction of Jerusalem and Temple in 586 BCE. Pulling from his abilities as a scientist and his beliefs as a Jew, he argued for the primacy of finding meaning in life, even as he confronted the horrors of the Holocaust firsthand.

Chapter 3

Viktor Frankl and the Search for Meaning

The truth is that among those who actually went through the experience of Auschwitz, the number of those whose religious life was deepened—in spite of, not because of, this experience—by far exceeds the number of those who gave up their belief.

—Viktor Frankl, *Man's Search for Ultimate Meaning*

The finding that a sense of purpose in life was strongly associated with both resilient and recovered status is in line with the theories of existential writers such as Viktor Frankl, who first postulated that a sense of meaning and purpose influence how individuals cope with stress.

—T. N. Alim et al., "Trauma, Resilience, and Recovery"

But in the big sense ... what we all wanted was meaning.

—Sara Miles, *Jesus Freak*

Centuries after the destruction of Jerusalem in 586 BCE, another Jewish writer also faced a desperate situation and found meaning in it not only for himself but also for others. Psychiatrist Viktor Frankl (1905–1997) prefaced his theoretical works with his experiences as a prisoner in the Holocaust death camps of Auschwitz and Dachau. Because his theoretical work—developed some years before World War II—focused on the search for meaning in an individual's life, Frankl believed that his experience in the camps complemented, if not validated, his ideas. He emphasized that even if he had not survived, he would have lived in a way that searched for meaning. In fact, he faced death almost every day. Frankl seemed to be arguing for psychological survival as a way of maintaining our humanity and integrity in whatever circumstances we find ourselves.

As a young psychiatrist in Vienna, Frankl was familiar with Sigmund Freud's writings, but he later associated himself with one of Freud's breakaway disciples, Alfred Adler. Frankl eventually developed his own psychological approach, called *logotherapy*, which might be interpreted as therapy for meaning. He objected to other tactics that he believed undermined an individual's capacity to respond to the challenges of life. Although he used some techniques common to other therapeutic approaches, as well as some he developed before he was sent to the camps, he emphasized ideas often associated with philosophy and religion. He felt free to talk about the importance of conscience as a faculty for determining meaning and the power of love to help a person act in a way that achieves meaning. Psychiatric symptoms were not to be distinguished so much as explored for their opportunity for growth through self-transcendence. In that way, anxiety was not to be feared; rather, it was to be embraced as a signal to pursue meaning by actively facing the demands of one's life experience and overcoming any sense of victimhood through one's actions and attitudes. Unlike other theorists, Frankl was forced to test his own approach in the direst of circumstances—World War II concentration camps—and thereby became a credible witness to the theories and approaches he offers us.

Fortunately, Frankl lived another fifty years after his liberation from the camps. In addition to continuing his writings, he became the center of an international and multidisciplinary professional group that reflected on and supported his work, as well as tested it through experiments. Although logotherapy is perhaps not as influential now as when Frankl was alive, his work stands as an important contribution not only to the field of mental health but also to religion, as psychologist Ann Graber argued in *Viktor Frankl's Logotherapy.*

Frankl's ideas can help address the religious crisis that arises as new scientific evidence undermines the Jewish Scriptures' historicity. For believers and scientists alike, these discoveries demand a reevaluation of what the Jewish Scriptures were all about. Believers may see in this newer construction of Jewish history a different kind of miracle: religious sentiment provides the engine for survival and development. For scientists, the question is, more specifically, "What is this religious dimension all about?" Frankl's psychological theory addresses the latter question because it is built on an assumption that we are endowed with the capacity to make sense of our existence. Other psychological theories may emphasize the role of beliefs in human construction of reality or the use of interpretation as a way to become more reality-based. However, Frankl argues that meaning is the key to understanding human behavior and the primary motivational force for human beings.[1]

Frankl's thoughts and personal example can guide us if we fully embrace the possibility that the most powerful stories of the Jewish Scriptures—those involving Abraham, Moses, and Joshua—are best seen as fiction. How do we respond when there is no external evidence of the sojourn in Sinai or Joshua's rapid conquest of Palestine? How do we remain religious if some of the basic stories that tell of God's intervention in history have been mistakenly believed as historical? Frankl's writings encourage us to see these stories more as a subjective search for meaning than as an objective record of God's interventions. Using his approach as a way to develop another perspective, we can see the stories as a creative effort to find meaning in a desperate time in Jewish history. Frankl's theory not only offers a lens through which we can view others' heroic struggles, it also raises questions about the source that empowers that struggle.

Suffering and Meaning

The Jewish writers of the Persian period had to make sense of their predicament. Here, Frankl's work can also be helpful because he noted that one vehicle for finding meaning in life is suffering—although he was quick to point out that he was not arguing for suffering unnecessarily.[2] He also believed that if people can remove the source of their suffering, they should do so, but that suffering is part of life, and the challenge is to make it meaningful. Again, Frankl had excellent credentials to substantiate this discussion. He offers his own life experience as textual proof of his arguments; he points to the human capacity to respond to life's vicissitudes, no matter how dire. He described Freud's work as a will to pleasure and Adler's as a will to power, whereas his own work advocated for a will to meaning. For the Persian era biblical writers, finding meaning involved transcending their present state in a burst of religious thought and behavior that influences us even today.

The writers of Ezra and Nehemiah explained people's suffering as a consequence of their own sinning. Their view of history allowed them to see beyond the global politics of the times and instead focus on God, who transcended history and whom they had offended deeply. In fact, in the stories of Moses and Joshua the people had been warned that they would be punished if they ever disobeyed God's commandments. With their desolation reframed as punishment, the people were encouraged to make amends to God, who again assured them that the promises of greatness for them would be fulfilled. These amends became quite substantial: they involved the Jews separating themselves from foreigners, maintaining the commandments, following the prescribed rituals, and rebuilding Jerusalem and the temple. This new understanding of suffering allowed them to create their own empire, separate from the one that claimed them as subservient. Instead, they would be servants of God.

In the writings identified as Deutero-Isaiah, chapters 40–55 of the Book of Isaiah, the Jewish people are asked to see their suffering as a process of refinement, tested like silver in the fire (48:10) and now redeemed not with money but through God's graciousness (52:3). Behind their suffering is a consoling god who will restore their past greatness and make them the envy of all nations. However, that section of Isaiah, sometimes described as the Song of the Suffering Servant, is where the idea of suffering achieves an almost mystical quality. Although Christians see it as prefiguring Jesus's suffering, biblical scholars usually understand it as a description of the Jewish people, or perhaps someone who lived during their return from exile. The poetic passages suggest that in God's eyes, suffering is meaningful. In its most mystical moments, the poem describes the suffering servant as reborn and achieving some great status. The writer in the Persian period asked people to see behind the suffering and desperation of their condition and imagine a loving god who cared for them, appreciated their suffering, and would restore them to the greatness promised of old.

The Consolations of a Loving God

The introduction of a loving god can be another powerful vehicle for obtaining meaning. As Frankl would attest, the salvation of humanity and the discovery of meaning in life can be achieved by loving another.[3] In the death camps, he found that he was strengthened by and even found peace in contemplating his beloved. He also argued that in truly loving another person, we encounter that person as he or she really is. In such encounters, loved people are made aware of their potentialities and given the opportunity to actualize them. The Persian era Jews' writings and rituals made the love of God so palpable that they were motivated to keep alive the hope of achieving greatness, despite the crushing burdens of their existence. In Deutero-Isaiah and

Nehemiah, God's great and everlasting love is proclaimed regardless of the circumstances of the times. This new meaning challenged people to separate themselves from others and live lives of the highest integrity, sacrifice, and discipline, and also contained the promise that those people would populate God's kingdom on Earth. The history of the Jewish people in the Persian era is a testament to the transformative power of love.

Scientists may have experienced this power personally, but it is another matter to look at love scientifically. Psychiatrist George Vaillant has tried to do just that in his book *Spiritual Evolution*. He quotes both laboratory studies and his own longitudinal research to advocate for love's powerful and evolutionary value, and for the other positive emotions that are not studied scientifically. Vaillant maintains that a positive emotion like love is part of our evolutionary heritage and is a main contributor to what we understand as spirituality—and spirituality is critical to our own evolution as humans. He closes his book by suggesting that "having love for all people and compassion for all religious beliefs will reflect a cultural evolutionary advance."[4]

How does love transform? For both Frankl and the religious writers of the Persian era, conscience preceded love. Frankl saw conscience as a capacity to identify the choices that an individual faces in a particular challenge, as well as the natural consequences of such choices. Love was the capacity to implement those choices through actions that would generate meaning through self-transcendence. The religious leaders of the time seemed to follow this two-step process. First, they appealed to people's conscience—namely, the idea that the people had suffered because they had sinned. The second step was motivating moral behavior by emphasizing that, if these sinners repented, their merciful and loving god would forgive them and restore their status as the chosen people. The Jews' response was truly remarkable because it led to the writings, rituals, and practices that more or less identify religion in the Western world. Moreover, as archaeologist and biblical scholar William Dever has acknowledged, the ideas and practices stemming from this time of suffering led to the traditions and values that we hold most sacred in the Western cultural tradition. Dever makes the case that many values—such as the absolute worth of the individual, the rule of law, and belief in progress—can be attributed to the biblical tradition.[5]

Self-transcendence

Frankl insisted that true meaning is found, not primarily by withdrawing into an introspective investigation, but rather in an active encounter with life's circumstances, specifically: "(1) by creating work or doing a deed; (2) by experiencing something or by encountering someone; and (3) by the attitude we take towards unavoidable suffering."[6] Such sentiments run counter to a philosophy that emphasizes self-actualization through the development of one's interests and talents. Instead, Frankl held that self-actualization is a by-product of the search for meaning. He challenged us to be other-directed at a time when self-interest and inner direction hold sway. He urged us to be heroic in an atmosphere of fear. His writings are peppered with brief hagiographies of secular saints who found meaning on death row, started an ambitious project while suffering from a terminal illness, or developed an attitude-changing insight during the final months of their lives.

Behind all this prodding and challenging was the man himself. Frankl was such a promising psychiatrist that both Freud and Adler invited him to write articles in their respective journals, even though those publications upheld differing views of psychoanalytic theory. Yet in both his life and his work, Frankl demonstrated how concern for others was the bedrock of his theory. In 1941, he refused to pick up his visa at an embassy in Vienna—even though his decision meant certain arrest—because doing so would mean leaving his parents behind in Austria. He survived almost three years in the concentration camps, and then returned to his work with such vigor that he earned a doctorate in philosophy just a few years after he was liberated. For the next fifty years, as the founder and voice of the logotherapy movement, he wrote some thirty-two books, published in twenty-nine languages—one of which, *Man's Search for Meaning,* was rated in 1991 as one of the ten most influential books in the United States by the Library of Congress. His work was recognized with numerous awards and honors from all over the world. Frankl is admirable not only for his intellectual prowess, but also for the moral integrity that he exemplified in his life and argued for in his writings.

Frankl and Religion

Frankl saw himself and his followers as engaged in an ongoing dialogue with religion. He held that part of the unconscious was spiritual, and that this spiritual core was the inspirational source "for our artistic inspiration, our religious faith, our beliefs, and our intuitions."[7] Yet his understanding of religion was broad enough to include atheism and agnosticism because he saw religion as a human phenomenon—namely, the search for meaning that springs from the spiritual unconscious that is present in all people. He saw his theories validated when psychometric instruments were developed that could test the importance of the search for meaning. Although an individual's belief in life's meaningfulness was highly correlated with positive outcomes and negatively correlated with the fear of death, that correlation was not dependent on whether the person was religious.[8]

Independent of organized religion, Frankl perceived a spiritual dimension—the search for meaning—as a basic component of human existence. Although he believed in some absolute truth, he also noted that our finiteness as humans prevents us from grasping it. So, although he thought that religious sentiment could be developed and articulated in various ways, he was critical of the denominational in-fighting and competing claims for truth among the various religions. Perhaps more important, Frankl maintained that the search for meaning is, by definition, an individual one—each person must confront life's demands on his or her own and create meaning in the process. Religion can be described as a search for ultimate meaning, but Frankl believed that ultimate meaning is beyond the scope of the individual mind. However, he seemed to leave open the possibility of a life beyond this one. In his efforts to understand the meaning of suffering, he entertained the idea that another dimension existed, in which "the question of an ultimate meaning of human suffering would find an answer."[9]

At this point in the conversation, the scientist is likely to part ways with the psychiatrist. Frankl seems to be proselytizing for an innate capacity that points to a transcendent source because it can be found within all of us. While he is not backing a particular religion, he is advocating for those activities, such as altruism and meaning-making, that are inherent in religion. He is supporting, if you will, the idea of a religious dimension that can be experienced and expressed in a variety of forms and that ultimately takes form as an individual creation developed in response to the challenges of one's life.

Although scientists may balk at Frankl's invitation to observe the religious impulse as something to be explored and followed, they may find the psychiatrist's critique of religious dogmatism refreshing. In particular, the open-endedness and antidogmatism inherent in Frankl's view of religion can be starting points in critiquing one aspect of the Jewish belief system that developed during the Persian era.

Meaning-Making Can Be Dangerous

Frankl's skepticism of religious dogma tempered his profound respect for religion. His approach represents a middle ground that both accepts and criticizes religion. Similarly, we might find the powerful and inspirational writings of the Persian period awe-inspiring and truly appreciate the writers' creative capacity to find meaning in the midst of profound suffering. At the same time, we can investigate particular dogmas and positions that are the end products of such a process. Because finding meaning often involves putting aside some information and privileging other information, a particular conclusion or point can always be suspect. Even more important is how helpful or how dangerous the meanings resulting from this search are.

One problematic meaning-making effort has to do with the status of Jerusalem, the supposed heart of God's coming kingdom. Modern scholarship has both questioned Jerusalem's historical accuracy as the center of a united kingdom and undermined Jewish claims to that city. Finkelstein and Silberman argue persuasively that David was a legendary tribal chief,[10] and that Jerusalem was the center of a small city-state inhabited by various tribes. Present-day Israel has chosen to ignore the reality-based, 10,000-year-old history of Jerusalem and has instead focused on a biblical tradition that identifies the city as belonging rightfully and exclusively to the Jews. The reality is that Jerusalem was inhabited some 2,000 years before David's supposed conquest, and for almost the same amount of time by other peoples after Jews were forbidden to enter the city following the Bar Kochba revolt in 135 BCE. Still, Jerusalem invokes such religious fervor that the biblical story will likely win out over the more scientific explanation. Yet that creation of a mythical past has tragic implications for present-day Israel, in addition to persistently confounding the peace process in the Middle East. Biblical scholar Keith Whitelam pinpoints that connection between past and present: "The loss of an indigenous Canaanite or Jebusite voice in the past is paralleled by the loss of the indigenous Palestinian voice in the present."[11]

Meaning making can conceivably be a harmful process. When adaptation is used to hide the truth or harm others, the process is self-serving and not self-transcending. When someone adopts another's religious views without doing the hard work of integrating and claiming those views, the views' religious meaning will likely have little permanent value. In addition, people who construct their meaning-making efforts by closing themselves off to important and available information will also suffer consequences. Holding on to religious views based on supposedly historical data can undermine religion itself. The middle position is to sustain the traditional values and insights that have been so meaningful to our Western culture and simultaneously take in information that relativizes those traditions. Frankl's work suggests that we become anxious as we approach such a venerable religious system. However, he would also have encouraged us to face and even embrace that anxiety, as opposed to giving in to it, avoiding it altogether, or settling on a solution that creates even more problems.

Search for Meaning/Journey of Faith

Frankl has suggested that we are not so much engaged in a search for meaning as we are challenged to find it in the situations that confront us. He thinks that in responding to challenges, we become aware of our own spirituality, our capacity for self-transcendence, and the opportunity to find ultimate meaning in life. The new information that undercuts the historicity of our favorite Bible stories presents us with a similar demand. We are free to ignore this particular demand and remain in a comfort zone that dismisses either religion or the new information. What can motivate us to action is a belief in our own capacity to find meaning despite the confusion and uncertainty that normally accompany a time of change. We can also find encouragement in the idea that we are trying to pass on to future generations a powerful tradition now free from its historically determined circumstances. As we step back from such a process, our efforts seem somewhat similar to the powerful religious transformation that occurred in Yehud.

How we respond to the demand is an individual choice, one that cannot be assigned to us from on high. However, some data suggest that Americans are moving away from a more dogmatic and denominational position and toward one emphasizing responsibility and right behavior.[12] In such a context, organized religion also faces a demand that challenges it to respond creatively—not only to the new information in recent Scripture studies but also to the new information that people's idea of religion is itself changing. Further, this demand challenges organized religion to move away from a content-heavy message and create instead an environment that values the process inherent in an individual's search for meaning. That environment could do no better than to begin with Frankl's idea that at our core, we are all spiritual beings who are capable of self-transcendence in our responses to the demands of our everyday lives.

Frankl and the Scientist

Frankl would have defended his fellow scientists' right to be independent, even their right to say no to God. Yet he was also convinced that science needed to evaluate and therefore transcend itself and see the consequences of its activity. This need has become more apparent today as we struggle with specific moral issues, such as abortion, stem cell research, and capital punishment. Additionally, Frankl argued for humanity's need to accomplish tasks as a community, a need that is also more obvious today in global issues such as climate change. Yet he believed that such a common effort would be possible only if people were "united by a common will to a common meaning—in other words, by an awareness of common tasks."[13] Although Frankl considered himself a scientist, he would have asserted that science itself is not in a privileged position to comment on the existence of ultimate meaning. Instead, he would have urged scientists to understand the importance of moving beyond science to entertain the richness of meaning making. Indeed, quoting Wittgenstein, Frankl noted that to believe in God is to see that life has meaning—and he encouraged scientists to embark on a religious journey.

That the therapeutic effort Frankl outlined overlaps with a faith journey is no coincidence. He was not afraid to explore a spiritual dimension in his work, and spiritual directors continue to use his approach in their pastoral ministries. In addition, Frankl's own character and life history may have enhanced his work's appeal. His experience in the concentration camps inspired him to speak out against what he saw as postwar materialism and what he described as the idolatry of science. He continued the prophetic tradition, challenging us to see as harmful what we may unthinkingly accept without question. His work also contained a powerful moral dimension: he taught us that the search for meaning requires difficult choices and self-discipline; it is an ongoing process that continues until the moment we die. Evolution is not just about whether we have common ancestry with the ape. It is about our personal evolution, as recorded in our own spiritual journey.

Frankl's life and work attest to the human need to find meaning, even in the midst of dire circumstances. He reminded us that our psychological and spiritual survival are threatened, as well as challenged, in these difficult moments. He asked us to look not outside ourselves for help but deeper inside ourselves to find the creative power that enables us to make sense of our surroundings. Frankl translates the Greek word *logos* as "meaning." Implicitly, he may be offering us another credo:

> In the beginning was meaning.
> And meaning was with God.
> And meaning was God.

Part II

The Christian Journey to Faith

Christianity's founder and hero is Jesus Christ. However, that name summarizes the mystery at the heart of the religion: Jesus, the object of historical research, and Christ, the object of belief. Modern scholarship's tendency to explore the humanity of Jesus creates significant tension with those who believe in the Christ of faith. Yet that tension can be productive and even creative because it mirrors the pulls of opposite values that we are challenged to manage in our own human journey—individuality and community, for example.

A similar tension is to be found in the story of Christianity's origin in the first and second centuries. Modern scholarship has reconstructed the arduous growth and polymorphous shape of a movement that painfully emerged from its Jewish roots and then went on to clash with the larger Gentile world. Yet this more scientifically based construction is in conflict with a more idealistic narrative that claims uniformity over diversity and divine power over fallible human effort. Although such tension is never resolved, a more realistically based appreciation of early Christianity's painful evolution can not only be inspiring but also can protect us against those who would build their own truth claims on inaccurate history.

The impressive development of Christianity into both local and worldwide communities can inspire us to find a real connection with others who are likewise on a journey of faith. Community and individuality are opposing values, but we have evolved by finding ways to develop and preserve both, even though some tension remains. It may not be easy, but we can, like President Barack Obama, find a community that uses that tension creatively and in a way that gives meaning to our own deep-seated needs for both individuality and community.

Chapter 4

The Jesus of History and the Christ of Faith
Dissonance and Dialectics

Interest in the "historical Jesus" has continued
unabated since the Enlightenment. Each year new
books and magazine articles appear, the media offer
new programs, and since the 1970s, college courses
on the topic have been overflowing in enrollment.
No single picture of Jesus has convinced all, or even
most, scholars; all methods and their combinations
find their critics as well as their advocates.

—Amy-Jill Levine, *The Historical Jesus in Context*

For me, therefore, a Christianity or kerygma minus
the historical Jesus of Nazareth is ultimately vacu-
ous—not Christianity at all, in fact.

—Edward Schillebeeckx, *Jesus: An Experiment in Christology*

Dutch theologian Edward Schillebeeckx published his 700-page book *Jesus* in 1979, followed the next year by his 900-page book *Christ*. His
work graphically demonstrates that Jesus is not the same
as Christ. Rather, two identities have been merged into the
familiar compound, Jesus Christ. The first part of that name
refers to a historical individual reconstructed by scholars,
although the reconstructions continue to be debated and
overall consensus remains unlikely. In this chapter, I rely
on the reconstructions of scholars such as Raymond Brown
and John Meier, who attempt to reach a middle ground
in the debate. Nevertheless, the various portraits of Jesus
focus on the likely words and deeds of a pious Jew living

in an occupied country and bringing his own faith to bear in an attempt to find meaning in such a difficult situation. *Christ* comes from the Greek meaning "anointed one," which in turn comes from the Hebrew term we know as *messiah*. The term *Christ* has expanded beyond its Hebrew roots and has come to mean not just a special agent sent by God for a particular purpose but the source and object of faith—a portrait drawn by believers. We are faced with two dialectically opposed concepts: a man of faith and an object of faith, a human being and a divine being. Explaining how these two concepts can be joined into a new entity has preoccupied thinkers for centuries, writes theologian John Hick, but these theoretical explanations (e.g., one person, two natures) are increasingly seen as inadequate.[1]

Why bother with the challenging work of distinguishing Jesus from Christ? One reason is that without some understanding of the historical Jesus, *Christ* can be an ambiguous concept. Christianity, the religion that bears that name, can be filled by a variety of interpretations, which can be self-serving or even destructive. Preachers routinely tell us what Jesus wants us to do or make claims that Jesus has called them to a particular work or mission and ask for our support in Jesus' name. In the United States, Jesus and Christianity are so much a part of our culture and national discourse that Americans are especially vulnerable to individuals or groups who would claim Jesus as their figurehead, declaring their own political vision as inspired by him. Such a vision can become destructive, as pointed out by investigative reporter Jeff Charlotte in his book *The Family: The Secret Fundamentalism at the Heart of American Power*. He argues that an idealized view of first-century Christianity has been used as a cover to justify policies that have harmed others and a moral philosophy that allows its elite to justify its own unethical conduct.

For the skeptical believer, understanding the historical Jesus and his relationship to the Christ of faith is more than self-protection. It is a mark of intellectual honesty: religious claims, including our own, are to be investigated even if they leave us with a certain tension and ambiguity. Working through such tension is part of the spiritual journey. More than that, the human journey is one that progresses dialectically as we struggle with opposing values: authority or independence, individuality or community, self-care or altruism. To some extent, we struggle to keep our dreams alive while we face the realities and surprises of everyday life, working to avoid the pit of cynicism or the escape into denial.

The historical Jesus would have had a similar struggle because he was attempting to keep alive the dream of a just and merciful god even as he lived in a world marked by injustice and even oppression. If faith, to use the definition offered by scholar Dominic Crossan, is a "theologically-based interpretation of history's meaning,"[2] Jesus sustained that faith by immersing himself in his own Jewish traditions and practices. In commenting on the Gospel of Luke, scholar Raymond Brown notes that the gospel begins and ends with the temple. Brown interprets Luke's beginning and ending in this fashion as a way of stating that Jesus lived his whole life within the confines of Judaism.[3] Jesus was a Jew who preached in synagogues, worshiped at temple, argued about dietary laws, and was considered a rabbi by some.

He also exhibited characteristics of many Jews of his time who were concerned about the dramatic disconnect between God's grand promises to the Jews and their desperate, seemingly hopeless condition in Palestine. Although the gospels downplay his relationship to John the Baptist, Jesus was one of his followers. And John the Baptist was an apocalyptic prophet—that is, someone who is so concerned about the state of the world that he believes and preaches that it is about to end in some dramatic and traumatic fashion. John's baptism ritual was meant to be a preparation and identity marker to help faithful believers in those last, most difficult days. Although Jesus may have softened John's

message somewhat, he seems to have been imagining that
God's kingdom was arriving in the very near future; in fact,
he may have claimed that the kingdom of God was beginning to break into the present. His emphasis, therefore, was
less on the ending of this world and more on a new beginning that marked the fulfillment of God's promises.

Like other religious leaders of his time, Jesus offered a
solution to the religious-political-economic crisis in those
turbulent years in Palestine before the Jewish revolt that
began in 66 CE. Less than a hundred years before the time
of Jesus, it seemed as though the promises God made the
Jewish people were about to be fulfilled. They had their
own kingdom and some autonomy under the Hasmonean
dynasty (142–63 BCE) whose members were descendants of
the Maccabees, the family that led the ultimately successful revolts against their Hellenistic rulers. However, when
the Romans conquered this modest kingdom in 63 BCE,
things began to change. For a while the brilliant and ruth-
less Herod the Great offered them some measure of autonomy and national pride, especially by rebuilding the temple.
Yet even before Herod's time, pious Jews were struggling
with this apparent failure of God to establish a kingdom in
Israel. Where was their god? What could they do to hasten
God's coming?

Different groups had different answers, different theologically based interpretations to history's meaning. To
oversimplify a bit, the Sadducees and the members of the
Jerusalem elite believed that this was as good as it could
get, so they focused on temple worship and tried to create space in this world for God's presence. The Pharisees
hoped to spread their particular religious practices throughout Palestine, believing that God would establish the kingdom if all the Promised Land were inhabited by believing
Jews following the correct way to uphold the faith. The
Essenes, whom we now know more about since the discov-

ery of the Dead Sea Scrolls, believed that most other Jews were wrong and, along with the Gentiles, would be condemned when God came. They alone were the true chosen people who would purify themselves to such a point that God would recognize their achievement and intervene. After Herod's death, revolutionary groups developed in the hope that they could achieve God's kingdom by force and that God would be with them as they fought to regain their ancestral home. These positions, of course, intersected and varied within themselves, but they all began with the belief that God would intervene to establish a kingdom among God's chosen people. Their programs were solutions to the terrible dilemma created when the facts on the ground conflicted with the promises from Heaven. These promises were kept alive in the sacred readings the Jews heard at festivals and in synagogues or were referenced in the words of preachers, teachers, and prophets such as John the Baptist. While all this religious activity heightened the dissonance, it also offered the raw material from which Jesus offered his own solution.

Jesus preached that his teachings and actions, especially exorcisms and healings, were signs that God's promises were beginning to come true. He likely chose twelve special followers to be the rulers when this new kingdom came into being, echoing the story of the twelve tribes who supposedly formed the original kingdom of Israel. Some scholars argue that Jesus taught them a prayer that called on God to establish God's kingdom on Earth as it was in Heaven—not because of people's piety but because of God's own power. Although Jesus knew the rules, followed the traditions, and celebrated the feasts, he also believed that the religious establishment was increasingly unnecessary. As biblical scholar John Meier summarizes, "Jesus the eschatological prophet was acting out the role of the eschatological Elijah, even as he both proclaimed the imminent coming of God's rule and made that rule a reality even now by his miracles."[4]

The Jesus of history was a Jewish prophet whose faith in God was so powerful that he developed a solution to the religious crisis of his times and offered his fellow Jews hope that God would remain faithful to them. He believed that his own life and ministry were powerful signs that God had not abandoned the people, but was still vitally connected to them. His specific actions, such as exorcisms and meals open to all, were meant to help others believe what he did: that God's kingdom was breaking into this world. Many of his followers saw his utter faith as a practice to emulate. Even at the end of his life, when his solution seemed flawed and his program a failure—even when his followers were abandoning him—Jesus did not surrender his faith, and he still believed that God would welcome him into the kingdom.[5] If, as Meier argues, Jesus realized he was wrong about the imminent coming of the kingdom but still retained his trust in God, we have another powerful example of the extraordinary faith of Jesus.

This brief portrait of Jesus emphasizes something about him that we tend to forget: he was a man of great faith. Although there will always be a dispute about his understanding of himself—what did he know and when did he know it—Jesus was so convinced of God's merciful love that he proclaimed it through his words and actions, even when he experienced failure and was sentenced to death. Such hard-core faith can be uncomfortable to emulate. In our efforts to create a more palatable Jesus, we make him into a proto-feminist, early ecologist, or would-have-been-protester against nuclear weapons. Likewise, asking "what would Jesus do?" also takes us away from the historical Jesus. Arguing against such approaches, Raymond Brown protests that Jesus was a first-century Jew who had no idea or frame of reference for addressing modern problems.[6] But the most common way we soften Jesus' raw and unyielding faith is by mixing up and blending the Jesus of history with the Christ of faith.

Separating the Jesus of History from the Christ of Faith

Scholars construct the Jesus of history, a man of a particular age, and theologians tend to describe the Christ of faith, an icon for all the ages. Actually, the term *Christ*, or *messiah*, preceded *Jesus*: it was a title that had been developed in the Hebrew Bible and that had gained more popularity in Jesus' time. We find the term used in the Dead Sea Scrolls and other writings such as 1 Enoch, a favorite book of the Essenes and one that was quoted from in the next to last book of the New Testament, the Epistle of Jude. Over time that term was expanded by both Jewish and Christian writers, although their respective religions ultimately defined the term in dramatically different ways.[7] Despite the claims made in the gospels, it is unlikely that Jesus thought of himself as the messiah, but rather more of a prophet, as noted in Meier above. However, in Christian circles, that title moved beyond its Jewish roots to become the faith-inspired portrait of someone who was not only God's anointed or chosen one but was himself God come to Earth to save humankind through his passion, death, and resurrection.

As messiah changed to Christ, the term lost its Jewish moorings and instead became more defined by the Greco-Roman culture. Several scholars have pointed out similarities between the evolving understanding of Christ and the existing myths of heroes and gods in that Gentile world. Equally important is that the term clearly evolved. Earlier philosophers, such as Justin Martyr in the second century, held that Christ was subordinate to God but created in God's likeness. Justin and many of the early Christian philosophers used the philosophy of Plato to explain the identity of Jesus Christ. That idea of subordination to God was kept alive even until the fourth century by the influential priest Arius and his followers, as well as versions of Christianity that flourished for several centuries in what was the eastern part of the Roman Empire.[8] In the ecumenical councils of the fourth and fifth centuries, the doctrine of the Trinity enabled Christ to be identified with God, along with the Holy Spirit. Such a formula ensured that the historical Jesus quietly disappeared, to be replaced by Christ, the revelation of God that could be made relevant for people of every time and place.

Although he still might be called Jesus, he became a multifaceted icon that through the centuries could be soldier or pacifist, teacher or poet, powerful ruler or servant to the needy.[9] The historical Jesus has not only been overwhelmed by the theologically inspired Christ, but for all practical purposes has been replaced by a culturally driven image. This replacement has been nowhere more evident than in the United States. Recently, historian Richard Fox[10] and religious studies professor Stephen Prothero[11] wrote books describing how a culturally based Jesus evolved in response to the needs and interests of particular times, beginning in prerevolutionary days and extending to a modern Jesus portrayed as a celebrity in plays and movies. In that sense, we have a Jesus filled with the projections of particular times and circumstances in our evolution as a country. We are left with a very attractive, relevant, and available Jesus, but one who bears little resemblance to the Jesus of history. However, for many believers, the cultural Jesus may be similar to the Christ of faith in the sense that we use our culture and present circumstances as the context for understanding the alternative universe that we associate with the divine and to whom we pray for inspiration and guidance.

The real problem in separating the Jesus of history from the Christ of faith is how to make the former relevant or even appealing to us. In many ways the reconstructed Jesus is not that attractive. He is quite conservative in his morality, demanding in his requirements for discipleship, and wrong in his signature belief that the kingdom of God was breaking into this world. However, if we push through the powerful Christ of faith to the vulnerable Jesus of history, we find a story that can be just as inspiring. To do so means to let go of a familiar story that may have served us well and to begin investigating a somewhat different one. In this new story, Jesus is important, but not because he founded a new religion. In fact the assumption that he began a movement we now know as Christianity is arguably untenable from a scientific perspective.[12] Jesus is significant because his tremendous faith offers us the opportunity to appreciate what the process of faith is all about. However, if we are to appreciate his faith journey, we must take away or at least bracket the notion that he was God and therefore had no need of faith. That is difficult to do because we have been conditioned by religious education, stories in the New Testament, and even culture to see Jesus as supernatural, as God. So before looking at Jesus' own journey of faith, we try to free him from his identity as Christ, the object of faith.

A sermon is not a lecture, and therefore a preacher might be excused for not distinguishing between the Jesus of history and the Christ of faith. It is understandable that the average parishioner will also confound the two portraits and come to believe that the historical Jesus actually said or did things that modern scholarship would attribute to the believers who followed him and who retrojected such actions into his lifetime. A case in point would be the scholarship of John Meier, who reviews the miracles of Jesus and identifies many of our favorite stories as coming from the post-resurrection experiences of the disciples, rather than incidents that can reliably be traced to the lifetime of the historical Jesus.[13] Likewise, Raymond Brown observed that modern writers occasionally confuse the Jesus of history with the Christ of faith and attribute to the historical Jesus activities, such as founding a church, that are actually faith-based conclusions.[14] Although sermons and Sunday school maintain the confusion between history and faith, church teachings reinforce the confusion at a more fundamental level. For example, despite the work of such Catholic biblical scholars as Meier and Brown, the catechism of the Catholic Church fails to distinguish between the historical world reconstructed by scholars and more symbolic one developed over time by the followers of Jesus. Anyone looking up "Jesus" in the catechism's index will find the words, "*See Christ.*"

To sort out the confusion, we need to do our homework. That means entering into the ongoing discussion about the historical Jesus and the history of the early church. In his book on the crisis in the American Catholic church, Peter Steinfels argues for the importance of educating ourselves in the faith. He calls for a spirituality of lifelong religious learning, much like the Jewish tradition of Torah study, "as the birthright and obligation of all who can pursue it."[15] If we turn to the portrait of Jesus as carefully drawn by middle-of-the-road scholars like Meier and Brown, we find someone who was deeply immersed in his religion and lived it in his daily life. As suggested, Jesus faced a crisis. In facing it, he entered a process of discernment, a journey that attempted to reconcile his deep faith in God's promises and the reality of living in an occupied country. What follows is a construction of what his faith process might have looked like and how we might apply it to ourselves.

Jesus' Faith Journey and Ours

Value the faith

Jesus was quite passionate about his faith. It was the source of his prayer life and guide for his devotion and action. Like others who had opinions about correct religious behavior, he argued, sometimes heatedly, when he engaged with those who disagreed with him. In some instances he appeared more conservative, for example regarding divorce, while in other disputes he was more liberal, for example regarding what was allowable on the Sabbath. A closer look at these arguments shows that Jesus had his own understanding of correct conduct based on his role as a charismatic prophet who was announcing the coming kingdom of God. Along with his lifestyle, he was outlining the right way to live in this world that brought one closer to God and closer to one another.

We can begin our own faith journey by being grateful, for example, for how many have fought and struggled for that belief system we understand as Christianity. We can also respect those who have been helped by this belief system to live more loving and responsible lives. We revere those whose belief has been a source of wisdom that supports and guides generations. How can we forget those impassioned few who suffered great hardships to leave behind a world that was safer and more just? At a level that is difficult to calibrate, Christian faith has entered into our culture, and it silently influences the way we think and act.

Face the conflict

Like his fellow Jews, Jesus was challenged to reconcile his faith in a merciful god who promised freedom with his experience of living in an occupied country. He would have empathized with the anxiety and confusion demonstrated by his fellow believers as they desperately sought to reconcile faith and fact. To make matters worse, any religious program that was seen as threatening to civil authority was likely to be suppressed, something Jesus would have witnessed with the imprisonment and execution of his mentor, John the Baptist. He faced the conflict with a passionate faith that gave him the courage to act and the confidence to insist that their god was with them, even in this time of uncertainty.

When we began to appreciate the differing portraits of Jesus, we are thrown into our own crisis of faith. How do we reconcile this new information with the traditional belief system we have inherited and held on to for such a long time? What do we do with the information? Where do we go with our belief system? The conflict arises when one has both a strong belief system and an accumulation of information about the historical Jesus that challenges that system. Those with little faith will see the new information as confirming what they always suspected: Jesus was only a man and therefore marginally important, if that. Those who refuse to engage the new information or do not search for it are likely to remain in their traditional belief system, at risk of being stunted in their faith development. The third possibility is to proceed somewhat on your own, much as Jesus did: faith means working out your own path.

Take responsibility for change

Jesus offered his own faith-inspired solution to the serious conflict he experienced. While he stayed within the Jewish religion, he argued that moral behavior took priority over the important but complicated rules about ritual purity that served as identity markers for the Jewish people.[16] While he called for moral behavior to reach the highest level, he also declared that sinners should be forgiven, not seven times, but seventy-seven times. He lived out his belief in a merciful god by dining with outcasts and making concern for the poor a cornerstone of his ethics.

It is unlikely that the scholars will suddenly agree on any consistent and coherent portrait of the historical Jesus. All these portraits have elements of interpretation, and often betray the belief systems of the portrait artists themselves, a phenomenon that is likely unavoidable. On the other hand, official church authority is not always helpful when an individual attempts to resolve conflicting pulls between the

Jesus of history and the Christ of faith. There is a natural reluctance to examine new information that is more scientific than theological. As in Jesus' own time, religious authorities are compromised and conflicted. Any impetus for addressing the tension between the Jesus of history and the Christ of faith is more likely to come from an individual's study than from an organization's pronouncement.

Toward a more global solution

It is difficult to argue that Jesus came to preach to everyone. On the one hand, he did emphasize the more inclusive elements of his own religion, as for example in contrast to the more exclusive position taken by the Essenes. Also, following the prophetic tradition, he urged his fellow believers to return to the most basic articles of their religion, namely, a trust in a merciful god and a commitment to justice, especially for the poor and marginalized. While the prophetic tradition also seemed to have room for Gentiles in God's kingdom, Jesus did not appear to offer a global message to Jew and Gentile alike. "The weight of evidence remains clear: that Jesus, during his mission, did not encourage his disciples to think of any missionary outreach beyond Israel."[17]

Jesus is pictured as open and forgiving to others, but his ideology as a Jewish reformer impinged on and thereby limited his vision when it came to Gentiles. If we closely examine the faith of Jesus, we learn that any faith-inspired vision can be limited by historical circumstances, the power of culture, and the finiteness of being human. The intensity of faith, rather than freeing us from error, may blind us to its existence. We all struggle to free ourselves from perspectives that once guided us but now may be limiting and harmful. Yet these very limitations support the view of faith as a process that can undergo change as it is informed by challenges from other valid viewpoints, as well as from significant life experiences. Additionally, the study required to understand the Jesus of history can lead one to question and doubt: it can in itself be another catalyst in one's faith journey.

Scholars and the Faith Journey

Scholars who have reconstructed the historical Jesus sometimes give their reflections on the impact such study has had on their own faith journeys. In a volume edited by Charles Hedrick, thirteen religious scholars offer differing descriptions of how their scholarly investigations influenced their spiritual development.[18] Generally, their stories describe journeys that took them away from a more conforming and exclusive perspective to one that embraces what is worthwhile in other beliefs and practices. Additionally, they speak of a personal transformation, as though their investment in the work was never purely academic. The search for the historical Jesus was also a transforming search for the divine within themselves. And in their journeys they became especially sensitized to the marginalized, those so often outcast and shunned by our society. It is as though the study of the historical Jesus brought them in contact with the more numinous Christ of faith. Two other scholars, Luke Johnson and Elaine Pagels, tell similar stories.

Catholic theologian and biblical scholar Luke Johnson imagines a faith journey that identifies structured beliefs as more of a starting then an ending point. In *The Creed*, he argues for a return to the creed as a more basic form of Christian identity, almost like a new baseline from which faith can be renewed. He argues that the official church has gone beyond the creed and claimed too much. Yet he is proposing more than a simple return to an earlier age. He takes the position that the creed constructs a mythical worldview that, as such, cannot claim higher validity over the worldviews of others. His emphasis on religion as a mythical world, and his heated criticism of religion's misuse of its authority challenges us to think independently. He closes his book with a strong hint that believing is an ongoing dialectical process. In his understanding, a Christian is one "who knows the difference between the nonessential and the essential, who is free to think and imagine boldly within the strong and flexible framework of faith, and who is open to wisdom from any source, confident that wherever there is truth, it is from God."[19] He argues that intellectual honesty is a hallmark of the faith journey.

Elaine Pagels found a deep connection with a Christian community, even though her own faith journey was not identical to those of the other members. In the opening pages of *Beyond Belief,* Pagels describes a crisis of faith occasioned by the severe illness of her young child. Although she had not participated in organized religion for some time, she was attracted to a particular church community somewhat by accident. What attracted to her to the congregation was the experience of a community of supportive and helpful individuals who were undergoing their own struggles and searches. In that experience, professions of faith seemed superfluous, if not irrelevant, to the community that gathered there.

Pagels, a professor of religion at Princeton University, wonders about the Christianity that existed and defied persecution before there were creeds. At the end of her book, she argues for the need to make choices about the larger Christian tradition. She writes, "Most of us, sooner or later, find that, at critical points in our lives, we must strike out on our own to make a path where none exists."[20] She is describing a process, both religious and psychological, in which an individual in a community setting and with regard to the values of that tradition nevertheless embarks on a unique spiritual journey.

These scholars remind us that we are challenged to take a broader perspective than the historical Jesus did. We are encouraged to see one's religious view in relation to other faiths and other searches for meaning. Doing so means working to achieve a deep respect for others, their ideas, and their own searches for truth. Yet such a perspective introduces tension and ambiguity in the journey of faith. And what motivation can there be to stay with an elusive process marred by doubt rather than to settle on a definitive position that promises security? The short answer is that we are human beings. The struggle to reconcile opposing values may be an important characteristic in our own development as individuals—an evolutionary challenge, if you will.

A Closer Look at the Journey of Faith

Whether we are believers or seekers, we are hardwired to pursue an evolving, conflicted spiritual journey. For believers, theologian James Fowler offers a progressive, six-stage theory of "faith-knowing" that builds on psychological theories of human development and constructs a religious dimension to human growth that can evolve from earlier, more primitive stages to one that is more comprehensive and inclusive. Both formed and limited by one's developmental stage, religious concepts evolve from the child through the adolescent and finally to the adult. Yet even religious adults remain conflicted as they try to balance the differing pulls in their lives. Fowler leaves developmental psychology and invokes grace as a catalyst for a seventh stage. The few who reach this level seem to transcend conflict and embrace both God and others in a wholehearted manner. [21] Seekers might appreciate how psychologist Michael Basseches has modified Fowler's theory to emphasize more of an evolution of human values, rather than traditionally religious ones. Both emphasize the increasing challenges involved as individuals search for meaning in their lives. They would also hold that spiritual maturity can only be reached after one has gone through successive stages in which one works through more limited and conformist views so as to embrace the value in other positions without surrendering value of one's own. However, this more global solution does not automatically come with age. Just as a college provides a supportive environment in which students grow intellectually by engaging with different ideas, someone on a faith journey could benefit from a community that offers a similar support for engaging new information that challenges beliefs.

In both of their works, these scholars emphasize that growth—psychological or spiritual—comes from the struggle to work through the tension caused by opposite pulls. For example there is a pull toward individualism and an opposing pull toward community. If a person is too individualistic, a connection to community can be lost, but if one is too identified with community, individual identity can be swallowed up in an unthinking allegiance to the larger group's beliefs and attitudes. If a scientific community influences the work of a scientist by fostering allegiance to a particular paradigm, as historian of science Thomas Kuhn would argue, how much more will a religion, political party, or nation influence the beliefs and attitudes of their members?

Like Fowler, psychologist Michael Basseches argues that this struggle between individual and community values is played out on a more global scale at higher stages of development. He describes as fundamental to the human process a "collective pursuit of shared human values."[22] He argues for a pursuit of truth as a "collective good that transcends the individual,"[23] and he envisions a process of dialectical thought that becomes more complex as an individual develops a more comprehensive way of managing conflicting positions while simultaneously holding on to basic human values.

Yet if the process has a global dimension, it must also involve interacting with others. Basseches's work can be helpful to anyone who is trying to sustain some valuable truth and not fall into mere relativism, but at the same time engage in conversations with people and ideas that represent viewpoints different from or even contradictory to one's own. In fact, precisely by engaging in a dialogue with such differing positions, we grow intellectually and spiritually, developing a more complicated and inclusive way of understanding.

Yet Basseches points out that such a process can overwhelm people and lead to a backward movement, or at least a kind of paralysis in which one refuses to accept the challenge of new information. He states that what is needed for progress is an "optimal mismatch" that challenges but does not overwhelm. "An environment which offers optimal mismatch, combined with general supportive features, which promise to socially affirm the integrity of individuals while they bear the risks of putting aside ways of looking at things that they have previously relied upon in order to build others, is likely to provoke development."[24] We can readily imagine a family or a school that provides the supportive context that allows a person to develop. Sadly, we can also imagine a community or environment that stifles such development. Basseches argues that psychotherapy can address such stunted development by providing a safe place in which an individual can effectively address the conflicts that have limited psychological growth.[25]

The Dialectical Process as Therapeutic

Building on the work of Basseches and others, psychologist Marcia Linehan has developed a particular approach to clinical problems, which she calls dialectical behavioral therapy.[26] She recounts a particular dilemma in which a therapist is working with a suicidal patient who begins to describe growing distress from suicidal thinking. The therapist, concerned about the patient's safety, may push for more intensive care. The patient, who is struggling to become more autonomous, resents the therapist's intrusion and resists seeking more care. A quandary emerges, in which the therapist's goal of protecting the patient is in conflict with the patient's goal of remaining autonomous. A power struggle can develop, which might lead to the patient's hospitalization or attempted suicide. Linehan suggests that what is critical in such a situation is the introduction of dialectical thinking. The patient, and obviously the therapist, would come to appreciate that the goals contradict each other, but that neither is absolutely true. The way is then open to negotiate for a common goal that respects the legitimacy of both positions and attempts to find compromises. Translating Basseches's work into the therapy situation, Linehan suggests that a new synthesis can be developed, one in which these two goals do not conflict.

While psychological or spiritual growth is an individual process, it can be part of a much larger struggle in which conflicting values are pitted against each other. For example, in the Catholic Church after the Second Vatican Council, the hierarchy was concerned about the safety of doctrine, whereas the laity was concerned about autonomy. These two positions became increasingly polarized, and neither side was able to appreciate that an ever-accelerating power struggle was developing. A graphic example of that power struggle is described in the book *Double Crossed*, by Kenneth Briggs. Briggs points out that orders of nuns were developing their own independence in the years prior to and just after Vatican II. With increased freedom, they began experiments that troubled the hierarchy, which then attempted to slow down the growing momentum toward change. The clash was irresolvable, and the inability to think dialectically when faced with this conflict between authority and independence is at least part of the reason the number of sisters has plummeted in the United States.[27]

The conflict between authority and independence played out on a national stage in the above example is likely reflected in the lives of many believers. Such tension is heightened because we are aware of just how power can be abused. For example, in the Catholic Church the sexual abuse scandal has clearly shown that the official church has abused its power by covering up crimes and sheltering perpetrators. Yet the same misuse of power is played out when the church suppresses the work of scholars offering arguments that challenge its privileged position and the faulty historical evidence on which it is based. As noted by Catholic Scripture scholar Johnson, the effort of the Catholic Church to defend its own hierarchical form of government, as well as its position on "celibacy and a males only priesthood, is breathtaking in its arrogance."[28] We can understandably distance ourselves from a church that refuses to examine its own truth claims in the light of new information. Like Pagels, we can stay connected to religion and appreciate that our fellow parishioners support our faith journey, even if it differs from theirs.

The individual faith journey, although lonely at times, is in solidarity with the journeys of others, in particular with the faith journey of Jesus. We can be inspired by the religious journeys modeled by many scholars, including Pagels and Johnson. Our efforts can be validated by the psychological descriptions of life-long spiritual growth outlined by Fowler and Basseches. They remind us that engaging in the conflicts that challenge us can be both life enhancing and therapeutic. We are cautioned that differences can lead to impasses, but the insights of Linehan's dialectical perspective offers hope for some resolution. And while the journey is an individual one, it is always in context: it assumes some kind of relationship with others or even a community. Finding a helpful community is a problem, but perhaps not the most serious one. The real challenge to spiritual and psychological growth may not rest in any external barrier or hindrance: we all struggle with an internal prohibition against changing and evolving.

The Inner Struggle
to Change Our Thinking

Although he focuses more on political ideology than religion, psychologist John Jost argues persuasively that we are all ideologues.[29] Citing the results of surveys and psychological experiments, he describes how people's ideologies influence the choices they make, even if they are unaware of or cannot articulate a specific belief system. An individual's belief system—which begins in childhood, according to one longitudinal study—appears to be almost hard-wired and "plays an important role in distorting as well as organizing information."[30] Jost hints that religious beliefs may show similar patterns. His research indicates how difficult it is for individuals to change, let alone be aware of, their own deep-seated way of thinking. His work indicates just how problematic it is to follow one of the most basic teachings of the historical Jesus.

Jesus called on the people to repent, an idea captured by the Greek word *metanoia*. Raymond Brown translates that same word into the phrase "You have got to change your way of thinking."[31] John Meier concludes that in his parables and self-descriptions, Jesus "meant to tease the mind of his audience into active thought, to pose uncomfortable questions instead of supplying pat answers."[32] Surely something we can take from the historical Jesus is this challenge to break through our conventional thinking and develop a more complicated global perspective that tries to see things from the viewpoints of others. The Christ of faith also challenges us to change our way of thinking, specifically calling us to answer the question of who he is for each of us. Even Albert Schweitzer, who minimized the importance of the Jesus of history, goes on to describe, in the often quoted ending of his book, a Jesus who would engage us in the tasks of our own time. Schweitzer describes the process in which followers of Jesus will come to know him: "He will reveal Himself in the toils, the conflicts, the sufferings which they shall pass through in his fellowship, and, as an ineffable mystery, they shall learn in their own experience Who He is."[33]

The tension between the Jesus of history and the Christ of faith is in its own way a case study in the larger issue of human development. The Jesus of history is a man of tremendous faith, whose struggles to live out his faith can still inspire us. More than that, many scholars who study him report a transformation in their own lives. They describe going beyond divisions and limitations to embrace a deeper understanding of themselves and their relationships. They report being connected to a power that can lead to a fuller life, one that is connected not only to the lives of others but in some mystical way to the universe itself. The effort to reconstruct the historical Jesus can benefit our own psychological and spiritual growth. If, as philosopher Kwame Appiah argues, our highest goal and basic moral responsibility is to make a good life and thereby respect others doing likewise,[34] then our efforts to investigate the Jesus of history and to grapple with the Christ of faith may be a significant way of contributing to such an accomplishment. If we appreciate that our own solutions are subjective, we would be inclined to appreciate that others are entitled to their own searches and the meanings they give not only to their life experiences but to their understanding of life itself.

Additionally, understanding the distinction between the Jesus of history and the Christ of faith is necessary to appreciate how Christianity developed from its historical Jewish roots in the first century to its increasingly Gentile makeover in the second. How did the pro-Jewish Jesus begin a movement that morphed into an anti-Jewish religion in such a short period of time? Even more puzzling is how a

Jewish prophet who saw himself as calling his people to renewal in expectation of the coming kingdom of God could miraculously become the founder of something quite different. Appreciating the tension between the Jesus of history and the Christ of faith can help us understand the burst of creative energy that led to the genesis of the new religious movement that became Christianity. To that dynamic and mysterious transformation, we now turn our attention.

Chapter 5

The Miraculous Conception of the First-century Christian Community

Try to conceive of a mental world so rich with ideas, prophets, factions, priests, savants, and god-drunk fanatics that it was the equivalent of a night-sky kept alight by thousands and thousands of fire-flies, brief lived, incandescent, luminous. That's what Yeshua and Saul witnessed.

—D. H. Akenson, *Saint Saul*

Nevertheless, it is clear that the author of 4 Ezra and presumably his readers did consider that the sack of Jerusalem in 70 CE and the enslavement and exile of many Jews thereafter were grossly inconsistent with theological views on the election of Israel and the significance of the temple.

—P. F. Esler, *The First Christians in Their Social Worlds*

The recent, historically based views describing the development of early Christianity might be even more earthshaking than the new information about the historical Jesus. As with Jesus, this new understanding starts with the context in which Christianity was born, namely, the Jewish religion of the times. Try to imagine a religion with multiple Jerry Falwells seeing the hand of Satan everywhere, with stories involving science fiction characters and comic-book heroes, and overlaid with Amish-like customs and behaviors, and you begin to appreciate the diversity of the Jewish religion in those exciting yet dangerous times in the first two-thirds of the first century CE in Palestine.

Just as Jesus lived within that system, his first followers were Jews who claimed that polymorphous Judaism as their religious home. These early Jewish followers of Jesus, although sometimes experiencing prejudice and even persecution, knew the stories, debated the law's meaning, and followed some version of the ritual whose foundation was temple worship. True, they had their own version of Judaism with Jesus occupying a significant role, but the religious environment, with some exceptions, could tolerate the many versions and factions that claimed to represent the faith, such as the group at Qumran revealed in the Dead Sea Scrolls.

There came a time when these Jewish Christians were expelled from their own Garden of Eden: their parent religion could no longer tolerate them. Given the ultimate success of this rejected group, it is natural to idealize their rough beginnings. As they figuratively and, in times of persecution, literally fought for their lives, we imagine their courage and self-discipline. As they preached to crowds of unbelievers, we marvel at the power they unleashed on the world. And their faith in the risen Christ transformed them into a resourceful and loving community. The idealization of the early Jesus movement can serve us well. We can be inspired by their efforts, and our conflicted faith can be strengthened when we remember theirs.

However, such an imagined portrait of these early followers of Jesus can cover over the more realistic picture that has begun to emerge in recent studies: the story behind the story can be equally inspiring. If we believe that God works in this world, we owe it to ourselves to understand what that work looks like. If we ignore the more realistic description of early Christianity, we are vulnerable to holding an inauthentic faith, one that can do harm or, perhaps worse, miss the workings of God in our lives and the lives of others. Did the death of Jesus call forth a burst of divine power that miraculously gave birth to Christianity? Such a supernatural explanation misses the all-too-natural description of how Christianity came to be born. If there is a divine power, research about early Christianity would suggest that the power worked in a very messy and unpredictable manner, much like everything else in evolution. The fossil record of Christianity reveals its false starts, dead ends, and the ultimate survival of something Jesus probably would not recognize.

So how did this tiny branch of Judaism break away from the massive tree that was its parent religion? And how did it successfully replant itself? To answer that question, we must first disabuse ourselves of the more traditional explanations. Jesus did not have the establishment of a church in mind. His apostles were not organizational men hand-picked to establish a breakaway religion. As argued by John Meier, the calling of twelve was another symbolic gesture by the prophet Jesus that pointed to the coming kingdom of God, not the birth of a new faith.[1] Likewise, there was no document of truths that Jesus left for the many preachers who would do missionary work in Palestine and beyond: he instead focused on providing the practices that would distinguish his followers from the other groups within Judaism. We know that he stood for no divorce and was against all oath taking. It is likely that when he quoted Leviticus, "You should love your neighbor as yourself," he meant what the original Jewish authors intended: only his fellow Israelites. Meier goes on to suggest that we may have lost much of what Jesus articulated as his brand of Judaism because his Torah-based arguments for particular practices would have seemed so strange and odd to Gentile audiences that such specifics were left out when the gospels were written.[2]

Yet in those first years after Jesus, there was one major theme that characterized the religion of these differing communities: their Jewish god was the main character in their story. Raymond Brown argues that in the first two chapters of the Gospel of Luke, we find embedded in the narrative Jewish-Christian hymns that with minor changes could be recited by believing Jews today. These hymns or canticles not only contain words and phrases from the Hebrew Scriptures, but also follow the style of contemporaneous compositions found in 1 Maccabees and the Dead Sea Scrolls.[3] They celebrate the wondrous works of God, but their sometimes awkward placement in the narrative strongly suggests that they predated the gospel and were sung or recited in these early Jewish communities of Jesus' followers. The Canticle of Mary, commonly known as the Magnificat, closely imitates the song of Hannah in the book of Samuel. The song of Zechariah praises God for sending a prophet who has come to prepare the way for God's coming.

Brown also points to the Gospel of Mark, written for a Gentile audience, where Jesus is questioned about the first of all the commandments. His reply is a paraphrase of the great Jewish prayer, the Shema Israel, found in the book of Deuteronomy: "Hear, O Israel: The Lord our God, the Lord is one; you shall love the Lord your God with all your heart, with all your soul, with all your mind, and with all your strength" (Mark 12:29–30; cf. Deut. 6:4–5). Brown argues that this gospel passage demonstrates that even in preaching to the Gentiles, the basic thrust was to inform potential converts about the heart of the Jewish religion.[4] The group of Jesus' followers remaining in Jerusalem, and more importantly, the missionaries from this group, insisted on following Jewish practices, including circumcision. For them Jesus was a Jewish prophet who came to announce the coming of God's kingdom.

Again, how can we understand how this new movement pulled away from the orbit of Judaism and begin a new one centered on Jesus? The gradual evolution to Christianity is analogous to the evolution of the human species: a common ancestor but many species ultimately leading to something more familiar and adaptable. In fact, it makes sense that the multiform, passionate Jewish religion of the times would naturally spawn an equally diverse Christianity, or Christianities. The traditional view of a single Christianity proceeding uniformly from the time of Jesus was seriously challenged by the discovery of early Christian documents at Nag Hammadi in the 1940s. Since then, other documents have come into play and scholars have called our attention to the diverse literature and the various communities that produced them. In 2003 Bart Ehrman authored two books, *Lost Christianities* and *Lost Scriptures,* which summarized what the earlier versions might look like. Scholars continued to emphasize different properties of the communities as ways of explaining and understanding the dramatic variety in what we would now call early Christianity. In 1984 Raymond Brown argued against those who projected an idealized version of Christianity, in which Jesus had directed the establishment of the church and the apostles uniformly carried out his directives. Instead, various communities had differing forms of leadership and organization.[5] Likewise, Howard Clark Kee emphasized how various communities developed their own identities based on differing but powerful religious imagery and ritual.[6] John Dominic Crossan saw at the heart of these early Christianities the conflict between the more radical itinerant preachers and the more conservative householders.[7] Before them, James M. Robinson and Helmut Koester argued in *Trajectories through Early Christianity* (1971) that there was no uniformity of belief, but ambiguity and conflicting approaches not only at the beginning of Christianity but for some time into the future. All of this makes sense when we remember that Jesus was a Jew and not interested in starting another religion. His followers preached their own version of Jesus in response to the needs of the people they addressed. Communities developed and fleshed out the meaning of the message for them in their individual and group faith journeys. Christianity was conceived in Judaism but was born in many differing and often conflicting forms.

Religious Imagination

The new information about the conflicted beginnings of early Christianity reveals a story as equally revealing and inspiring as the more traditional one that believes orthodoxy was there from the beginning. It was not just the persecution and prejudice that made things difficult: they could not agree on Jesus' identity. These Jewish followers of Jesus began to develop their own view of their leader and celebrate his memory using material available to them. They appropriated all the descriptions in their religious writings given to those favored by God, even though such various ideas would not only cause confusion because they lacked consistency but would also eventually prove inadequate because they could not contain their evolving beliefs.[8] He was a prophet announcing the coming of God's kingdom; he was God's Messiah ushering in that kingdom; he was a holy man through whom God worked wonders. He was so close to God that he was with God even before the creation of the world. In their small groups they reflected on his life, and also on his felt presence within their community—those faith-based connections with him they experienced in visions and rituals. Missionary preachers proclaimed the good news about Jesus, and those listening came away with their own images, perhaps inspired by mystical experiences. These early communities developed various, differing portraits of Jesus. "As in the first century, so today: no one's Jesus—and no one Jesus—suits everyone."[9]

However, in the letters of Paul, written some twenty years before the destruction of Jerusalem, we begin to see someone trying to rein in those creative descriptions of Jesus and address the consequences of differing images and beliefs. His letters were mostly topical and in response to specific problems; therefore, they do not easily admit of a systematic construction of Christian belief. Yet despite the range of specific issues, Paul evidences the gradual moving of Jesus to center stage. God is still the main actor, of course. God raises Jesus from the dead and takes him to Heaven. God will eventually send Jesus to establish the kingdom of Heaven on Earth at the immanent end time. However, Paul is not talking about the Jesus of history. He is exclusively concerned with the Christ of faith, the Messiah: About half the references to the Messiah in the New Testament can be found in Paul's letters. Paul attempts to bring some unity to the disparate pushes and pulls of the various communities by emphasizing the crucial importance of Jesus the Messiah, Jesus the Christ.

Paul tried to bring some unity to the process of reimagining Jesus as the Christ. Although his insights were not always respected, Paul continued to enhance the identity and importance of Jesus Christ, while still attempting to remain connected to the Jewish religion. We can see his desperate balancing act in his letter to the Romans, where he emphasizes the value of the Jewish religion, suggesting that Gentiles were simply a wild branch grafted onto the tree that was the Jewish people. On the other hand, the small communities associated with Paul contained Gentile members and so would not emphasize all the traditional Jewish practices. Paul believed that Jesus' crucifixion and resurrection meant that the old legislation that served as identity markers for Jews should not be required for Gentile converts.[10] He imagined that the risen Christ would be the foundation for a new community that would unite both Jew and Gentile. More than that, he believed that the success of such hybrid communities would soon bring about the return of the Messiah and the inauguration of God's kingdom on Earth. Yet Paul introduced a significant evolutionary change when he approved of Gentiles becoming first-class citizens in the groups he established. The question was whether the movement could absorb these new recruits with their different religious concepts and moral codes or whether it would be fatally crippled by them. Their growing presence could introduce dynamic centrifugal forces that could not only shatter any hope of unity but possibly kill the movement through conflict and turmoil.

One Death, Two Rebirths

The increasing centrality of Jesus as Christ and the growing number of Gentile converts were not the only factors that pulled the fledgling group away from its parent religion. Something else happened to make matters worse, at least initially. Jesus' Jewish followers, like most of their other fellow Jews, looked to Jerusalem and the temple not only as a place of worship but also as a pledge that God's promises to the people would be fulfilled. They believed that Jesus Christ would return to Jerusalem at the end time in fulfillment of their Jewish Scriptures. Only when we can appreciate how Jewish those early followers of Jesus were can we begin to understand how problematic the destruction of the city and the temple in 70 CE was for them. One way of emphasizing their Jewish identity is to remind ourselves that these early followers would not have espoused the major beliefs we associate with Christianity. They would not have an orthodox view of the Trinity, in which the Second Person became man through the power of the Holy Spirit. Jesus did not rise from the dead, but rather was raised by God. Finally, no church had been established nor gospels written. In other words, the apostles could not have said the Apostles' Creed any more than Jesus could be a Christian. They were Jews who believed fervently in the promises that God made to the people.

As Philip Esler notes in the epigraph above, the Romans' destruction of Jerusalem was not just a social and economic disaster; it was also a religious one, because much of the religion was based on anticipation of God's fulfilling promises to the people. The keystone of those promises was the absolute centrality of Jerusalem and its temple. Jerusalem was the holy city, and the temple was the most sacred place on Earth, from which God would ultimately rule an earthly kingdom. After the events of 70 CE, faith and fact collided for believing Jews, including those who followed Jesus. As both groups struggled to find meaning and direction after the disaster, each developed a different identity, although both claimed they were continuing the same traditions. With the temple and the land gone, a small group of Jewish scholars in the city of Jamnia, just north of Jerusalem, re-constructed a version of the Jewish religion that focused on interpreting their sacred Scriptures, much in line with the tradition of the Pharisees. Without temple or priesthood, they emphasized rituals that could be performed at home. Eventually, they chose the writings that were acceptable and began a process of study and commentary that would be the source of their identity and a connection to their past.

Another group of scholars spread out among various communities collected and edited stories about Jesus, bas-ing their reconstruction of the Jewish religion on his ex-panding identity. Their task was not simply to write a biog-raphy but to argue that through Jesus, God had continued the plan and would fulfill the promises, despite what had happened to Jerusalem and the temple. They were the new Israel and their task, at least initially, was to imagine how Jesus revealed a new chapter in God's plan. Imagining that they were continuation or even a successor to their parent religion, they still used the Jewish Scriptures and rituals, al-though radically recontextualized to give them a new mean-ing. With no direction from a central authority available, small communities began a desperate effort to find out who they really were.

The scholars at Jamnia had a slightly easier task because, in a sense, they had a home-field advantage. They were members of a well-established religion, Judaism, respected by Gentile nonbelievers who valued the antiquity of a religion because it was established closer to the time when the gods ruled the Earth. They already had their Scriptures, which did not mention Jesus, and used their authority to discount other writings that they believed were not consistent with their new identity. Also, some of the disparate voices, such as those belonging to the Sadducees or the Essenes, were silenced by the destruction of Jerusalem and Qumran. Likewise, the scholars did not have to integrate Jesus' followers into their fold. Although it was some time before they gained more comprehensive authority over their fellow Jews, they offered scholarly tradition and pious practices as a basis for a viable alternative to a destroyed, temple-based practice.

Jesus' followers were faced with a much more difficult challenge. After the destruction of the temple, they lost not only the physical center of their religion but also the first community in their far-flung community of communities: that special group in Jerusalem under its leader, James. They also lost their early heroes to martyrdom, such as Paul and Peter, and soon those who knew firsthand about Jesus would die. Their creative efforts to connect with their parent religion were rejected. More and more, they had to choose between following Jesus or following the new version of the Jewish religion emerging in Jamnia. Jesus didn't offer much help—for all his questioning of his Jewish religion, he seemed quite satisfied with it. He celebrated the feasts and knew enough about the rules to offer his own interpretations of some ritual practices and codes of conduct. As a reforming prophet, he objected to religious practices that he perceived as betraying the spirit of the law, but he never objected to the law itself. Although he may have called for a reform of his religion, he never indicated that he wanted to start his own, nor did he write or dictate anything for posterity, as other religions' founders did. Finally, of course, he was executed as a criminal. How could they put a positive spin on that?

Religious Imagination in a Community Setting

Christianity as we know it today survived its birth and moved into early infancy by following the dynamic pattern outlined by Paul. Although the foundation was the story of Jesus and the religious experience of his followers, the thrust was the formation of a community with baptism as the initial rite of passage. Jesus' shameful death was reimagined as atonement for all who would follow him. Their belief that he was raised from the dead meant that he was still alive in their communities. They celebrated his presence in a special meal that was inspired by the story of his Last Supper with the apostles. For most of these communities, the outline of Judaism was unmistakable: they took from their parent religion their Scriptures, practices, and moral precepts. Yet inside this superstructure of an infant religion was the powerful force of a community that continued to define itself in an increasingly hostile environment. In an early church document known as the Didache (late first or early second century CE), we can read of their rigorous discipline as well as their growing self-awareness as the movement separated from both their Jewish and pagan neighbors.

Yet more challenging than hostile neighbors were the internal dissensions and disputes faced by the small and scattered communities. Early preachers like Paul expected the second coming shortly. He thought that believers who were still alive would meet Jesus Christ in the air along with those followers who had died, and then return to a changed Earth. That speculation, known today as the moment of Rapture, has become a significant dogma for some fundamentalist Christians fervently focused on the end of the world. As the promised event apparently came to be delayed, some followers became anxious and confused. Some may have left the movement. It is likely that the epistle to the Hebrews was written to encourage followers who were thinking of leaving and returning to the Jewish religion to stay in the movement. As we can see in Hebrews, which was written by an unknown early follower, the solution was to emphasize the role and status of Jesus, whom the author also refers to as Lord or Christ. Still, as more emphasis was placed on the person and role of Jesus, there was no real uniformity either in the teachings or in the communities that placed him at the center of their rituals, preaching, and behavior.

Predictably, the lack of leadership and direction spawned a variety of communities that must have felt even more on their own after Jerusalem's destruction. The early Christian-Jewish movement was made up of relatively small groups that gathered in homes to celebrate a weekly memorial of Jesus, and perhaps met more frequently when they had various communal problems to address. Some may have also gone to synagogues on the Sabbath. The relative autonomy of these small groups made it quite difficult to achieve uniform conformity, even in the same city. In later New Testament writings, we see instances of fierce rivalry among the house churches. In 3 John, the writer takes to task a certain Diotrephes, the leader of another house church across town, who is antagonistic to the writer's teachings. In Revelation, the author chastises six of the seven churches to which he writes, accusing them of listening to false teachers and failing to live up to their original commitments. Although these house churches may have accepted Jesus as the Messiah, they probably interpreted differently what that meant. Contrary to the story of uniformity romantically described in Acts of the Apostles, there was little quality control prior to 70 CE, and even less immediately afterward.

No Quality Control

The history of these early house churches was bound to be somewhat idiosyncratic because they were originally part of a Jewish religion that tolerated differences. Conceivably, they developed along a spectrum ranging from predominantly Jewish to predominantly Gentile. Shaped by the local culture and influenced by the local leadership, these small gatherings established their identities, including their separation from Judaism, "one church at a time."[11] A closer look at this history suggests that no one was really in charge, and quality control was therefore minimal. Although Peter always heads any list of the apostles and is said to have been the first to witness the resurrected Jesus, the extent of his actual authority is not at all clear. In Matt 16:18–20, the author has Jesus say to Peter that he is to be the rock on which the church will be built. However, as Meier points out in his careful construction of the "historical" Peter,[12] the special authority Jesus gave him, which is recorded in Matthew 16, is not historical. A more likely scenario is that the early church later attributed this influence to Peter. Meier also points out that two chapters later in Matthew, similar power is given to the church as a whole—even with the same phraseology. In the early part of Acts, Peter enjoys a certain leadership status, but halfway through the book he disappears, for all practical purposes having been replaced by Paul. Traditionally, Peter is also is believed to have been Rome's first bishop—the first pope, so to speak. However such a status-enhancing tradition must be a retrojection, because the office of bishop did not exist in Rome until some 100 years after Peter's death.[13]

If Peter's authority is confusing, the rest of the apostles' situation is even more nebulous. The twelve apostles were primarily a symbolic group calling to mind the founding twelve tribes of ancient Israel. Most of these apostles remained in Jerusalem, waiting for Jesus' return, when they could become leaders of the new Israelite kingdom. In Acts, Matthias was chosen as the twelfth apostle to replace Judas, who had disgraced himself by betraying Jesus and then, according to Matthew, by committing suicide. However, no one was picked to replace James, the son of Zebedee and brother of John, who was killed some ten years later (Acts 12:1–3). They believed that there was now no reason to replace the apostles because they would rule in the future kingdom, not in the present world.

We know that various factions, communities, and preachers clashed with one another—the evidence of their conflict shouts at us in the letters from the Christian Scriptures. But more significant is that the compromises between Jews and Gentiles that Paul and Peter envisioned could not last. These two heroic figures' status and influence may have kept alive the early movement's connection with the Jewish religion, but any capacity for rapprochement died with them. The vision of a Jewish-Gentile church could not be sustained. The ending of Acts, in which Paul turns to the Gentiles, is in one sense historically accurate: it echoes the turning away of Christians from their parent religion.

The authority of the twelve, who were to rule over the new kingdom, dissolved when that kingdom failed to appear. In the Gospel of John, written toward the end of the first century, the word *apostle* is not even used. The hope for a second coming of the Messiah in the near future slowly disappeared. Many of Christianity's early followers returned to the Jewish religion because Christianity could not deliver on its promise. The letter to the Hebrews reads like a desperate attempt to speak to these wavering converts by emphasizing the value of Christianity over that of Judaism. John's gospel emphasized that Christ was already present in the community, perhaps seeking to undercut the Christians' focus on a future return.

In 62 CE James, Jesus' brother, was killed by order of the high priest Ananus despite his best efforts to form a version of Christianity that would remain under the umbrella of Judaism. Other Christians saw James as a hero and tried to keep his vision alive. However, these Jerusalem-based communities could not keep up with the development of Christian thought, particularly concerning Jesus' identity, and they eventually fell into a no-man's-land between Christianity and Judaism and lost contact with both groups. Before fading from history, they were labeled Ebionites and declared heretics by the more mainstream church of the second and third centuries.

The Johannine community that John's gospel lionized also began to break apart. The theme of Jesus as the vine and the followers as branches equally connected to him was powerful in theory, but did not work out in practice. With no central authority structure to mediate conflict, the egalitarian community began to fragment. The Spirit that the Johannines had once invoked to protect the disciples against persecutors was now called on to protect the true believers from the renegade Christians. Here again, the center could not hold, and the community disappeared from history; some of its members drifted into what was later called Gnosticism.[14] How did Christianity survive?

Keeping the Connection
to the Jewish Religion

The Jesus movement survived its infancy because of the religious imagination of its members and the thrust for community inspired by the life of Jesus. However some credit must go to the writers, just as the scribes of old contributed to the formation of the Jewish religion. Out of the disarray that characterized Jesus' followers in the last third of the first century came the four documents that were ultimately accepted as the authoritative writings that described who

Jesus was. The four gospels highly valued the traditions of their parent religion. Their stories and references made no sense outside their Jewish context. Yet they also described in narrative fashion the struggle with the painful separation they experienced in being rejected by their parent religion. Out of that pain, they developed narratives that took much from Judaism but refashioned it to fit their new communities. Although the gospels were about Jesus, they simultaneously rewrote the Jewish story of a god who made everlasting promises to the Jewish people.

As was fashionable at the time, the gospels were presented as having been written by prominent followers of Jesus, but they were actually written or edited by individuals, probably Jewish Christians, whose identities will always remain hidden from us. Yet for the struggling Christian communities scattered across the Roman Empire, these anonymous writers provided a new form of leadership that did not offer directives so much as provide a structured religious experience for the listeners (most Christians could not read). These stories of Jesus were constructed from remembered incidents and sermons but were shaped in such a way as to include various communities' particular needs, problems, and concerns.

As the Christians who heard these stories recounted in their weekly gatherings, they could imagine themselves as part of the narrative, especially because it seemed to be written and spoken for them, and Jesus Christ would come alive for them. When the community gathered, these new narratives played an important role in the developing Sunday ritual. Portions of the gospels may have been used as lectionaries, with a particular section chosen for each gathering, perhaps following the Jewish liturgical calendar.[15] The gospels became community documents that united people in celebrating the great work that God had done in and through Jesus. In their own way, the four gospels channeled and structured the religious imagination of the early

Christians. Although we may not get some of the allusions and references to the parent religion, the gospels insisted on an organic connection with the Jewish religion and its Scriptures. Modern scholarship reminds us that Judaism's imprint was clearly visible in the gospels. Luke begins with an infancy narrative that seems to be peopled by characters straight from Hebrew Bible stories. Zechariah and Elizabeth are stand-ins for Abraham and Sarah, who, like the couple they reflect, are without child until God intervenes and grants them a son: John the Baptist. Mary recites a hymn so similar to Hannah's at the birth of her son Samuel (1 Sam 2:1–10) that nowadays we might accuse her of plagiarism. In Matthew's gospel, Joseph interprets his dreams and helps his family survive, just as another Joseph, son of Jacob, used his dreams to survive in Egypt. In the flight to Egypt, Jesus avoids King Herod's massacre of young boys, just as Moses averted a similar slaughter that Pharaoh initiated.

The Gospel of Matthew seems to be saying that, starting in his infancy, Jesus relived all of the great Jewish stories and claimed them as his own. As the gospel stories continued to develop, their authors saw reflected in Jesus' life story the Jewish writings' references to an imminent messiah. Ultimately, the gospels both borrowed heavily from the Jewish religion and subverted it. Somewhat like the Essenes, the gospels' followers reinterpreted the narratives and transformed the rituals to define and validate their new community. By constructing a Jesus who embodied God's older prophecies, the early Christians established him as God's final revelation. Like other Jewish reform groups, including the Essenes of Jesus' time, they claimed to be the true Israel.

An Inspiring but Ambiguous Jesus

The Jesus of the gospels burst the boundaries of Judaism and proclaimed a global solution for all the problems of humanity and a new meaning for life on Earth. If we place the gospels in the chronological order in which they were written, Mark comes first, followed by Matthew, Luke, and John. That sequence reveals the gradual evolution of the Jesus of history into the Christ of faith. Mark's Jesus is clearly human—embarrassingly so for the writers of Matthew and Luke. For example, Mark's Jesus twice attempts to cure a blind man, as though struggling with the cure, but in Matthew and Luke, it happened effortlessly.

Mark's gospel also reveals Jesus' own frailty. He is notably angry and frustrated with his disciples. He is frightened as his death draws near and prays that he might escape his fate. His true identity remains hidden, acknowledged only by the demons he exorcises and the Roman guard who supervises his crucifixion. In this gospel, we hear the voices and concerns of a community that struggles to maintain its belief in Jesus at a time when this belief may be dangerous. Yet from its beginning with John the Baptist to its end at the empty tomb, the gospel pushes its followers to answer one question: who was this Jesus?

Mark's gospel set the narrative precedent for Matthew and Luke. However, all were doctored according to their own theological purposes, as well as the demands of their communities. Matthew emphasizes Jesus' connection to Jewish history and its prerogatives in the infancy narrative, but by the end, Matthew's Jesus shatters the barrier between Jews and Gentiles and becomes all-powerful. He instructs his followers to make disciples of all the nations by baptizing them and teaching them to observe all his commands. Matthew's community needed an authoritative teacher who could both privilege Jewish heritage and simultaneously introduce Gentile converts to Jewish traditions. This gospel reflects a community that says, "Yes, but ..." to the Jewish religion. Yes, scribes and Pharisees are to be respected, but Jesus is greater than Moses. Yes, to be born Jewish is significant, but faith in Jesus is more important. Matthew, the only gospel to speak of an organized church (Matt 16:18 and 18:17), is insistent that a new community, composed of both Jews and Gentiles, has now been formed. His people are evolving away from the hybrid communities formed by Peter and Paul.

The community that Luke sprang from seemed to be more at peace than those of Mark and Matthew. This group's mission was to understand for itself Jesus' message and vision regarding the coming of God's kingdom. In this community, the look and feel of that kingdom had changed to become one that privileged the poor, sought justice, and celebrated neighborly love. The Gospel of Luke reflects a faction that has moved beyond the hope of an imminent second coming and now looks to itself and its own behavior for a sign that the kingdom has come. By emphasizing a more interior kingdom, the followers of Luke made another significant advance in the evolution of Jesus' original preaching. There was no impending cataclysm to be feared, no political upheaval to await. In this gospel, Jesus says, "For, in fact, the kingdom of God is among you" (17:21). Similarly, the case against Judaism is closed. The temple was destroyed—no more needs to be said. The Pharisees, who entertained Jesus in the beginning of the gospel story, condemned him by the story's end.[16]

Although it was written some time after Luke, the Gospel of John reflects a community that is in fierce if not violent conflict with the synagogue, as well as in opposition to other groups with differing understandings of Jesus. The Johannine understanding of Jesus is precisely what activated such divisiveness. For this community, the kingdom of God announced by Jesus in the other gospels has all but disappeared. Instead, the entire focus is on Jesus himself. In the beginning, Jesus, the Word, is with God. Jesus has come to Earth so that all who believe in him can have life; then he leaves Earth and returns to the "Father's" kingdom, where he awaits those who believe in him. It is as though the kingdom has been replaced by this new life, which grants immortality and is now accessible to all believers. Because all members of the community share in this life, the people project a strong egalitarian if not antiauthoritian stance. The all-too-human portrait of Jesus captured in Mark and airbrushed somewhat in Matthew and Luke has almost entirely disappeared. Yet at least early on, the Gospel of John was suspect, especially in Rome, and it was many more years before it gained acceptance. Ironically, by that time the Johannine community had split up and disappeared, the largest group having "drifted off into Gnosticism."[17]

(Super) Natural Selection

The Johannine disappearance can help us understand what was different about the communities that survived. The communities reflected in Mark, Matthew, and Luke maintained some connection and familiarity with the Jewish religion. This approach allowed the communities to stay connected to much of the religious thinking, literature, morality, and even ritual that Judaism had developed and refined. Like young adults emancipating themselves from home, these communities had valuable resources that they could revere but also use or adapt as new circumstances developed or challenges arose. For example, the early communities kept up the Jewish practice of fasting but changed it to occur on different days of the week and included it as part of preparation for baptism. The moral behavioral code that the Jews established, as well as individual responsibility for choosing correct behavior, also found a home in these Christian communities. Their Jewish background gave them more than just a head start.

Unlike John's followers, the groups associated with the other three gospels maintained a connection with the historical Jesus. Their Jesus was a reforming prophet who spoke out against injustice and showed deep concern for the poor. The Jesus of John's gospel was not as focused on these social justice issues. Likewise, the itinerant preachers who traveled from group to group modeled in their lifestyles not only a radical trust in God but also an identification with the many poor and marginalized members of society. Even though other individuals were not expected to follow these preachers' lifestyle, they were challenged by example to express their own forms of care for the impoverished and marginalized. A second reason, then, for the survival of the non-Johannine groups was that they represented a nonmilitaristic, countercultural alternative to a mainstream society that was at times oppressive and unjust.

However, the itinerant preachers did not challenge just religious followers; they also challenged one another. Paul lists a number of positions or offices within these communities: "And God has appointed in the church first apostles, second prophets, third teachers; then deeds of power, then gifts of healing, forms of assistance, forms of leadership, various kinds of tongues" (1 Cor 12:28). Paul also adds that in their assemblies, individuals play various roles, but he cautions that all roles should be focused on community building (1 Cor 14:26). Although Paul cautions those who speak in tongues to restrain themselves a little, we can imagine a gathering in which individuals almost competed to push rightness and morality. Perfection was not limited to the elite, as Greek philosophy would have it.[18]

Also unlike John's community, the other groups survived because they developed forms of leadership, as well as a process of resolving disputes, that could keep them unified. The citations above from 1 Corinthians describe an organization composed of various responsible individuals who could foster a community's evolution. The leader of the ritualized meal, the Eucharist, was likely the head of the house in which this service was performed. If a member of this type of society sinned, another member would try to get him to repent. If that did not work, the concerned person would call on others to try to convince the deviant member of the error of his ways. As a last resort, the entire community would take up the cause (Matt 18:15–17).

Modeling themselves after the synagogue's organizational structure, many communities had a group of elders or presbyters who set policy. Another office, outlined in the Dead Sea Scrolls, was that of overseer, an administrative position we now know as bishop.[19] At least in their earliest stages, communities survived because of a diffuse and flexible structure that shared responsibility for such diverse functions as rituals, teaching, and administration. Such a diversity of leadership could have its problems, but it could also invest many in the group with a sense of ownership within that community and a vested interest in its survival. Such an investment could only further motivate the members to embody positive ethical values.

A community that demonstrated such high standards of ethical living was no doubt attractive to many people searching for a way to lead virtuous lives. Likewise, these followers' generosity toward others would be quite attractive to those who felt empathy and compassion for the less fortunate. Sociologist Rodney Stark argues that Christians' heroic compassion for the victims of plagues in the second and third centuries contributed to the movement's expansion. However, the community's pressure on its own members to lead highly moral lives, and the concomitant rigorous process of fulfilling this obligation, bound the members tightly to one another and to the beliefs and behaviors they shared. As social psychologists have noted, uncomfortable experiences can foster positive feelings toward others who have shared similar experiences.[20] Extrapolating from such findings, it is likely that the sacrifices necessary to join a group despised by the dominant culture, the ongoing cost of participation, and the examples set by peers who validate the worth of such a trial would all tend to justify hardship and create a close bond with fellow members.

Survival through Communitas

Another powerful psychological force may have been at
work in these early Christian communities that miraculously
survived the loss of their original leaders and their connection to the Jewish religion. Psychiatrist Richard Almond
argues that an important component of any therapeutic
community is a sense that members are responsible for one
another, as well as for the overall functioning of the group.
Such shared responsibility engenders a way of relating that
emphasizes direct interpersonal communication while at
the same time lessening the powers of more traditional roles
and lines of authority. Building on the work of the anthropologist Victor Turner, Almond calls this egalitarian quality
"communitas."[21] Turner arrived at this concept by studying particular cultures' healing rituals and noticing how traditional roles were usually suspended during those events.
This intermission did not lead to anarchy, because specific
behavioral norms were also part of these rituals. In both his
research and his clinical work, Almond attempted to introduce communitas as an ongoing element in a therapeutic
community.[22]

Arguably, the early Christian communities could survive the loss of leaders because they developed a group process that contained an element of communitas. Although
such groups were vulnerable to more charismatic leaders
who did, in the earlier stages, take them in one direction
or another, a series of norms evolved that reflected the historical Jesus' teachings. Inspired by the story of Jesus they
heard preached by their leaders and saw lived out by fellow
members, these believing communities also became healing
communities. Members could find respite from the fears
and anxieties that came with the world they had inherited,
and they could imagine bringing into existence another
world that promised safety, justice, and love. Their success
as self-reinforcing communities was a sign that that a new

world was possible. Although the believers lived in the present world, they challenged and supported one another to act in a way that would make them worthy of entering another one. Although many other social, philosophical, and religious groups were likewise competing for members, the Christian factions were especially attractive because they cared for one another, as well as for others who were not part of their community. For the Christians, the element of communitas not only focused on healing individuals but also addressed healing this world.

The Christian Community from an Evolutionary Perspective

If we can put aside the unhistorical belief that Jesus started a new religion, we can find revealed for us an inspiring account of how God may have worked in this world. The Jesus movement was deeply indebted to the rich treasury of traditional Jewish values and practices, and then found a way to survive and thrive when it separated from the parent religion. Part of that survival strategy was based on the encouragement of religious imagination channeled somewhat by the early writings of Paul and the evangelists, but nevertheless allowing for some diversity in belief, practice, and structure. Perhaps most important, the movement tapped into an innate and powerful human force—*communitas.* The new model or paradigm suggested by recent information about the founding of Christianity changes the emphasis from a top-down, hierarchical model to a bottom-up one that tolerates diversity within community. Additionally, this new information suggests an evolutionary process as various versions of Christianity emerged, flowered, and then died out. This new model with its background narrative of a challenging, sometimes harsh evolutionary process has relevance for us today. The point is not to wish nostalgically for some golden age of the past. Those early communities evolved during a specific historical niche that is long gone. But the values they modeled can inspire us even today, as we face our own evolutionary crisis.

Today's Evolutionary Survival Crisis

The list of global crises continues growing, to the extent that we can become numbed by the many dangers we now face: terrorism, climate change, scarcity of drinkable water. Other problems seem resistant to our best efforts at resolving them: international conflict leading to war; unequal distribution of wealth leading to intractable poverty; widespread immigration leading to suspicion of other cultures. Social scientists Stanley Greenspan and Stuart Shanker see a catastrophe of global proportions unfolding, but they view it within an evolutionary context.[23] Although they are like other authors who outline stages of human development, they differ in the sense that they ask how people can grow psychologically in a way that will equip them to work on such global issues. The authors argue that for individuals to fulfill such a goal, they must develop emotional, social, and intellectual capacities that can help them appreciate the critical importance of interdependency and the idea that the basic unit of survival is global. These individuals would not be forced to give up their own identity or their allegiance to family and other groups; they would simply have to be willing and able to operate on several levels, seeking the compromises and solutions necessary to achieve some stability.

Groups can likewise be characterized by how adaptive they are in managing the predictable crises in their own development. Greenspan and Shanker stress the importance of groups, beginning with the family but continuing to larger institutions, because groups in these environments can nurture and advance what the authors describe as individuals' functional emotional development. Groups must also struggle to maintain some balance between their individual goals and the larger group's goals. Ideally, the collective, like the individual, would see itself as part of a global group that is the basic unit for survival. Both individuals and groups would be guided by a new morality concerned with the needs of the weakest.

Although an appreciation of evolution may motivate individuals and groups to make decisions that will facilitate global survival, Greenspan and Shanker recognize the need for cultural and religious support that "fosters both a personal core and a shared sense of humanity and reality as part of an ethic of shared survival."[24] Evolution is an opportunistic process: most of the species that once inhabited the Earth are now extinct. Like many other authors, Carl Sagan argued that the human species could likewise become extinct unless we recognize and act on our connectedness to others. "If we are to survive, our loyalties must be broadened further, to include the whole human community, the entire planet Earth."[25]

If Christian and other religious communities are to support and contribute to the growth and survival of the human race, they would do well to model the meaning and power of community and communitas. Following such an example does not mean that Christians should abandon their concern for poor and marginalized people; in fact, Greenspan and Shanker would argue that such a cause is essential to human survival. What this idea means is that Christianity would also support a view of humanity that emphasizes the basic connectedness between peoples, and their critical need to interact with others, despite significant differences. Early Christianity may be unique in the sense that in its history, it evidenced a charisma that enabled it to overcome differences among people in a kindly manner while simultaneously challenging a more fear-based culture that over-valued military and political power.

The challenge for the church today is not simply to accept evolution but to see it as part of the process of faith, for individuals and also communities. Rather than privileging its own survival needs, the church can embrace those of others; rather than focusing entirely on maintaining its own traditions, it can support the preservation of all traditions that contribute to the common good. It can once again strive to create a new kind of community, one in which serious differences are tolerated for the sake of that larger good. In such a revitalized version of Christianity, both members and the larger society would be challenged to develop moral behavior that might enable us to survive as a species. We are all, Christians and non-Christians, part of a unique cosmic process in which change is the only constant and extinction is always a possible outcome.

It will not be easy. As Christianity moved from infancy in the first century to its adolescence in the second, it revealed something in its founding that tended to stress right thinking over right behavior. Like the warrior god found in Joshua, an angry god began to emerge in the Christian movement that became equally harsh. Identity became dependent on specific beliefs and the penalty for not believing became a serious crime. How that developed is the focus of the next chapter.

Chapter 6

The Development of Second-century Christianity
From Paralyzing Trauma to New Identity

> The second century in many ways shaped the future
> of the Christian Church. It is the time in which the
> church definitively breaks with the synagogue, the
> time in which Christians reach out to the pagan
> world surrounding them, and the time in which the
> New Testament canon is essentially formed.
>
> —Sebastian Moll, *The Arch-Heretic Marcion*

> Opinions will vary on when the basic structure of
> the church was in place. The year 100 seems too
> early, since its organizational structure and founda-
> tional documents were still in the process of forma-
> tion; some date within the course of the second cen-
> tury would appear more accurate, and an estimate
> would depend on what one considered constitutive
> of the essential nature of the church.
>
> —Roger Haight, *Christian Community in History*

Just as it is difficult to construct the Jesus of history, it is difficult to reconstruct the church of history, and the tension between the Jesus of history and the
Christ of faith is replicated and paralleled in the beginnings
of Christianity. On the one hand, the "view that Jesus in-
tentionally founded the church as the autonomous institution it came to be is no longer common among exegetes
and historians."[1] In its earliest stages, the historical church

appears quite Jewish and utterly dependent on the Jewish religion for its meanings, rituals, and stories. Sometime in the second century CE, however, Christianity began to develop a new identity as an independent religion based on a new story about God's work in this world and a more exalted role for Jesus.

Although it may seem artificial to distinguish the Jesus movement of the first century from that of the second, some general patterns mark a difference. The later writings of the New Testament, such as the epistles to Titus and Timothy (ca. 100 CE), are concerned with fitting in with the larger culture rather than challenging it.[2] The leaders tended to be Gentiles rather than Jews. Second-century Christian heroes such as Justin Martyr attempted to describe their faith in philosophical terms. Others such as Ignatius of Antioch pled for more uniformity and stressed the need for a strong, hierarchical organization. Of course, it grew larger. Even some Roman pagan writers took notice of it, although disdainfully. There were sporadic persecutions as the movement failed to be granted the exemption from emperor worship that was given to the Jews. In fact, Judaism seemed to be left behind.

The faith-based description of this change originates with the Acts of the Apostles, which some authors such as Richard Pervo[3] and Joseph Tyson[4] argue was written in the second century. The traditional description leaves out important elements that could help us not only to appreciate what faith is all about, but also to see its relevance for our own time. An alternative view is to use new information and psychological theory to reconstruct those valuable but hidden dimensions of the story. And this retelling of the traditional story does not lead to the destruction of faith, but rather toward a more authentic version of it. Additionally, in reexamining second-century Christianity we can appreciate the effects of trauma that can still be seen in the church today. First, we go to the traditional story.

The Story in Acts

The Holy Spirit is the main character in the New Testament book, Acts of the Apostles. The mythical story of Christianity's origin offers a solution to the centuries-old Jewish concern as to how God is going to make good on God's promises and restore God's kingdom. The problem is solved when God inspires the frightened followers of Jesus to write a new chapter in Israel's history. These followers believe that their hero's shocking death and unexpected resurrection are a new revelation that God is fulfilling the promises made to their ancestors and that God's kingdom is actually entering this world.

In this story, the followers were so empowered by the Holy Spirit that they proclaimed through words and deeds a message that was so compelling that great numbers of their fellow Jews joined the movement. When an early conflict arose regarding Greek-speaking members, they experienced the Holy Spirit guiding them to make organizational adjustments that solved the problem. Later, when Gentile converts joined the movement, the Holy Spirit again prompted the compromise that allowed them to integrate successfully.

When Peter disappears from the story halfway through the Acts of the Apostles, Paul takes his place seamlessly, underscoring the relative insignificance of the human actors in this God-driven drama. At the end of the book, the Jews' refusal to become more involved in the movement is described as a failure for them and an opportunity for the Gentiles. Rome had replaced Jerusalem as the center of the new movement. This inspirational story is one of single-minded success and miraculous growth—and it is not historically accurate.

New Information

The movement to a more Gentile church was neither as clear nor as smooth as the official story would have it. For example, in Acts the first dispute in the early church about the requirements to be placed on Gentile converts ends with a creative compromise between James, speaking as the leader of the Jerusalem church, and Paul, speaking for the Gentiles. Scriptural scholar Raymond Brown would say that the actual compromise was quite different. Missionaries from Jerusalem required their converts to follow Mosaic law, but Pauline missionaries would not adhere to such restrictions. The real compromise was that each group had its own territories; when different missionaries worked the same turf, problems occurred. For example, the Jerusalem brand of Christianity was more traditionally Jewish, and was headed by members of Jesus' own family. First his brother James then other family members occupied positions of authority, leading the house churches in Palestine into the second century.[5] About that time, the individuals in that community called Ebionites were eventually condemned as heretics because they upheld a version of Christianity in which a nondivine Jesus was a prophet who taught them to live in common and support the poor. What worked in the first century did not in the second.

Probably the most important catalyst for the separation of Christianity from Judaism was the Jewish revolt that began in 66 CE and resulted in the destruction of the temple four years later. Until that time, Judaism represented a larger umbrella that tolerated a range of disparate positions. For example, James, the brother of Jesus, continued to worship in the temple while he was head of the Jewish Christian community in Jerusalem. Also, the Roman authorities wanted order and simply did not tolerate disruptions springing from internecine warfare. When James was killed in 62 CE by the order of the high priest Ananus, the Romans removed the priest from his position. According to legend, Jesus' followers did not participate in the revolt of 66 CE; they left Jerusalem and waited out the war in Transjordan. Although the story may be a metaphor that points to a parting of ways between the parent religion and its offspring, it likely branded them as traitors in the minds of some Jews. Certainly after that point the Jewish religion became more circumscribed and more hostile toward Christians. Jewish religious authorities would reject their separated brethren, turn them in to the Roman authorities, curse them in their prayers, and eject them from their synagogues.

Though there may have been clear boundaries between the two religions, especially in the minds of their respective leaders, followers of both often got along well and even prayed together at times. There was certainly conflict, but there were also many areas of mutual respect. For example, in Antioch, the city where the followers of Jesus were first called Christians, the followers of both religions seemed to be on good terms. In fact it was much later, in the fourth century, when the bishop there, John Chrysostom, went on a rant in a series of sermons demanding that Christians no longer pray with Jews or fast on the same days they did. A closer reading of history shows that many rank-and-file Christians often continued to appreciate the value of their parent religion, much to the dismay of their leaders.

The Struggle for Identity

While Christianity began to develop its own identity after the fall of Jerusalem and destruction of the temple in 70 CE, its first efforts to define itself were not promising. Some converts reverted to the traditional Jewish religion when Jesus failed to return. Paul's dream that Gentiles would be grafted onto the tree of Judaism did not come true. The mother church of Jerusalem fell into decline. The community of the beloved disciple splintered, and the majority joined the movement we call Gnosticism. As the original leaders faded into memory, no consistent voice or strand of Christian orthodoxy remained. The movement was rudderless in its first few generations. Its small and far-flung house

churches tried to stay in contact by writing and sharing letters. However, in their struggle to survive, they frequently
turned on and attacked one another for failing to live up to
certain traditions or for abandoning certain practices.

Of course, the search for identity took different paths,
some more successful than others. As religious historian
Stephen Spence writes, "The church in Rome was not the
church in Jerusalem, which was not the church in Corinth,
which was not the church in Ephesus, and so on."[6] Each
church had to work out its own identity in the clash of differing religious values and the context of local circumstances.

Yet for an identity to be psychologically successful,
it must be described in a narrative that makes sense. The
Christian story had to make sense of failure, especially the
failure of its supposed founder and its rejection by the parent religion. As the movement evolved in the second century, it developed a new narrative that legitimated its origin
and privileged its followers. This new and overarching story
also provided the basis for a Christian identity to organize
its members and to attract new ones. Yet at the heart of the
story would be the pain and humiliation suffered by both its
hero and his early followers.

Trauma Theory

One lens that can help us explain and understand the second-century birth of this more recognizable Christianity
comes from clinical psychology. In particular, a growing
understanding of the effects of traumatic experiences can
be a powerful analogy that allows us to appreciate the evolution of the Christian movement into something beginning to resemble an institution. Psychologist Chris Brewin
writes of the dramatic changes that can follow a traumatic
experience.

It is...striking that survivors of trauma frequently
experience a sense of disconnection and alienation

from their families and friends, lose their trust in other people and institutions, comment that they will never be the same person again, and report dramatic shifts in their fundamental values and reasons for living. These observations offer an important clue that trauma does not just affect beliefs but also identity.[7]

For example, the traumatic events of the terrorist attacks of September 11, 2001, on the World Trade Center in New York and the Pentagon in Virginia spurred Americans to reorder their belief systems concerning the nation's vulnerability and the way others viewed the United States. The devastating experience prompted citizens to respond in ways that showed their country was still strong and unbowed by threats. The nation reaffirmed that sense of itself as powerful and acted in a way that attempted to master the traumatic experience. However, when the military response included the invasion of Iraq and the overall effort also included behaviors, such as torture and the denial of certain human rights, that Americans found inconsistent with other aspects of national identity, such as a sense of justice and fair play, some people desired a response that was more consistent with those other qualities. Although difficult, there was an effort to move past the shocking incident while learning from it. A response to trauma can be a process that involves recalibrating and even remodeling the building blocks of an individual or social identity that is shaken by the traumatic event.

Yet trauma is often not an isolated experience. Frequently, victims are not able to escape from an environment in which they are experiencing harm. The traumatic events the Christians experienced included their parent religion rejecting, cursing, and sometimes persecuting them. A second experience was persecution by the Roman authorities, including the martyrdoms of important leaders such as Justin, Polycarp, and Ignatius. Finally, Christians were forced to witness the suppression of the second-century Jewish revolts in 115 and 133, an experience that involved immense loss of life and apparent diminishment of the Jewish religion. Yet the movement, even as it experienced these traumatic events, found the power not only to redefine itself but also to compete successfully for new members. To master the trauma, Christians had to rewrite history, reconfigure old practices, and develop new identity markers that connected to the old and legitimated the new.

After the destruction of the temple in 70 CE, Judaism reinvented itself at Jamnia. There, a duly ordained judge named Johanan continued a court of law under the old name of Sanhedrin. He ordained disciples and thus claimed an unbroken line of authority dating back to pre-70 CE Jerusalem.[8] Taking a page from the rabbis' playbook, Christians began to create a parallel story. Jesus had ordained the apostles as bishops and had given them his teachings, the deposit of faith. Like the rabbis, Christians in the second century could claim a legitimacy of succession and integrity of teaching. With such small numbers and recent origins, Christians tended to overemphasize the bishops' role as the key link and first proof of legitimacy. At the beginning of the second century, Ignatius of Antioch claimed that the local bishop was appointed by God and should be viewed as such by other members of his church. Shunned by the rabbis, the Jewish Christians instead created a powerful rationale and vehicle for authenticity.

The Christian narrative needed to make sense of the sporadic persecutions and ongoing oppression the Jewish and Gentile Christians endured at the hands of the Roman authorities. Those who were tortured and executed were identified as heroes who suffered and died as witnesses to their faith. Rather than a program of revolts, Christians developed a cult of martyrdom. The Eucharist took place at the tomb of the martyrs as these new heroes became intimately connected with the cult of Jesus, who was seen as dying a heroic death in obedience to his Father. With the cult of martyrdom came an understanding and appreciation of Christian suffering. Linked with Jesus' suffering, martyrdom identified Christians as longing for another world. At the same time, it drove home the point that Christians were not like the Jews, who were fighting for a place in this world.

Jews suffered terribly after the revolts of 115 and 133. The vibrant Jewish community of Egypt was practically wiped out after the so-called diaspora revolt that began in 115, and more than half a million Jewish men are estimated to have been killed in the revolt that Bar Kochba began in 133. Thousands of others died of starvation or were sold into slavery.[9] The Romans severely punished the Jewish survivors as a way of warning other would-be revolutionaries that disobedience would be soundly crushed. The Jews lost privileges and could not enter Jerusalem, which became a Roman city. On the other hand, Judaism's weakening may have enabled the Christians to expand their distance from their parent religion.

A New Story of Origin

Any credible religion had to have its own sacred writings. In the first century, when Christians referenced Scriptures, they referred to the Jewish writings. But as the number of Gentiles in the Christian movement steadily increased, the search was on for different writings that could provide a less Jewish and more Hellenic frame of reference, as well as become the foundation of a new story of origins. In Rome in the mid-second century, the theologian Marcion proposed a uniform book of Christian writings, or canon, which would exclude the Jewish Scriptures and instead include the letters of Paul and the Gospel of Luke, minus the first few chapters, which rooted that gospel in the Jewish Scriptures. Marcion's new origin story called for a radical break with the Jewish religion by proposing that Jesus revealed a god of love who rebelled against and superseded the Jewish Scriptures' evil god. Marcion's theology was challenged, but it was quite popular in the second century: his insistence on exclusively Christian Scriptures was widely supported. His proposed canon also challenged others to create their own collections.[10] Although they were not formalized until later, the ground rules for identifying truly Christian writings were being developed.

Another man's work toward the end of the second century crystallized and focused the Christian story's sporadic and awkward evolution. Irenaeus of Lyons was no stranger to trauma. His mentor, Polycarp, was martyred by being burned at the stake in 155 CE. Ten years later, the congregation Irenaeus served was persecuted and decimated, with many members martyred in a public spectacle. When Irenaeus was asked to become the leader of the survivors, he was challenged to define true belief more precisely. He was determined that the faith his fellow Christians died for would not be undermined by divisions within the movement. In his writings, notably *Against Heresies*, he pushed for wider acceptance of John's gospel, which contained the most powerful arguments for Jesus' divinity. The Roman Church had resisted this gospel because it was seen as undercutting Peter's authority—an authority the Roman Church claimed for itself. Irenaeus also challenged the position of Marcion and others who sought to cut themselves off from the Jewish Scriptures. Instead, he proposed a more expansive narrative that began with God's self-revelation to the Jews and selection of them as the chosen people. Irenaeus then interpreted the prophetic writings as predictions that the Jews would renounce God's revelation in Jesus and forfeit their role as chosen people.[11]

The new Christian writings were meant to evidence the idea that a new chosen people had been called into being through the self-revelation of God in Jesus. Irenaeus emphasized the historically inaccurate Acts of the Apostles as the true story of Christian origins and as proof that the Holy Spirit continues to protect the church from error. Despite multiple and disparate versions of early Christianity, Irenaeus promoted a "deposit of faith" that had remained consistent since the apostles' time. He mistranslated the Hebrew Scriptures, misrepresented earlier Christian writers, and ultimately rewrote history. Yet he offered a coherent narrative and persuasive argument for an orthodoxy that became the outline of Christianity as we know it. As noted by one scholar, this story endured more or less "until at least the 19th century."[12]

Irenaeus provided the overarching superstructure that united both Jewish and Christian writings by positing history as an opera in three acts. First came the creation, fall, and extensive Jewish prologue to the incarnation; followed by the redemptive coming of Jesus; and then his return, which signaled the end of the story. Irenaeus could hear the replaying of melodies that connected otherwise disparate pieces in this work of art. Sometimes it was an individual, such as Eve, who reappeared as her opposite, the Virgin Mary. Other times it was a phrase. Isaiah speaks of washing away filth from the daughters of Zion; John's gospel describes Jesus washing his disciples' feet. These parallels were proof positive for Irenaeus that God was the author and conductor of this magnificent drama. Telling this divine story was an invitation for all people to respond in true faith and right behavior to such a generous god.

Church historian Wayne Meeks describes this narrative as a moral drama that was new to the world at that time. "If anything may be said to be unique in Christianity's contribution to Western ethical sensibilities, it is this dramatic history of everything and all peoples, centering on the erratic response of God's elect people to God's speaking and acting, and culminating in the calling to account of every creature for what they have done in God's world."[13] The prophetic vision of the Jewish Jesus had been expanded into a global worldview that found a prominent, powerful place in Western civilization. How did that happen?

To some extent, the moral drama that Irenaeus presented was a solution to the traumatic experiences of the second century. Revolts, plagues, and persecutions fueled people's anxiety, especially as the Roman Empire was beset with internal problems and external threats. As opposed to Christian apologists who primarily used Greek philosophy to defend the movement through rational argument, Irenaeus was a pastor who told a moving story, even if it was not always intellectually satisfying. The gospel according to Irenaeus offered Christians the opportunity to participate in a great narrative that gave their life circumstances an alternate meaning and gave them a new identity as contributors to the story. In particular, martyrs were seen as contributing to the fulfillment of the story as they witnessed its authenticity through their own sacrifice.

Who Interprets the Story?

In opposition to Marcion, Irenaeus suppressed the many theological difficulties present in the Jewish writings and instead proposed that the Jewish Scriptures were basically a proto-Christian book that prefigured and supported what he considered basic orthodox beliefs. Trinity, incarnation, and the coming of Christ at the end of time were all ideas that could be found in the Jewish writings if one knew how to read them. Yet the narrative's most important subtext was the apostles' role and identity. Irenaeus made a case for a pristine deposit of faith given by Jesus to the apostles and handed off to their successors. These traditions were contained in the various churches founded by the apostles

and their successors in an unbroken line. Yet the church in
Rome that Irenaeus believed Peter and Paul had founded
had a special significance among all the churches. Irenaeus
wrote that every church must be in agreement with it. He
insisted on a system of quality control that included orthodox belief, common narrative, and legitimate authority.

Armed with often specious arguments, Irenaeus attacked those he saw as living outside the fold, condemning
them for their refusal to see what he saw. He declared that
only those who remained within the fold would become a
new race that in the fullness of time would eventually as-
cend to Heaven to be with God for eternity. Yet Irenaeus
claimed no special status for himself, declaring simply that
he was one of a long, unbroken line of bishops who traced
their ancestry to the apostles. Irenaeus rewrote history to
fashion a religious identity that could be passed on to future generations. Later, in the fourth century, his narrative
became the backbone of the creed that was developed at
Nicaea and expanded at Constantinople.

A Story with an Edge

Christianity's second-century response to abandonment,
persecution, and violence was truly original, even if it borrowed much from its parent religion. Yet the adaptation of
Jewish practices and rituals had an edge. As Jews separated
themselves from Gentiles, Christians separated themselves
from Jews, so the fasts were on different days and the rituals had different meanings. Gentile Christians did not possess that more intimate connection to the parent religion
that earlier followers felt. The violent suppression of the
Jews after the bloody revolts of the first and second centuries suggested to some that the Jews were being punished:
the ancient religion was becoming less admired. Whatever
practices and traditions the Christians had taken over from

Judaism no longer needed the defense, initially supplied by the author of the Hebrews, that Jewish ritual had been superseded by the work of Christ. Instead, the growing separation invariably led to disparaging any connection to the parent religion, despite the obvious similarities in tradition and practice. Christians would claim to find God in the details that separated them from Judaism. Yet also hidden in these differences would be the hostility and pain associated with the trauma they had experienced.

As it freed itself psychologically from the Jewish religion, the Christian movement faced an identity crisis but responded with ingenuity and creative adaptation. Membership increased from an estimated 7,500 adherents facing extinction in 100 CE, to a thriving movement of more than 200,000 by 200 CE.[14] Although those numbers are debated, we can see the broad outlines of a fragmented tiny movement in the first century that expanded to something much larger and coherent in the second. Understandably, this progress idealized the second century as the time of heroes who stood in direct lineage with Jesus and his apostles. Such idealization represents a natural stage in human development, just as a child needs to idealize parents as a buffer against the frightening challenges of the world. But idealization can have a noxious underside. Marcion's slamming of Judaism as a lesser religion with a lesser god has continued into our own time.

To return to the analogy of the trauma victim, we can appreciate both the creativity of surviving the past and the idea that past solutions are now problems for us. The iconic Jesus can be misused to justify prejudice, oppression, and even war—the very forces his followers struggled against in the second century. The process of idealization itself can lead to an all-or-nothing bifurcation of reality into the artificial realms of good and evil. Denying Christianity's own Jewish roots can lead Christians to maintain a supersessionist position that isolates their religion from not only Judaism but other religions as well.

Problems with the Story

Second-century solutions cannot be expected to work in the twenty-first century, and new information destroys many of the assumptions that undergirded Irenaeus' narrative. The twelve apostles were primarily symbolic positions that pointed to the restoration of the twelve tribes of Israel, which would occur when God's kingdom arrived on Earth.[15] According to Raymond Brown, most of the apostles remained in Jerusalem, waiting for Jesus' return.[16] The early house churches employed a variety of organizational structures, with the role of the bishop evolving over time; Rome may not have had a traditional bishop until the second century.[17] Fragmentation, not unity, was the hallmark of the movement in its earliest stages. To look backward in time, as Irenaeus did, and see a powerful strain of orthodoxy is to do more than simply commit violence against history. It means committing violence against people who do not hold the same beliefs, judging them on the stories they tell and not on the lives they lead. In the crucible of traumatic and world-changing events, a movement survived by claiming a privileged status that offered consistency and hope in a time of upheaval, but at a price.

Returning to the scene of the trauma can lead to a greater appreciation of Christianity's inspired and creative expression of religious experience. It can also lead to a greater appreciation of the connection between Judaism and Christianity, without creating a zero-sum game in which one has to lose for the other to win. The goal of revisiting the trauma of Christian beginnings is also an invitation to revisit the trauma of Jewish beginnings. A new consensus might emerge that both faiths were outstanding ways of expressing religious experiences and are vehicles for such expressions even today. However, the implication—namely, that each is a rewrite of history composed in a time of trauma—is one that both religions would find extremely difficult to accept.

Facing Problems with the Stories

Judaism and Christianity each have an Achilles' evil. Each religion holds that certain events happened in history, events that are foundational to the religion itself. In Judaism, the foundational event was the exodus from Egypt, the formation of people in the desert under Moses, and the conquering of their homeland under Moses' successor, Joshua. Similarly, Christians claimed that Jesus not only challenged the Jewish religion but also began a new religion of which he was the center. Neither origin story can be maintained in the face of historical scrutiny. However, what remains for both religions is an appreciation that each story contains an expression of spiritual triumph in the face of nearly overwhelming crises. Still, both stories may have an edge because they contain the terror and trauma that was with them at their beginnings.

Can This Story Be Rewritten?

If religion is to survive in our times as something helpful and not toxic, what form will it take? Organized religion in the twenty-first century seems to be moving in a more fundamentalist direction. For some Jews, violence in Israel is justified by a historical claim that privileges the Israeli ownership of the land and justifies their unjust treatment of their fellow Semites. Some Christian fundamentalists support a virtually idolatrous view of the United States as a vehicle that will bring Christianity to a godless world, even if such an approach involves war.

In Catholicism, the move toward fundamentalism is visible in the pontificate of Karol Wojtyla, who took the name John Paul II. Like a modern Irenaeus, Wojtyla experienced significant trauma. The painful deaths of his family members and the horrors of World War II challenged and then reaffirmed his faith. As Pope John Paul II, he tried to steer a middle ground between the more progressive and more reactionary elements in the church. Like Irenaeus, he was a pastor who sought to provide a uniform story, even if it meant suppressing views that did not quite fit into his. His emphasis on orthodoxy blocked many of the liberal changes that many Catholics expected after the Second Vatican Council, but his openness to the world and other religions seemed to sustain some of the council's momentum.

Yet for all of his brilliance and talent, John Paul II's story about history and the church's role in it faltered in real time. Initially, he articulated a need for human freedom that became a galvanizing war cry in the ideological battle against communism in the 1980s. Unfortunately, he could not adapt his message to the struggles against the repressive regimes of Central and South America to any similar effect. Moreover, he was especially distressed when his native Poland became more secular and less attentive to his vision. His mystical belief that once Poland shook off communism the country would lead a spiritual renewal in Europe was destroyed. Like a trauma victim, John Paul II began to see the world as a dangerous place where materialism and rampant capitalism produced a culture of death that threatened to overwhelm a more spiritual life. In the face of such perceived chaos, the pope, like Irenaeus before him, clung to an imaginary doctrine of orthodoxy as a solution.

In his encyclical *Veritatis Splendor,* John Paul II articulated the need for the faithful to give their assent to the pope's declarations. He tried to justify a view that presented complex moral conflicts in black-and-white terms, a position that most moral theologians have seen as resisting moral theology's more recent developments.[18] Just as Irenaeus identified teachings as being simply the continuation of the deposit of faith, John Paul II saw his writings as exemplifying Christianity's changeless truths. Like Irenaeus, John Paul II needed to block out or reject other voices that told different stories.

Can We Live with a Distorted Story?

We can speculate about the role of traumatic experiences in the development of a rigid orthodoxy that claims for itself the status of eternal truth. How much does the experience of psychological harm lead to a rigid defensiveness if it is not resolved? Irenaeus' path is uncertain, but "the adult Karol Wojtyla would keep his own counsel and almost never entrust to other mortals the traumas of his life."[19] On the other hand, it may be that the moral strength and personal determination formed in a time of survival are attractive to many who feel so bruised and alienated by their own life experiences. The clarion call for revenge and the reassertion of U.S. power were almost universally supported after 9/11. Yet even here, trauma may have led us to a more irrational sense of our own entitlement to make war, as in Iraq in 2003.

Among other things, the development of orthodoxy in Christianity's history suggests a certain irrational element, no matter how rational the arguments supporting orthodoxy may be. Past battles are fought again in the present. Questions are perceived as attacks, and other perspectives as dangerous. It is naive to assume that people will easily give up what they consider to be hard-won truths. When a friend of John Paul II presented him with arguments in support of birth control, the pope reportedly replied that he could not change what he had always taught.[20] It is as though a religious perspective needs to embrace eternal truths, assuming these exist.

For both John Paul II and Irenaeus, orthodoxy brought with it a passionate concern for assent and a near obsession with error. What remains is a closed belief system that claims superiority over other systems. A contributing factor to such orthodoxy is a history of traumatic experiences that were courageously resisted and led to a willful identity that resisted accommodation. The intensity of that vision both attracts and repels. On one hand, it offers a powerful and unwavering ideal that can motivate people to lead heroic lives and, in doing so, accomplish wondrous things. The pope deserves credit because his leadership was significant in Poland's survival and the communist empire's break-up. Yet a closed belief system also cuts out other thoughts and experiences that are perceived as foreign and perhaps dangerous. Irenaeus condemned other Christians who could not accept his views, even if they led honorable lives. John Paul II suppressed progressive movements springing from the Second Vatican Council because he feared they would drift away from what he considered orthodoxy.

A More Ambiguous Story

In this information age, we are all too aware of social injustice and the fragmentation of society itself. To assume that morality and community will easily appear through a simple appeal to our better natures would be naive. Yet the experience of trauma may be a catalyst for someone to lead a more spiritual life. The experience of alienation can motivate someone to participate in a community. An awareness of injustice can lead a person to work for a more just society. Focusing on individual responsibilities may assist people in becoming less frightened about the world and more concerned with what they can do to create a better one.

Such behavior could be embedded in a new, more ambiguous narrative that values the process of self-discovery
and individual responsibility that is nourished, rather than
stunted, by the tradition someone holds. The Vatican II
document *Nostra Aetate* cautiously began a narrative that
identified connections with other religious stories. Valuing
these other stories can lead to an appreciation that these
truly human texts express, in ways both powerful and limited, the creative responses of particular peoples in particular circumstances. However, any attempt to privilege a particular story above others is like the creation of a false self
after a trauma experience: it is helpful for the moment, but
inadequate in facing future difficulties.

On the other hand, such an ecumenical perspective
introduces ambiguity by relativizing any individual narrative. A person's own story is an ongoing process, as changes
demanded by new information and maturation add new
chapters and revise old ones. A community is a place where
like-minded people share their stories and sometimes find
the common threads that can be used to create fabric for a
larger narrative. Community leaders are challenged to live
out their own stories while they nurture the developing stories in their community. The goal is the development of a
particular religious sensitivity that values the awkward process involved in forming a religious identity.

Such an awkward process can be sabotaged and short-
circuited by the traumatic experiences and partial resolutions that can be seen in the lives and work of Irenaeus
and John Paul II. Although we can appreciate their cry for
unity, we can also acknowledge that such a desire creates
winners and losers, the privileged and the "less than." The
test is whether the journey to faith can reconcile the anger
and grief associated with trauma so that one's religious
boundaries are open to the values of other traditions, even
those appearing to be in opposition. In such a journey,
past traumas are worked through so that future challenges

can be approached unencumbered by the partial solu tions of the past. An analogy might be seen in the lives of those parents who were once abused as children but have broken the pattern of trauma and provide a different and healthy experience with their own children. Likewise, the journey to faith can lead to a community that relates differently, not only to each other but to the world at large. In this individual journey, one is challenged to find a community that treasures its traditions and still remains open to the thoughts and practices of others. The following chapter is offered as an example of what such a journey might look like.

Chapter 7

Barack Obama and the Journey to Community

> There is no selfhood apart from community, no faith
> apart from community, no destiny and no vocation
> apart from community.
>
> —James Fowler, *Becoming Adult, Becoming Christian*

It's cool to be spiritual, but not so cool to be religious. Being spiritual allows you to claim a meaningful value system without having to be tied down by any of those messy, embarrassing incidents that dog organized religions nowadays. According to research published in 2008 by the Pew Forum on Religion and Public Life, the number of religiously unaffiliated individuals in the United States is increasing.[1] Nationwide, the percentage is 16.1; among certain states, particularly Western states, that number is higher. This statistic represents a trend among Americans ages eighteen to twenty-nine in particular: one out of four people in that age range claim to be unaffiliated with any particular religion. By the time the next Pew Survey is taken, more Americans may be unaffiliated than belong to mainstream Protestant religions. When so many Americans embrace such a "cool" position, in which they cast off the mantle of organized religion in favor of a more nebulous, less challenging version of spirituality, are they losing the opportunity for community?

The previous two chapters outlined the role of community in the development of Christianity or, more accurately, of the Christianities of the first and second century of the Common Era. The same may be said for the earlier discussion of the story behind the story of the Jewish Scriptures. In that case, pushing through the inspiring narratives about Abraham, Moses, and Joshua revealed the heroic story of struggling people trying to survive on the outposts of a powerful empire. Although different scribes and their communities battled with one another in the province of Yehud, it was in the service of living up to their identity as the chosen people. We can see that an individual's journey of faith, as least as outlined in what we know about those who wrote the Scriptures, takes place in the context of a community grappling with a crisis. In addition to one's individual faith journey, we can also see a parallel process—the journey to community.

The more recent, science-based reconstructions of both Judaism and Christianity show that these religious movements were characterized by diversity: the norm is not only for many religious communities but also for some diversity within a community. So the issue is not finding the right community but finding one that supports an individual journey. Additionally, the members of these communities challenged one another to lead moral lives and be concerned for others. Yet as these diverse groups evolved, many simply disappeared. The Essenes did not survive the Jewish revolt, and the community that honored the Gospel of John disappeared into Gnosticism. Or it could be something more mundane. The community I belong to experienced problems during a time of transition, and many left the congregation. Yet even if it is temporary, a community can offer the comfort and challenge so important for one's religious journey.

The Example of Barack Obama
Spiritual but Unaffiliated
The life of Barack Obama exemplifies how one's religious search is paralleled by a movement toward community. As

he pointed out in his memoirs, *Dreams from My Father* and *The Audacity of Hope,* his mother imparted to him a unique spiritual heritage. A bright and curious woman, she sought out, in an appreciative way, what others might consider foreign and perhaps inferior. She took her son and daughter to explore different places of worship, thereby suggesting that these religions were all valuable in some way. As an anthropologist, she possessed a global vision that deeply respected other cultures. Through her example, she challenged her son to look beyond the narrow confines of his world and see value in the stories of others. Obama's legacy enabled him, at a relatively young age, to develop a tolerance for others as well as a global awareness that transcended the narrow boundaries of a local community or religion. In this way, he was not unlike a growing percentage of young Americans who are unaffiliated with traditional religion, but may consider themselves spiritual.

Yet *spiritual* does not necessarily mean *individualistic.* It is difficult not to see that we are all vitally connected. That knowledge comes, first of all, from an appreciation of common problems, such as the difficulties of the global, interdependent financial market, the vicissitudes of which seriously affect international corporations as well as millions of individuals. Then there is global climatic change. We are increasingly conscious that our efforts to develop and sustain our economies include burning fossil fuels on a vast and accelerating scale, thereby damaging our shared environment. The idea of global terrorism means that the world is threatened by extremists who seek change through violent means. Global trade creates interdependency as goods and services are moved from place to place. We look at our shirt labels to find the brand name and also the country where the garment was manufactured. The Internet provides access to information, views, and experiences from literally everywhere and can broaden anyone's horizon. In fact, the intricacy of worldwide problems and the constant availability of information can be overwhelming—occasionally so much that people are prompted to seek security by retreating to a more limited and individualistic worldview.

On the other hand, awareness of our interconnectedness with others and with our world can result in an almost mystical experience, difficult to put into words, which may hearken back to the blissful feelings of infancy. Freud described this experience as an "oceanic feeling," and argued that it was the basis for the formation of religion. Our awareness is heightened by the work of scientists, who continue to make astonishing discoveries. Our sense of awe, clothed as it is in today's more scientific garb, can still be the beginning of a truly religious experience, just as our earliest ancestors may have been awestruck at the beauty of their world. The difference is that today we are more aware of our integration with the world and the consequences of our actions within it, while they looked to the controlling powers of heavenly beings. We can arrive at a worldview that is horizontal and egalitarian, rather than vertical and hierarchical.

Taking Responsibility for Change

For Barack Obama, taking responsibility for change meant becoming a community organizer after graduating from college. His dream of helping others nearly evaporated as he tried and failed to find work as an organizer. He had nearly given up when he was offered a position in Chicago, sponsored by a coalition that included several churches, to organize people, mostly African Americans. As can happen, his effort to help others change helped him change. His experiences cemented his sense of purpose and commitment to work in the public sector. However, he was not just learning about himself; he was also absorbing new information that challenged the humanistic value system he had inherited from his mother.

While we all are aware of problems in the world, as well as conflicts within ourselves, we tend not to take responsibility for problems until we reach a point of discomfort, a dis-ease with the way things are going. We want to scratch the itch, and so we do something—it could be small or dramatic, a gesture or a life change. Additionally, the more complicated the problem and more dramatic the change, the more ability and resources are needed to tackle them. One would need a certain amount of optimism that change can happen and that the effort is worthwhile. Finally, accepting accountability would mean accepting the need for the hard work and self-discipline that such an enterprise demands. Such a task can be overwhelming, so it is helpful to step back and get a better look at the problem.

Taking in New Information

Information doesn't necessarily come from an outside source. Reflecting on our own feelings and intuitions can be extremely helpful, even if doing so is at times uncomfortable. Obama's discomfort stemmed from appreciating that something was missing. Although he had developed a principled life, thanks to his mother, he did not belong to a community with shared traditions in which he could ground his deepest beliefs. In the lives of the people he worked with in Chicago, he witnessed a religious dimension that had taken root in a community and that had become a guiding force as the community addressed nearly intractable problems. The religion he came up against challenged people to live more deeply in the world and embrace their African American identity, rather than allowing them to escape from either. As he processed these observations, Obama was ready to move to the next step.

Movement is part of the religious experience. According to Luke Johnson, precisely this tendency toward action distinguishes the religious experience from a good feeling that we enjoy, but that does not motivate us to change.[2] Psychologists have noticed something similar in studying the difference between a spiritual experience and one of beauty. Although both are characterized by a sense of awe, only the former contains the discomfort that can lead to positive change.[3] The new information that revolutionizes our understanding of the Bible can provide that kind of religious experience. (I know it did for me.) On the one hand we experience freedom. We do not have to believe the hyperbolic stories of biblical heroes or miraculous events that went against our modern sensibilities. And the stories behind the stories revealed people more like ourselves. On the other hand, we could experience some discomfort. What do we do now? Even if we haven't read all the new books, religious individuals seem to be more belongers than believers. And in that sense there is a growing divide between the professional ministers who proclaim certain beliefs as truths, and the laity who are increasingly making up their minds. Independence rather than obedience is becoming the default position. Yet if we consider the conflicts in the Jewish communities after the destruction of Jerusalem in 586 BCE and the uncertainties of those first-century Jewish Christians who left their religion to search for something not yet known, we can appreciate that our own journeys will be rocky. Taking in new information meant engaging in a process with no end in sight.

Although new information can be overwhelming, we have some choice regarding what we look for. We know, for example, that a certain TV program or radio personality slants the news and comments in a particular direction, and we can choose whether to tune in. The same is true of newspapers, the Internet, and forms of entertainment that we opt to attend or ignore. This is not to say that in this postmodern era there is a clear choice of objective versus subjective material. More than being what we eat, we are what we consume intellectually—soaking up new information does not mean that we can easily or intuitively decide between information that is valuable and not valuable, and then accept only the former. How can we develop the tools to filter the immense amount of information confronting us on a daily basis?

What may make accomplishing this feat even more difficult are the information and beliefs we already possess. New knowledge about global difficulties and possible solutions can run up against our own security needs or our preconceived ideas about how things should be. To further complicate matters, the world itself is in flux—change, not permanence, is the hallmark of our times. To take in new information is to tolerate a process that we can never fully appreciate, because we are in the midst of it. At the heart of that process is a certain tentativeness because we realize that the information is incomplete, and our own biases get in the way. Yet the spiritual experience almost demands a movement toward some kind of faith, be it traditional, homegrown, or some mixture of the two.

Accepting a Belief System

Obama's more personal and intuitive spiritual journey led him to a faith in a particular religion, the congregation of the Chicago Trinity United Church of Christ, whose pastor was the Rev. Jeremiah Wright Jr. Although he describes having had powerful religious experiences when listening to Wright's sermons, Obama claims that his decision to be baptized was more choice than epiphany. Embracing a traditional faith did not mean he shed the doubts and questions he had inherited—rather, faith and doubt could now coexist within his belief system. He found in biblical stories a context for African Americans struggling in Chicago, for his own journey, and ultimately for the larger world: "Our trials and triumphs became at once unique and universal, black and more than black."[4]

James Fowler suggests that faith's more advanced stages require believers to embrace a particular religious view. His catchy phrase "the absoluteness of the particular" means not that a specific religion has cornered the market on truth, but that the opposite is true.[5] Somehow, if only momentarily or partially, the infinite reaches out to the finite in the participant's religious experience—this tension between the particular and the universal is what undercuts any given religion's exclusive claim on truth.

The gift to organized religion of a searcher like Obama is that he personifies the tension between the universal and the particular. Taught to appreciate and learn from various spiritual practices, he was more likely to be inclusive and to respect the value of different religions, even if he did not accept them for himself. For example, he appreciates the work that the Nation of Islam has done for certain African Americans, but he sees the long-term weakness of such a religion. Because searchers have tried different brands, so to speak, they can articulate in a meaningful way the values and the attractiveness of the particular faith they ultimately choose without denigrating other religions.

However, Barack Obama argued that tolerance came from hard work: it meant embracing the debate on values that he believed would ultimately lead to some meaningful consensus. As part of that debate, he warned that doctrine and ideology not only blinded us to pragmatic and creative compromises but also prevented us from appreciating the values in the other's position. For him, the Golden Rule was more than mere relativism; it meant the more demanding call "to stand in somebody else's shoes and see through their eyes."[6] From a religious perspective, one test of his success as president would be his capacity to lead and foster a national dialogue about values that moves the country away from an ideologically driven stalemate and into real and empathetic consensus.

From Cool to Hot

Many in the growing number of religiously unaffiliated Americans could make a significant and enlightening contribution to more traditional religions. However, the searchers would have to move from cool observers to hot participants to make such a transition. When Obama began attending church services, Rev. Wright challenged him, suggesting that he might be worried that his attendance would seem too "feminine," or that some of his male peers would not accept it. But for Obama, going to church was meaningful on a deeply personal level. At the conclusion of *Dreams from My Father*, he recounts an episode at his dad's gravesite in which he tearfully mourned his father's mistakes and his grandfather's fear. In his reverie, he came to understand that these men suffered from a lack of faith— more specifically, a lack of faith in other people. Without this faith, they could not value the potential for helpfulness of others who saw the world in different ways. Instead, they became closed off and confused as they tried to manage their lives in fearful isolation. Faith in others, Obama implies, can be therapeutic because it can help us adapt to the challenges that change presents.

Earlier in the book, Obama touches on a similar theme when he describes how some African American professionals at Trinity said they had joined the church officially after they had avoided practicing organized religion for some time. At a certain point, they realized that something was missing: they had been cut off from themselves. Returning to church was not simply a spiritual enterprise, then, but one that also had psychological consequences. In this way, too, these individuals' decision to affiliate themselves with a particular religion was therapeutic, because doing so meant addressing the needs and feelings they could easily have suppressed as black professionals becoming successful in historically white industries.

If the challenge for believers is to think, the challenge for searchers is to *feel*. That means moving away from a "hip" lifestyle of spirituality without religion. It means recognizing the pain of isolation, whether you are grappling with change or with success. Do you feel that something is missing? Have you lost faith in others or yourself? If so, the experience can be uncomfortable, difficult to talk about, uncool. It is like the awkwardness that often characterizes a patient's first therapy session. The patient's decision to seek help usually affords some relief, but the idea of telling secrets to a stranger invokes anxiety. It's nearly impossible to be a "cool" therapy patient. Emotions experienced as uncomfortable and problems believed to be embarrassing are on display and sometimes heightened by the perception that the therapist is judging the patient. Yet those feelings may be precisely what the searcher must recognize and manage in order to embrace a more traditional faith. This parallel with therapy may also be reflected in the searcher's perception of being judged by a supposedly welcoming religious community and its minister.

The Struggles to Both Join and Stay in a Community

Adhering to a particular religion is also a turnoff for some people because it means living with mistakes, hypocrisy, and short-sightedness—not to mention the scandals and crimes—that the religion may evidence. Catholics are scandalized by the sexual abuse that some priests have perpetrated and the cover-up that some bishops have arranged. Fundamentalists must cringe as some high-profile pastors are pressured to backtrack after making racist statements.

A growing number of Jews have spoken out against Israel's treatment of the Palestinians. And Barack Obama left Trinity after certain inflammatory remarks made by Rev. Wright were publicized.

It's difficult to be cool and connected to an organized religion. Probably all religions—Christianity in particular— are about hope insofar as they tell stories of courage and compassion, usually with happy endings. The stories inspire us to believe in a better future. Obama wept at a sermon by Wright titled "The Audacity of Hope," which was itself inspired by a painting of a lone harpist playing a damaged instrument in a desolate place. In this story, Obama could see himself and the people he worked with. Despite the power of the political establishment in Chicago, he and they continued to organize people to seek redress against harmful policies and open up opportunities for employment in the hope that justice would be done and they would become better people in the process.

As sociologist Robert Wuthnow noted, religion is becoming less about beliefs that appeal to our intellects and more about the emotionally laden stories that ask us challenging questions and provide us with opportunities to discover meaning.[7] It offers a certain optimism that can support individuals in their challenges, a value system perhaps expressed in ritual or song, and, ultimately, a community of like-minded believers with some commitment to addressing more global concerns. Such a community may be less concerned with denominational issues, but can both challenge and support those working to move the world in a more life-giving and responsible direction. In this way, the particular religion would also be connected to the universal, even though the former would admittedly have its own faults and shortcomings.

If we cannot avoid looking at the world through a particular lens or filter, then joining a believing community is a way of deciding, or at least being mindful of, just what our filter is. By identifying with such a community, we declare that we view reality through the lens of a particular religious, mythical tradition. This is the leap of faith through which we commit to a way of living, even though we know that the tradition we embrace is limited by incomplete information and subject to error because of its cultural and historical determinants. We believe, but we also doubt. We embrace the tradition, but we are prepared to distance ourselves from those beliefs and practices that cause real harm.

We can see in the life of Barak Obama a religious journey that moves from an unattached, global belief to one that is attached to a specific, believing community. He began that journey with skepticism toward traditional religions, but with faith in people. When he felt an emptiness in his position, he moved toward a particular religion, not as a way of denying his more universal beliefs but as a way of expressing them. His story encourages those of us who are seekers to consider the importance of a community, flawed though it may be, as a vehicle that can carry and support us in our journeys. With change as the only constant in our lives, we are faced continually with new information that activates our survival instincts. How can we afford to look out for others when we must devote so much time and energy to caring for ourselves? Like Obama, we are tempted to enclose ourselves in armor and are reluctant to lower our defenses. Yet we can see in his story the value of opening ourselves up to the more emotional need to connect not only with others but also with the walled-off parts of ourselves. As social beings, humans develop those connections in a community setting. Experiencing discomfort can be an opportunity for seekers to risk joining a hopeful religious community.

The Challenge of the Journey

Patients are usually reluctant to enter therapy and are quite happy when it is over. Certainly, part of their hesitation stems from facing the hard work of looking at difficulties they have avoided and making changes that are uncomfortable. On a less than conscious level, our primitive survival instincts can thwart our potential to change—we may be convinced that we cannot disclose our vulnerability because the world is a threatening place. In fact, many entering therapy have simply reached a point where their discomfort is so high that the risk involved in attempting change becomes worthwhile. Yet it requires a special kind of courage to face the pain we have been avoiding for so long.

Change can also mean re-evaluating the core beliefs that have sustained us. And we may worry that without our faith guiding us, we will have no moral compass. We can also point to experiences when our faith gave us the courage to do something that prevented a downward slide into destructive behavior or achieved a recovery from such behavior. We can recall times when hard work in competitive situations was rewarding and opened up opportunities for our advancement and personal growth. Examining such traditional beliefs can provoke anxiety. In a panic, one imagines an either/or situation in which one is caught between the pull to stay with what has helped in the past and the attraction of what might be helpful, if not necessary, for the future. In such a state, it is difficult to imagine a synthesis that includes some values from a once helpful belief system, but also introduces elements of newly acquired information.

There is a story about an explorer who was progressing toward the North Pole. When he got his bearings at the end of the day, he discovered that he was farther south than he had been when he had started. Only then did he realize that he was on a large ice floe that was moving in the wrong direction. In the face of such power, one wonders whether it is even worth it to keep going. Why bother engaging in the demanding work involved in a progressive movement, personal or social, when everything appears to be going south? Why not simply focus on survival?

As he got to know the congregation at Trinity, Obama realized that it was a cultural community. Its members were part of a dynamic process in which the values professionals learned in school mixed with the experiences of those who had been educated on the streets. In that process, their particular identity was formed, strengthened, and maintained, often in the face of adversity. As a cultural community, the church challenged the values of the dominant culture, which overvalues wealth and material goods. Perhaps more important than its contributions to society or its advocacy for the downtrodden, the church offered a more psychological benefit: the formation of an identity more sustaining than the one Obama developed as a community organizer.[8]

Often, the process of joining a community involves the hard work and self-discipline required for learning new behavior. For Obama, that hard work was more emotional than intellectual. It meant becoming part of a community. We may believe that we are unable to sustain such hard work because we are so consumed with the demands of our everyday lives. And that may be true for some of us. On the other hand, we may simply be reacting to the perceived conflict between our own self-protection and the exposure involved in joining a community. Joining may be less about accepting a belief system or ideology and more about imagining the future through hopeful, shared stories of compassion and courage.

Community as a Support System for Managing New Information

To take in destabilizing information is to leave oneself open to anxiety. And that worry is like a hardwired alarm system that can raise our defenses and push back against the information as though it were an intruder. For Obama, some of the impetus to fight such anxiety came from religious leaders whose words and example led him to appreciate the value of faith.

There are at least two prerequisites for safely and pro-
ductively engaging in new information about the Bible:
one is individual; the second is social. The first involves the
courage to see. Obama tried to understand the religious
leaders who supported his community organization efforts.
Initially, such curiosity might have contributed to his emotional conflict as he contrasted his own belief in community
organization with that of these leaders and their dynamic
religious congregations. He might also have seen that he
was not abandoning his best values and beliefs, but finding a way to refine and enhance them in a community setting. He could also see something of himself in the other
members of the Trinity congregation. Therefore, a second
prerequisite would be some kind of formal or informal support system that can be a context and container for the psychological struggle involved in changing one's thinking.
Obama opened himself up to religious services and then
to a religious community. Although the struggle is an individual one, it does not have to occur in isolation.

Finding a good support system may be a challenge.
People look for a challenging but supportive environment
in which difficulties can be addressed nonjudgmentally.
They also search for a safe environment where they can be
vulnerable without feeling that they may be harmed. Finally,
there may be an intuitive element suggesting that a particular setting just "fits." (In a sense, searching for the right
environment is like searching for the right therapist.) If we
are to drop the cool, skeptical stance of a searcher and move
to the more emotional position of a believer, we are better
served not only by finding the courage to change but also
by possessing the common sense to find a safe place to land.

Whatever the landing, it might be neither long term
nor without challenges. Although very few of us will ever
have the opportunity to act on such a large stage as Barack
Obama, we can learn from his journey that the result does
not mean some new and more certain ideology: there are
always doubts and uncertainties. We likewise learn that faith

is a partial vision and a work in progress. Still, we can appreciate his courage to grow beyond his comfort zone in an effort to change both himself and society. Paradoxically, his larger-than-life efforts can help us lower our expectation about the consistency of faith or the efficacy of faith-based work. We can learn to tolerate our doubts and celebrate our partial solutions.

This chapter on the journey to faith sets the stage for the next section, part three, which addresses how a believer is both validated and challenged in the world. Given that beliefs can lead to both psychological health and deep concern for the world, one would expect that parallels to the faith journey can be described in nonreligious terms because religion does not corner the market in either the search for psychological health or the solution to worldly problems. On the other hand, given that faith is a messy and conflicted process, it is no surprise that nonreligious perspectives differ, sometimes dramatically, from more faith-based ones. After all, there are even dramatic differences within the spectrum of faith-based perspectives on a variety of matters. Despite some of these disagreements, the religious journey can be consistent with our deepest psychological strivings: religion can be healthy and worth our investment.

Part III

The Humanist Journey to Faith

Today, religious descriptions of the human journey must take their place with other explanations that come from science, philosophy, and art. These voices generate their own sets of terminology and assumptions to explain reality. Yet the differences between them can also offer some common ground because what was traditionally seen as religious—for example, narrative and ritual—can be viewed as intrinsic components of the human journey.

Of course, differences will remain, and the discoveries of science will be in tension with many traditions of religion. However, if such tensions can be addressed in a respectful conversation, both sides can develop a new appreciation for the possibilities and limitations in any human-constructed view of reality. If we are to evolve, we need more than reason; we need a mythical view that inspires us to face the crises of our times.

Former Soviet Union leader Mikhail Gorbachev exemplified such a mythical view when he understood that history was revealing the need for a more democratic form of governance that valued individual freedom and social justice in his own country, and a new commitment to peace by other governments. His growing understanding can be framed as a religious journey in which he faced the limitations of his communist political beliefs, and then worked through various conflicts to develop a more inspiring story about how people everywhere can join forces to resolve the evolutionary challenges of our times.

Chapter 8

The Biblical Narrative
What's Your Story?

As we know, a creation story never provided people
with factual information about the origins of life.…
In the ancient world its purpose was not to inform
but was primarily therapeutic. People would listen
to the recitation of a cosmological myth when they
faced impending disaster, when they wanted to bring
a conflict to an end, or to heal the sick. The idea was
to tap into the timeless energies that supported human existence.

—Karen Armstrong, *A Short History of Myth*

Here in the first decade of the twenty-first century
the story that becomes America's dominant narrative
will shape our collective imagination and hence our
politics.

—Bill Moyer, "A New Story for America"

When I pedaled my bike to church one afternoon, I never imagined I would be traveling to
another world. I was in the sixth grade at a local Catholic
elementary school, and the nuns there had encouraged
us to "visit Jesus" during the forty hours of devotion that
weekend. When I arrived, the only other occupants of the
church were two of the sisters, who had apparently been
there for some time. They almost immediately arrived at
the pew where I was kneeling, and one of them kindly but
firmly suggested I stay with Jesus until someone else arrive.
"We don't want to let Jesus be lonely." I was soon engaged
in a fairly relaxed but more or less one-way conversation
with the now very human and vulnerable Jesus. In this brief
encounter I had a sense of being called to service. I also

began to insert myself into the grand metanarrative of the Christian movement, that story of heroic altruists who continued the work of Jesus here on Earth.

Although I could not articulate it at the time, this experience opened up another dimension for me. For a moment, the everyday world I found so confusing, if not strange, disappeared and a new one opened up in which there was order, direction, and meaning. I was determined to become a citizen of this alternative world in which Jesus guided us to help those less fortunate ones trapped in an everyday existence where there was confusion and meaninglessness. I had been secretly called to help them, and I would remain at the ready until I was summoned to begin my mission. I returned home not just content but with a sense of validation. The real world mystified me. I even made mistakes on my paper route. This new world would be a lot easier. I just had to wait until Jesus gave me the signal. While I can smile about it now, I realize that that experience and the larger narrative into which I had inserted myself had profound effects on my own identity formation and, later in life, influenced my choices of spouse and career, as well as the values I modeled for our children.

Although the story of Jesus and the movement created in his name helped me lead a life with meaning and purpose, I now realize that story is more myth than history. On the other hand, I also recognize that stories can be powerful and even therapeutic. In this chapter, I take a closer look at the stories of Jesus in an effort to learn about their power, especially their power to transform. Yet transforming stories are not without distortion. Writers or listeners impose order and meaning that empowers as well as distorts the data.

How Beliefs Distort the Data

We know the stories of Jesus and John the Baptist from the four gospels, which were written by Christian believers. However, the Jewish historian Josephus (37–100? CE) wrote another version, in which the description of Jesus is quite brief and has been modified by later Christian writers according to most scholars. Josephus devotes much more attention to the story of John the Baptist. He gives us the juicy details of Herod's adulterous affair with his brother-in-law's wife; his own wife's escape to the kingdom of her father, Aretas; John's successful ministry and popularity; and Herod's execution of John the Baptist out of fear that John's popularity might spark a revolt. Josephus adds the postscript that when Aretas destroyed Herod's army, some of the Jews thought that God was punishing Herod for killing John. This writer gives the story of John more ink because it highlights the Jewish belief that their god is just and will avenge the deaths of faithful servants. Belief drives the historical narrative.

The four gospels, which were written at around the same time as the histories of Josephus, tell a dramatically different story of the relationship between Jesus and John. If we arrange these gospel stories in the chronological order in which they were written—Mark, Matthew, Luke, and John—we can see the Christian belief exerting more influence on the narrative over time. Mark has John baptize Jesus, and then reintroduces John a few chapters later to describe his death under circumstances that tend to shift the blame away from Herod to his wife, Herodias. Matthew's John baptizes Jesus under protest: "I need to be baptized by you, and do you come to me?" (3:14). Luke has Jesus being baptized, but apparently not by John. The book of John does not have Jesus baptized at all.

None of the gospels mention the defeat of Herod's army or the consequent belief that God caused that defeat to justify John's death. Placing the gospels in that order emphasizes the evolution of Jesus' exalted identity at John's expense. Such a belief actually commits violence to the narrative, especially if we accept New Testament scholar John

Meier's conclusion that John was Jesus' mentor.[1] Although in his ministry Jesus adapted the practices and teachings he learned from John, John's impact on him would be lessened, if not obliterated, in the gospel stories connecting the two.

Belief influences the storytelling, but the opposite is also true: a powerful story can shape our beliefs. The letters of Paul, written about twenty years after Jesus' death and almost twenty years before the first gospel was written, contain very few details about Jesus' life. Paul was a preacher and community builder who wrote to his fellow believers about the meaning and implications of Jesus' death and subsequent new life. Did he avoid a narrative format because he was not familiar with actual events of Jesus' life that would later be part of the gospels? New research suggests that Paul's writings do contain a narrative that might have formed the basis of his preaching and his belief system. However, Paul's narrative takes us to the realm of myth rather than history.

The Gospel According to Paul

Paul's letters are both inspiring and mystifying. The author of the New Testament epistle 2 Peter, who probably wrote in the early part of the second century, complained that the letters of "our beloved brother Paul" contained elements that were "hard to understand." The writer went on to warn readers that "ignorant and unstable" individuals were misinterpreting Paul's writings (3:15–16). As if to prove the author's point, in the middle of the second century, Marcion tried to develop a version of Christianity that was based primarily on Paul's letters, arguing that Paul was revealing a different god than the one the Jews professed. Apparently, ignorant and unstable people were not the only ones who struggled with the Pauline writings. Over the centuries, the learned and the normal sought to understand the writings, often arguing about the meaning of a particular word or phrase.

Paul scholar Richard Hayes argues that the letter to the Galatians contains a narrative substructure that puts in perspective one of the letter's often disputed passages.[2] Galatians is, in some ways, Paul's apologia as he defends himself against his enemies, who apparently put a full-court press on him, claiming that he did not preach an authentic gospel, was not properly authorized, and had neglected to impose certain requirements of Judaism. After defending his legitimacy to preach the gospel, Paul set up a rhetorical question about whether faith or works save us.

Hayes goes on to maintain that the discussion over faith versus works has overlooked the gospel narrative that can be teased out from Galatians 3:1–4:11 and that can also be found in other letters, notably Romans. Hayes asserts that when Paul talks about the salvific effects of faith, he is primarily referencing the faith *of* Jesus, not faith *in* Jesus. He comes to this conclusion not only by referencing other uses of the term in question but also by positing a narrative, or "gospel," that justifies his interpretation of the faith of Jesus.

In Paul's mythical story, the God of the Jews was seriously conflicted. On one hand, God was unbelievably merciful and loving; on the other, God could be so wrathful as to support the slaughter of women and children. Paul argued that in this story, it was Adam who started humanity on a downward spiral of sin and disobedience that ultimately placed God in a dilemma. How could the story move forward when God's chosen people were unable to overcome continual sinfulness, despite the pain of punishment and the rewards God offered for good behavior?

While Paul was trying to figure this out—or perhaps act it out in his persecution of Christians—he was transformed through a conversion experience, and in the process discovered how God solved the dilemma and moved the narrative

forward to another chapter. God sent Jesus into the world
to reverse the downward spiral of sin and do what ordinary
humans were unable to do: reconcile themselves to God.
Jesus, although innocent himself, vicariously took on the
sins of humanity and remained faithful to God, even though
doing so led to his crucifixion. Scripture scholar and theologian Ben Witherington III also sees the underlying narrative as a key to understanding Paul's writings: "God sends
Jesus forth as a *hilasterion* (i.e., propitiation). Some have
objected, does God propitiate God's own anger? The answer, however paradoxical, must be yes."[3] The dilemma was
solved: the crucifixion was the price to be paid for recon-
ciliation. In this story that Paul learned and then preached,
God rewarded Jesus for his faithfulness by raising him from
the dead and establishing him as the Messiah who would
return to restore God's kingdom on Earth (Acts 3:19–21).
A new age, a new chapter in the narrative, had begun.

In his writings, Paul was both fleshing out the story,
by seeing its foreshadowing in the Jewish Scriptures, and
simultaneously extracting rich meaning from the story's
relevance to all people, Jews and Gentiles alike. In making
his case for finding meaning in Jesus' death, Paul returned
to an earlier part of the narrative, the story of Abraham.
He noted that Abraham's faith in God is described as righteousness, which Paul saw as prefiguring Jesus' righteousness. Paul interprets the prophets—in this case Habakkuk—
as saying that God has promised to send a messiah whose
righteousness God will count as a fitting counterbalance
to humankind's unfaithfulness. In Galatians, and more so
in Romans, God is the focus and main actor of the narrative. It is God who finds the antidote to unfaithfulness and
disobedience by sending Jesus, whose faith and obedience
prove God's own trustworthiness and love, as promised
by the covenant. The death and resurrection of Jesus is an
"apocalyptic event" that demonstrates "God's eschatologi-

cal justice."[4] Paul believed that God would soon establish a
kingdom on Earth, but do it more safely now that, as Paul
wrote to the Thessalonians, Jesus would protect his followers from "the coming wrath."

Mythical narrative and belief can easily become locked
in an escalating and self-reinforcing spiral. For example, a
narrative suggests a belief that is then reapplied to the story,
which can then produce more beliefs, and so forth. That
escalating spiral has gone on for so long that the beliefs have
become inseparable from the narratives, perhaps making it
impossible to develop an accurate portrait of the historical
Jesus. But particularly for believers, the attempt to find a
more historically based Jesus may be a therapeutic process
in itself: the effort may help us correct the distortions that
our belief systems have constructed.

We can revisit the writings of Paul and appreciate that
he was a believing Jew who, after his conversion, was trying
to create a significant place in his religious worldview for
the person of Jesus Christ. Like other members of that first-
generation messianic movement, he believed that the faith
of Jesus was a key way of inserting Jesus into the larger narrative.[5] He struggled with a variety of explanations of just
how Jesus the Messiah fit into God's plan. He used conflicting metaphors to drive home a story that valorized Jesus'
ignominious death, while proclaiming the resurrection as
God's sign that a new age had begun. Such a process of
finding meaning and hope in painful and disturbing events
is reminiscent of what therapists do as they help patients
develop less harmful and more supportive narratives from
the events and memories of their lives.

Storytelling as Therapy

Although storytelling has a built-in distortion factor, expressing ourselves through stories is dramatically good for

us. Psychologist Kitty Klein identifies a number of experiments in which the construction of narratives is associated with improved physical health, psychological well-being, achievement, and cognitive functions, such as working memory.[6] Additionally, an approach appropriately defined as narrative therapy claims that this technique can successfully relieve the distress of trauma by helping people retell or reconstruct their stories in a way that leaves them less victimized and more empowered.

Rather than relying on a particular theory, a narrative therapist encourages patients to tell their own stories, placing particular emphasis on the role problems play in that narrative. Then the therapist, in collaboration with the patient, develops a narrative in which the patient has more control over those same problems. This approach is similar to that of other therapists, particularly Viktor Frankl. For example, Frankl tells of asking a depressed woman to tell her life story from the vantage point of her deathbed in a way that would give meaning to her particular life struggles. Although Frankl emphasized individual choice in constructing meaning, the narrative therapist might emphasize the role of co-construction of a narrative. In summarizing the successful treatment of a particular patient, a narrative therapist put it this way: "This life narrative was quite different from the one he had been trying to develop when he arrived. I had been an active partner in its construction, but it was no less his for that reason; he had guided me and I had guided him."[7]

Finally, a narrative therapist maintains that an individual's identity and sense of self can be changed dramatically in this process. Such an argument downplays the notion that an individual is mostly self-contained and autonomous. Reflecting postmodern and social-constructivist views, the therapist focuses on the creative and destructive processes that shape identity in social situations. The following is part of a letter that narrative therapists David Epston and Eileen Swan sent to an incest survivor who was experiencing serious psychiatric problems. The therapists constructed the letter together with other family members who had consulted with them. The patient had refused to attend the meeting.

> As a family, we have been an occupied zone, invaded and terrorized by our father-aggressor. But now we can and will recapture ourselves, our bodies, our dignity, and our pride. The best way to fight back is as a family because we have not spent all our strength. You did most of the fighting over the bad times and [are] perhaps the most weakened by it. We now would like to give you back some of our strength because we have more than enough. It is because of you we have become strong, the strong women we are, and we owe you a great debt. You have fought on your own for so long—now we will all fight back together.[8]

These psychological insights about underlying narratives, the co-construction of reality, and the social processes that shape identity can give us a deeper appreciation of the power of the religious narrative.

How the Religious Narrative Gets Its Power

For Paul, God is the main actor in the Bible, and God's conflict with creation needs to be resolved. God solves the problem by sending Jesus, whose faithfulness ushers in a new age open to Jews and Gentiles alike. The narrative that had been somewhat hidden in the substructure now becomes visible, as Paul describes benefits and opportunities available to those who align themselves with the faith of Jesus and who, in the process, have faith in him. He then invites the listeners to enter into the narrative and co-construct the next chapter of salvation history. Paul's gospel story may derive some of its power from this invitation to engage in its continuation. To be a follower of Christ is to participate in his mission and, in some mysterious way, be incorporated into him. Likewise, to insert our own stories into the ongoing biblical narrative is to fill those stories with added meaning. Narrative therapists explain it this way: "Stories are full of gaps which persons must fill in order for the story to be performed. These gaps recruit the lived experience and the imagination of persons. With every performance, persons are reauthoring their lives. The evolution of lives is akin to the process of reauthoring, the process of persons' entering into stories, taking them over and making them their own."[9]

When the aforementioned narrative therapists joined with a patient's family to co-construct a letter that offered a different narrative, the patient's life was retold in a way that changed her role from victim to heroine. This familiar plot echoes the story of Jesus, a victim-turned-hero in his followers' co-constructed account—the familiar story told every week in Sunday service, but applied to the present. As religion professor James Dausey states, "In its narration the story becomes alive to a new community, and its events transcend the past and move into the time of the participating congregation."[10] Again, the story's power lies not only in its description of Jesus' heroic journey, but also in its invitation to join that passage by inserting oneself into a story that is always under construction. As we become more aware of our changing identities, constructed and reconstructed as we interact with different people and experience differing life circumstances, the weekly service can remind us of our core values and encourage us to sustain them, even as we change.

While Paul was building on an older Jewish narrative, he was simultaneously constructing with his congregations another chapter in the narrative that now emphasized the present, rather than the past. In working free from that awful dilemma, God also freed human beings from a passive role in which they had no real power to do anything about the conflict. However, human beings' new freedom came with a responsibility to immerse themselves in the resurrected life of Jesus Christ. The retelling of the story draws us into Jesus' saving actions and invites us to take on his primary characteristic—faith. Hayes frequently makes the point that it is not our faith but our grafting ourselves onto the faith of Jesus that is salvific. He is not part of our story; we are part of his. Our faith does not set us free; his does. However, Jesus' faith was perceived as so powerful that some of Paul's enemies apparently believed that they were relieved of all responsibilities and bound by no laws. Paul objected to anyone inferring such meaning from the narrative and instead argued for a new ethic. Hayes suggests that, at least in Galatians, Paul was not proposing that we simply try to imitate Jesus Christ, or that our good efforts continue the work of redemption, which is a one-off event. Rather, the power of redemption itself fortifies believing Christians to live lives that echo Christ's.

From a narrative perspective, Paul and the other preachers of the gospel were inviting people to continue the next act of the God narrative. They were now players in the drama, fulfilling various roles and being carried along by its force. Though Paul focused on Jesus Christ's unique work, believers took on important roles in the story's retelling. Narrative therapists would say, "Every telling or retelling of the story, through its performance, is a new telling that encapsulates, and expands upon, the previous telling."[11] For many people today, the power of Jesus is primarily a backdrop: responsibility for our own behavior has become the focal point. In a 2001 survey, 90 percent of Catholics and nearly 80 percent of mainstream Christians were quite clear that it was not faith in Jesus, but their own good works, that would ensure their salvation.[12]

Narrative and Identity

Paul insisted that the gospel story was critical for the new believing communities because it fashioned and determined their identity. The phrases Paul used to describe himself are familiar to some: "It is no longer I but Christ crucified." An individual "puts on Christ" or is "baptized into Christ." Christians were expected to merge with Jesus' identity, and the community was to visualize itself as making up or fleshing out Christ's body. Although there was room for various roles within the community, its members were intensely interdependent. "Believers are and must be dependent on each other, not least because no one Christian has all requisite spiritual gifts to be an independent entity, a body of Christ, on his or her own. For Paul, just as there is no salvation outside of Christ, so too there is no salvation outside the body of Christ either."[13]

Paul's narrative may still have powerful pull. Philosopher Paul Ricoeur writes of his passion to find in a story or text "a world that I might inhabit and into which I might project my utmost powers."[14] In his epistles, Paul offered a powerful story and then invited Christians to immerse themselves in it. Although he suggested that Christians were to imitate Christ, he also pointed out that they were at a different point in the story than Jesus was, and that their faith was to be played out within their particular section of the plot.[15] Paul emphasized the more submissive traits of obedience and faithfulness, virtues he believed Jesus Christ exhibited. The narrative also conveyed the sense that Christians were all in it together, appealing to a sense of community rather than overvaluing individuality. No matter what challenges they faced, they would continue to bear one another's burdens in the same way that Jesus exemplified in his life (Gal 6:2).

During Paul's time, Christians were such a minority that he advised them to keep a low profile. They were to follow the laws of good government, even as he encouraged them to follow the higher law that bid them to love one another because they were brothers and sisters in Christ (Romans 13). For both theoretical and practical reasons, Paul insisted that Christians develop an almost common identity that sprang from the gospel narrative. As they put on Christ, they would become less like their old selves and more like their hero, whose faithfulness called them to a common destiny. Yet there was a danger here. Christians could discount the value of their own psychological growth by submerging their identities into the common identity provided by the powerful metanarrative.

Becoming a Hero in Your Own Story

Somewhere between Paul's call for a common identity in Christ and those theorists who propose an enduring and autonomous self—the rugged individualist—is the ground staked out by narrative therapists, who argue that a person's life story is co-constructed in such a way that identity or sense of self can change substantially over time. Narrative therapists Haim Omer and Nahi Alon, describing the "declining reality of the self," summarize much of the evidence opposing the concept of an enduring self that therapy is intended to uncover and restore. Instead, they take an alternative stance, quoting other theoreticians and experimenters, that one's sense of self is constructed.[16] The primary means of constructing the self is by developing alternative narratives that build on material left out of previous narratives. From a psychological perspective, we are all storytellers who rewrite our histories to make sense of and bring order to our lives.

In their book, Omer and Alon describe a case history involving an Israeli soldier who was exhibiting major symptoms of post-traumatic stress disorder. He was a ranking officer in a battle in which several of his men were killed and he was seriously injured. In recounting the incident, the now-retired officer blamed himself for not insisting on the kind of equipment and security procedures that would likely have prevented the soldiers' deaths. His stress was compounded because he could not persuade the board of inquiry to publicly address the high command's unwillingness to admit its error in ignoring suggested precautions before the engagement. The troubled patient was focusing on the parts of his narrative that highlighted or constructed a sense of himself as someone who had both failed his comrades and neglected to bring to justice those at least partially responsible for their tragic deaths. Blinded by this story, he became obsessed with matters of safety and justice in other areas of his life.

After an intensive but rather brief period of psychotherapy, the patient was able to recover the parts of his story that emphasized his own courage on the battlefield and his later attempts to achieve justice. Mobilized by this new narrative, he went public with his concerns about the battle and what he perceived as a cover-up by higher authorities. He experienced the healing power of his own efforts to shed light on the events and the consequences of avoiding serious preparations for it. Although he could not help his fallen comrades, he could provide valuable lessons for others preparing for battle. Though he still remembers the events that caused him so much suffering, he can sustain another perspective that engendered a sense of mastery over those events. Omer and Alon offer this summary of the man's reconstruction of his painful past: "The reconstructed narrative of Yoram's life made good sense to him now. He could recognize himself as the sinner who was trying to make good on his transgressions by public corrective acts. He was a hero with a flaw, but still a hero, and he had a goal and a mission, almost prophetic in scope."[17]

The authors' use of the word *prophetic* calls to mind those heroes of the Jewish Scriptures who spoke out against injustice. As was the case in Paul's letter to the Galatians, Omer and Alon's book betrays a narrative substructure that shapes and defines Yoram's reconstructed narrative. Admittedly, such an underlying narrative may be an artifact of Western psychotherapy. After all, no one goes to a therapist to be a better psychopath or to find more devious ways to harm others. Nevertheless, psychotherapy often involves reclaiming those more capable, if not heroic, parts of a person's story in an effort to offset damaging experiences that leave them feeling victimized and powerless. However, another element may be at work here.

The Challenge of
the Heroic Narrative

Paul's telling of the gospel story, with its emphasis on empowering individual believers through their connection to Jesus Christ, motivated many to define themselves in a new way. Paul proclaimed that they had received valuable gifts from Jesus' redemptive work and were now entitled to one another's support. Because they were now so empowered, he challenged them to change the world through virtuous living and to achieve that high level of obedience and faithfulness to which they were called.

Additionally, these converts were likely inspired by Paul, who underwent tremendous hardship and heroically faced challenges as he preached this gospel. In his letter to the community at Corinth, Paul claimed to have suffered more than the other preachers they knew. He wrote:

> Five times I have received from the Jews the forty lashes minus one. Three times I was beaten with rods. Once I received a stoning. Three times I was shipwrecked; for a night and a day I was adrift at sea; on frequent journeys, in danger from rivers, danger

from bandits, danger from my own people, danger from Gentiles, danger in the city, danger in the wilderness, danger at sea, danger from false brothers and sisters; in toil and hardship, through many a sleepless night, hungry and thirsty, often without food, cold and naked. (2 Cor 11:24–27)

How does a story give one so much power? Aside from the fact that we like to hear a story, which is not unimportant, a story can make us feel good and bring such benefits as improved physical and psychological health. From an evolutionary-psychology view, the power of stories is a bit of a mystery. Pascal Boyer claims that our minds comprise several inference systems that are always on the alert to draw conclusions that might be helpful, if not survival based: which plants are dangerous; which strangers can be trusted. Although we can never be absolutely certain, we need to make the best guesses we can, and our minds are designed to enable us to do so. Such a phenomenon is similar to what the Gestalt therapists have noted as our tendency to complete an incomplete figure. However, the narrative drive Boyer describes goes much deeper than that. From an evolutionary perspective, we may tell ourselves stories with different endings as a way to adapt to new situations and thereby survive and thrive.[18]

In this vein, stories play a critical role in our development. If we consider our own stories, we look into the past to find patterns and experiences that will enable us to move successfully into the future. We are similar to our ancient ancestors, whose stories about different tribes were built on past experiences that offered the best evidence about whether those tribes could be trusted in present and future interactions. We need only look at the Hebrew Bible for an underlying story that justified the interconnection of some tribes and called for shunning others. In fact, the entire "historical" narrative contained in the Jewish Scriptures is based on a construction of the past that gives prominence to the tribe of Judah, the supposed inhabitants of the Persian province of Yehud.

Although several disparate forces can empower a narrative, an important one for us to consider is the capacity to find powerful meanings by rereading the past in the light of present conflict. Paul did this when he experienced the cognitive dissonance that developed when his intense Jewish belief clashed with new information about the community he was persecuting. At first he was stunned by this new information that turned his world upside down: those he thought of as traitors to be punished, he now saw as witnesses of God's work in this world. Living with this community, he came to believe that the death and resurrection of Jesus Christ provided a new synthesis because it resolved the conflict between his traditional Jewish beliefs and his recent religious experience that God was working in this world in a new way. He turned to the Jewish Scriptures and found material that developed and validated the story of God's work in and through Jesus. He then preached this story to others, encouraging them to believe in this new narrative that emphatically challenged their own culture, while passionately arguing for a different lifestyle.

In developing his overarching story, or metanarrative, Paul was modeling for us the value and the effort involved in constructing such narratives. We have a built-in need to tell stories, especially our own, but it is not always easy to do so, especially when the past does not appear to be helpful in planning for the future. However, a good story may motivate us to change or stay the course, to forgive ourselves for the past or berate ourselves for old mistakes. In a conflict between narratives, the better story—or at least the one better told—almost always wins. Usually it is only afterward, when we can evaluate the consequences, that we can tell which one was more therapeutic. And we can discover that stories we once held as helpful are now blocking our progress.

When Stories Harm

Paul's comments about a "new creation" should be taken quite literally. Jesus Christ's death and resurrection not only marked the end of humanity's estrangement from God but constituted a new beginning in which believers could model a new way of living on earth. The new life Paul described was facilitated by the many blessings that he believed had now become available because of God's work through Jesus Christ. Paul encouraged new Christians to exhibit these gifts in their lives by living in peaceful harmony brought about by loving one another and bearing one another's burdens. He imagined that the power of God and the example of Christians would bring about the conversion of the whole world in a relatively short time. As a Pharisee, Saul believed that converting all the people in the land of Israel to the pharisaic practices would usher in the long-awaited day of the Lord. Renamed Paul, this former Pharisee imagined that widespread conversion to Christianity would signal a return of Christ to this world and the completion of this new creation.[19]

On that last day, Christ would also return as judge, and God's wrath would be unleashed on those who did not believe. Jesus' faithfulness had protected his followers against God's wrath, much as John's baptism promised to provide protection in the apocalyptic scenario he imagined. Even then, Paul saw signs that God was already singling out unbelievers for harm. In his letter to the Romans, Paul argued that the pagans' lives had devolved into such unlawful and unhealthy practices that they deserved death, along with anyone who approved such a lifestyle (1:18–32). Similarly, his opponents were often condemned in the harshest of tones. For all his enthusiasm and modeling of loving behavior, Paul could not escape the consequences of the wrathful God he evoked in the letter to the Romans and passed on to his Christian followers. A rival group may have turned him in to the Roman authorities while he was in Rome, where he was probably executed.[20] Some three centuries later, Christians used their new powers to visit the wrath of God not only on unbelievers but also on those whose Christian beliefs were judged as unorthodox.

The Jewish narrative adapted by Christians contains a fatal flaw. The story imagines a once-innocent people now cut off from their god because they sinned. Although inspirational, this story is in serious conflict with the more recent archaeologically driven conclusions that the Jewish foundational stories were mythical and not historical. The scriptural stories Paul believed in are now seen as latecomers to Jewish literature, narratives that were developed to explain the plight of the small province of Yehud/Judah in a larger scheme in which powerful empires ruled the world. The notion of God's wrath explained why Jews had been marginalized in these empires: they were punished for their sinfulness. Yet God's wrath also eventually trumped these empires' power in the past, and they believed God would do so in the future.

The narrative that Paul inherited and creatively made the best of is essentially a story of power. Who has it? How do you use it? What happens to those who don't have it? From a feminist perspective, mainstream (manstream) narratives are suspect because their power can be oppressive. Feminist writers challenge dominant narratives as oppressing certain groups and simultaneously privileging the role and status of others, notably males. Theologian Elisabeth Shüssler Fiorenza argues that if the underlying narrative describes Christianity as a reform of Judaism, the story tends to make Judaism a lesser entity and may even foster anti-Jewish sentiment. If Jesus is presented as a heroic individual, the narrative separates him from his followers and marginalizes not only their importance but also the importance of the social movement of which Jesus was a part. Fiorenza argues that in constructing the narrative of Christianity, a person should be aware of the potential for both exploitation and emancipation.[21] Feminist writers call for a way of looking at historical narratives that highlights the players' struggle for freedom against oppression. They tend to see history itself as a heroic march toward emancipation and human dignity.

One Solution: Multiple Narratives

Ultimately, we all have at least one story to tell and re-tell—our own. Psychologist Jerome Bruner describes this construction process as an ongoing one: through narrative we create and re-create selfhood.[22] We co-construct our narratives as we interact with others and their storytelling, all of us pulling material from our culture and the master narratives embedded there. Although we construct stories with others, sometimes using the same incidents, we often wind up with divergent meanings. We may be continually surprised that we can develop "multiple plots for the same course of events."[23] We may sometimes be aware that we consciously construct or reconstruct our own identity narratives, but we may not realize we are building our stories from the few master narratives that provide the general contours of our own thinking. The feminist critique is a reminder that although we may be awed by stories' brilliance and novelty, we are responsible for the consequences inherent in the ones we construct and the ones we inhabit. No matter how breathtaking or meaningful we find them, these stories likely contain traces of the evolutionary mechanisms that gave birth to them. Who is in and who is out? Who can be trusted? Who is to be marginalized so that others can be given center stage?

Another Solution:
Beyond Narratives

The themes of the biblical narrative are embedded in Western culture: good will ultimately triumph over evil. Heroic sacrifices will not be in vain. Everything is part of some larger plan, but we are granted only glimpses of it. Paul's countercultural story has become mainstream. Though such themes may remain alive in Western cultures, the biblical narrative that birthed them has been dealt a fatal blow. If this whole master narrative is suspect, what happens to our concept of God, the main actor and driving force in the Bible?

One possibility is that the superstructure of the story remains, but we create our own version of God. Sociologist Robert Wuthnow has noticed the increasing ambiguity in meaning when it comes to God. He sees people as making up their own beliefs leading to a question as to "whether their notions of God are actually oriented toward the supernatural or merely something higher than themselves."[24] Theologian Harvey Cox, speaking perhaps tongue in cheek, has argued that the Market has taken the place once occupied by God. He capitalizes the term *Market* as a way "to signify both the mystery that enshrouds it and the reverence it inspires in business folk."[25] One can only wonder if the recent economic crisis has led some to a real crisis of faith.

The challenges to the biblical narrative also call into question the usefulness of a narrative to describe God. On one hand, we are heavily programmed to use narration as a basic tool for understanding our world and our place in it. We plan our futures and find our very selves in the stories we tell. We try to extrapolate from our own stories some ultimate story of where we have come from and where we are going. We use our stories to find meaning, even ultimate meaning, in our lives. We would be highly resistant to any suggestion that we give up narrative—a tool that can make us physically and psychologically healthy in this life—as we consider and face what is beyond it. On the other hand, our present understanding of narrative challenges us to appreciate that it is constructed, malleable, and somewhat idiosyncratic. This new information challenges us to free God from the stories, those human artifacts that otherwise serve us so well in our daily lives.

If we cannot give up narrative as we ask ultimate questions, the next best thing might be to relativize narratives that seek to comprehend the incomprehensible, to borrow a phrase from Viktor Frankl. Narratives built on our evolutionary need to draw conclusions from limited data demand checking and rechecking, despite their power to make sense of things. For those of us embedded in the biblical narratives, new information about these stories can create an opportunity for us to reevaluate them. A more scientifically based position encourages us to see them as stories in which we are invited to be heroes in our own lives. We are also alerted to the possibility that our stories can create victims—ourselves or others. The journey to faith is a challenge to live in a world of many narratives and to be careful about stories that claim too much.

Chapter 9

Rituals
For Better or Worse

I am suggesting that ritual may be understood as practical wisdom, that is, *doing something*, performing some act that is believed to bring us into closer step with the ultimately real. A rite is for setting things aright.

—Loyal Rue, *Religion Is Not About God*

Liturgy leads us to the edge of chaos.

—Graham Hughes, *Worship as Meaning*

The distraught mother took her twelve-year-old daughter to a family therapist. The child seemed fascinated with fire and had been caught playing with matches several times. Her secret behavior was becoming more dangerous and recently only luck and an observant relative had prevented what could have been a disastrous fire. Fire setting was not only a serious psychiatric symptom; it was also one that could physically harm the child and her family. Serious interventions would likely be considered: intensive individual psychotherapy, medication, or even placement outside the home in a residential treatment center.

After some assessment, the therapist offered his recommendation and course of treatment. He concluded that the girl did not know how to properly start a fire and therefore needed training so that she could learn that particular skill. He advised the mother to set aside a specific time to teach her child how to start a fire. The lesson should take place in a safe environment; the therapist recommended using the fireplace. The mother should demonstrate how to light a fire safely and then ask the child to try it herself. The lessons should continue until the mother and child concluded that the little girl knew how to start a fire safely. Follow-up showed that the girl had learned her lesson so well that she stopped setting unsafe fires.[1]

Although psychotherapy was once called "the talking cure" and emphasized the power of developing insight, family therapists emphasized the power of action-oriented techniques in their efforts to change the dysfunctional patterns of behavior and communication they observed in the families they treated. In their 1992 book *Rituals for Our Times*, family therapists Evan Imber-Black and Janine Roberts summarized these techniques, calling them "rituals," and argued for their importance not only in psychotherapy but also in everyday life. They related an anecdote in which a two-generation family—parents and their adult children—struggled to celebrate their annual Christmas dinner after the sudden death of a younger adult son. Over the next few years, the celebration became especially difficult because of an unspoken rule that no one should speak of that deceased son.

Finally, one year, another son and his wife brought to the Christmas dinner an album of photographs that included several of the son who had died. At first, one adult daughter left the home, crying that the couple had ruined the Christmas celebration. After working through their initial shock, the parents gradually began to look through the album and reminisce about their son. The adult daughter soon returned and joined the group as they mourned and remembered their son and brother. Through tears and laughter, stories were told about his endearing foibles and noteworthy accomplishments. In the process, a rigid ritual was replaced with one that celebrated life.[2]

This new emphasis on ritual as being life-affirming stands in stark contrast with another, equally valid view— that rituals can limit and confine us. This latter view can be traced to the work of Sigmund Freud, who claimed that celebrating religious rituals was akin to his patients' obsessive-compulsive behavior. Obsessive-compulsive disorder (OCD) is a limiting condition that is often characterized by specific rituals that even those employing them see as ridiculous. A promising technique for helping those who suffer from OCD is the establishment of a counter-ritual using cognitive behavioral therapy. Rather than understanding or interpreting the patient's ritualized behavior, the therapist coaches the patient to replace limiting and harmful actions by gradually introducing counter-behaviors, alternative rituals that offer a more strategic way of managing anxiety. The anxiety lessens as the obsessive behavior loses its intensity.

The Power of Rituals

Sporting events are nearly awash in ritualized behavior. In football, a kicker might tap the shoulder pads of the holder three times before he attempts a field goal. Hometown baseball fans might turn their caps around when their team is losing, hoping their efforts will introduce a game-winning rally. Likewise, rituals are part of everyday life. Children seem to function better if they have a regular routine in the morning before school and a specific schedule for homework after school. Most of us rest a little easier at bedtime after we have gone through a nightly routine of checking the locks on the front and back doors. We don't ask "Do you want a cake for your birthday?" Rather, we ask "What kind of cake would you like?" Ranging from the trivial to the superstitious to the meaningful, rituals calm our anxieties, aid in our celebrations, and even make us more efficient.

On another level, rituals remind us that words are not enough. We feel an unspoken pressure to express our feelings through actions. Although we might take the idea to absurd lengths in our consumer society, we recognize that our words are better accompanied by something concrete.

On the other hand, we are naturally suspicious of a person who professes to care deeply for someone but does nothing about it. We can appreciate the truth of the saying "You talk the talk, but do you walk the walk?" Words and stories are simply not enough when a lot is at stake. In fact, words often seem to fail us in times of intense experience. After a particular meaningful action, we might say, "That says it all." Rituals can draw power from our evolved psychological makeup as humans: we want communication to be more than just words.

The role of ritual is so deep-seated as to be part of our evolutionary inheritance. Anthropologist Pascal Boyer explains how ritual behavior might have developed and why it would have such intense power. He argues that to survive, human beings needed to develop a way of assessing what food was edible and not harmful. He posits that over time, a cognitive system developed that could infer what was safe from what was dangerous. Although such an inferential system might have originally been focused on food, it could be applied to other dangerous situations. Boyer explains, "Contact with rotting corpses or with wounded or diseased people, ingestion of feces or dirt: these are avoided for good evolutionary reasons."[3] To underscore the importance of this inferential system, the possibility of contagion would be accompanied by strong emotional reactions. Just think of the face and sounds a mother makes when her child is about to eat something that he has just picked up off the ground!

If Boyer's theory is correct, we all have a built-in, highly charged concern about contagion that enters our normal process of planning for action. In fact, we don't even need an explanation for avoiding something—if other people do it, we are likely to follow. Boyer goes on to suggest that those who suffer from OCD may have an inferential system that is so active that it interferes with the normal planning process. He argues that recent evidence suggesting a neurological basis for OCD supports his theory.[4]

Quoting other authors in the field, Boyer suggests that this concern about contagion seems to be at the heart of most rituals. Participants are concerned about purity and avoiding pollution. Rituals demand a particular format, with designated words and gestures. Participants come to believe that the ritual must be performed correctly or else great harm will befall them. However, most rituals also have a social function. In general, suffering hardship while participating in a ritual tends to intensify the relationships among participants and loyalty to the group. Examples range from the initiation rites of "primitive" warrior societies to the humiliating tasks required to join a fraternity. Though the stated intent may be to gain secret knowledge, the real effect of the ritual is that these young men are now prepared to become involved in risky behavior that can protect or support a larger group. Boyer calls this phenomenon the "relational catch" of rituals. It involves a new way of relating to other people that is hard to describe but intuitively seems to be related to participation in a demanding ritual.[5]

This important relationship between hardship and the power of ritual is also supported by what social psychologist Elliott Aronson has called "the single most important study ever done in social psychology."[6] Aronson is referencing the 1959 experiment by social scientists Leon Festinger and J. Merrill Carlsmith in which subjects were asked to help the experimenters by telling others that an unpleasant task was actually pleasant. Half of the subjects were paid $1 to perform this activity; the other half were paid $20. Surprisingly, but consistent with the theory of cognitive dissonance, the $1 group came to believe that the activity was actually pleasant, overvaluing it as a way to lower the level of discomfort they felt when told to describe this supposedly pleasant experience. Their behavior was consistent with the theory of cognitive dissonance which holds that when belief runs into conflict with new information, some individuals may try to rationalize their position as a solution to the conflict. The $20 group did not need to employ such mental gymnastics because they felt adequately compensated and therefore experienced much less discomfort when told to describe the experience. That same year, other experimenters, following the same theory, demonstrated that people going through a more severe initiation ceremony to join a group say that they like that group better than those who undergo a milder initiation. The conclusion seems to be that we may bond with a group or stay engaged with it when the price of entry involves some ritualized hardship.[7]

Although these descriptions of ritual might help us appreciate that their power comes from dynamic but less-than-conscious forces within us, they tend to neglect the healing power contained in the stories of rituals that family therapists describe, in which anxiety is successfully managed by creatively using our natural tendency to employ rituals. The fire is contained in the fireplace. A Christmas celebration is not polluted by the memory of a dead son; it is enhanced by including those memories. I argue that one element present in reparative rituals, and in the counter-rituals that help someone suffering from OCD, is *courage*—the courage of a parent to face a child's problem; the courage of a young couple who rebel against an unspoken rule; the courage of an individual suffering from OCD to take the first steps in confronting massive anxiety. Turning to religion, I contend that people cannot appreciate religious rituals unless they appreciate the courage their performance exhibited, at least originally. In fact, a sort of desperate courage lies at the heart of rituals like Passover.

The Courage of the Canaanites

In her book reconstructing the history of the Passover feast, Tamara Prosic locates the beginning of this powerful ritual in the desperate circumstances of subsistence farmers living millennia ago in the area we now know as Palestine.[8] They were members of many different tribes, but following biblical traditions they are now commonly called Canaanites. In this land without major rivers for irrigation, life depended on rain, which came not year-round but in one season. Human life was sustainable in this land only if the rainy season began and ended at the right times. First, the rain needed to begin in the fall, and the ground had to be plowed and prepared for planting. If the rain did not come then, the family or village faced a drought, with only the food they had stored to keep them from starving. Second, the rain had to stop when the grains were just beginning to mature: continued heavy rain destroyed the crops before they were ready to be harvested, leaving the people with insufficient food for the year.

In those ancient times, the god of war, the storm god, was the all-powerful Baal. In their desperation to control their environment, the villagers developed a ritual to stop Baal in the spring, when his presence would be disastrous, but resurrect him in the fall, when his absence would do the same. Under the protection of night, the villagers dared to break the taboo that levied a curse on anyone who would harm the god. In a ritual, they killed Baal, symbolized by the lamb, and consumed the flesh entirely, so as to prevent him from exercising his power and bringing the disastrous spring rains. The bones of the lamb were not broken, but were buried carefully, so that Baal could rise again in the fall when they needed his rain to soften the ground for plowing.

Prosic rightly points out the tremendous anxiety associated with such a ritual. It was a life-and-death struggle. The Canaanites needed to both control the god and avoid offending him. The attendant apprehension in such an effort provoked a series of ritualized behaviors that bound the anxiety temporarily and became a source of massive concern should the ritual fail. If the storm god did not die, what had the people done wrong? If he did not return, had they performed the burial improperly?

The Courage of the Judeans

In the sixth century BCE remnants of the defeated Kingdom of Judah were allowed to return to their homeland, where a small province now called Yehud was carved out from the lands their king had previously ruled. While many of the inhabitants of the land had not been exiled, the now combined population may have totaled as few as 20,000 people, with about 1,500 of them living in the city of Jerusalem.[9] When the exiles returned, they brought with them the beliefs and rituals they had developed to preserve their identity during their years in Babylon—they had become more religiously observant than the people who had remained in Judea. They offered something to fill the vacuum left when the king, the focus of their religion, was no more. The returnees also had status because they enjoyed the support of the Persian empire. Finally, they had at their disposal the power of ritual itself. Archaeologist Charles Carter argues that at this time the concept of separation became especially important for determining ethnic and ritual purity. Rituals became the major vehicles for designating those who were in and those who were out. As though they had read the books on cognitive dissonance, the émigrés from Babylon introduced hardship as a part of a complicated initiation process that would lead to something new in the world. In Yehud, there would be "for the first time a bold attempt to construct a whole society and culture in the light of a religious faith."[10] And if there was one ritual that identified the story of hardship as integral to the formation of a new community, it was Passover.

The returnees transformed the agricultural feast of the Canaanites into one that celebrated their mythical beginnings as an ancient people. The book of Ezra tells of a special Passover celebration, the dedication of the second temple (Ezra 6). In this story, the returned exiles were joined by those who had separated themselves from other nations and purified themselves so as to belong to the God of Israel. Although Yehud was isolated and materially poor, an insignificant province in a vast empire, the new leadership produced religious literature, written law, and unique rituals that helped establish a community that could survive materially and spiritually, despite the hardships of the times. It is very likely that Yehud remained apolitical during its period of isolation. It did not rebel against the Persian empire; rather, it focused internally on consolidating its own identity.

The Passover ritual thus became a safe place in which to rebel. By recalling a mythic past in which a mighty pharaoh was destroyed by the hand of their god, the Judeans could vent their frustration and mock their conquerors without incurring the wrath of the empire. Under the pretext of celebrating a past triumph, the Judeans kept alive the hope of returning to glory in the future. Given this historical context, the Passover feast was part of a larger agenda that attempted to carve out a national identity and a national god. Along with religious literature and written law, Passover became a vehicle through which the Judean people could wait for the time when they and their god would change the course of history. Building on the rubrics of a primitive ritual, Jews defined salvation not as freedom from the physical world, with its danger caused by drought, but as independence in the political world in which they struggled to survive as a distinct people. The Judeans hoped that the Passover event, one reminder of their mutual past, would coax god into reentering history. Passover enabled them to think of the land they inhabited as truly their own—given to them by God, not by the emperor.

Rituals are meant to bring about what they seek to accomplish. However, this small Judean population, with its modest economy and non-existent army, had to postpone any hope for God's triumphant intervention until the distant future. To borrow from Freudian terminology, Yehud

was in a latency period. Just as Freud believed a child between the ages of eight and twelve suppresses the varied
conflicts that will ultimately burst through in the teenage
years, the Persian period can be seen as a time of relative
calm before the dramatic efforts at independence a few centuries later. The ideology and enhanced self-identity that
the Judeans formed during the Persian era ultimately placed
their nation on a collision course with the Roman empire,
as well as provided it with the strength to recover after the
disastrous revolts of the first and second centuries.

The Courage of the Early Christians

Passover underwent one more significant permutation. In
the years after the death of Jesus, his followers began developing the rituals that would identify them. And as can
happen in any attempt to separate oneself from others, the
boundaries would be dramatic and intense. In the ceremony of baptism, the initiates would ritually be buried with
Christ and then rise from the waters with a new identity—
immersion being the preferred form for the ritual. In the
Eucharist, they celebrated the enduring Passover sacrifice of
their hero. While these early followers were trying to maintain their connection to Judaism, their rituals so challenged
if not scandalized Jews that they would ultimately contribute to a religious identity that was separate from their parent religion.

As Gerd Theissen, New Testament professor at the
University of Heidelberg, points out, baptism challenged
the Jewish religion on two levels.[11] By including death and
burial as the new metaphor, the ceremony reversed the
ritual taboo associated with touching the dead to one in
which being buried with Christ brings a new and pure life.
The symbolic dying and rising in baptism was not only a
prominent image for Paul and his communities (Rom 6:4;

Col 2:12), but also known by others, for example the group in Rome.[12] The second challenge was that baptism broke down the barriers of ethnic purity that were established so forcibly by the Jews in the Persian era. In the Christian worldview, people were no longer separated into clean and unclean. "As many of you as were baptized into Christ have clothed yourself with Christ. There is no longer Jew or Greek, there is no longer slave or free, there is no longer male and female; for you are all one in Christ Jesus" (Gal 3:27–28).

Theissen argues that the Eucharist ritual was an even more intense crossing of the forbidden threshold that was baptism.[13] Whereas baptism broke a ritual taboo concerning cleanliness and separation, the Eucharist involved breaching moral taboos: the shedding of blood, the eating of another's flesh, and even human sacrifice. The ritual for this new Passover celebration provided a safe place in which Christians could symbolically reenact Jesus' violent death, as well as benefit from his sacrifice for them. The bread and wine, the innocence of a meal, hid and contained the naked aggression that was played out in the religious imagination.

Yet that aggression might well spark another level of anxiety that would be associated with a need to celebrate the Eucharist correctly. When the ritual was to be performed, that secondary anxiety was not so focused on who led the ceremony or even what words were said. Instead, there was a heightened concern that the participants be consistent and true to the goals of the ritual. In 1 Cor 11:27–32, Paul severely criticized the wealthy who would not share their food with the poor during the celebration. In John's version of the Last Supper, the author substituted Jesus washing his disciples' feet for his words over bread and wine to emphasize that service to others is this ritual's essence. The Didache, a first or early second-century CE manual on Christian instruction, warned that their ritual would be defiled if participants did not confess their sins or resolve their conflicts before the ceremony. In short, the apprehension around the ceremonies centered on the concern that they were creating a new people whose devotion and service marked the beginning of God's kingdom on this Earth.

The Courage to Be

The rituals of the early Christians were not just about breaking taboos. By claiming that people were purified by contact with the crucified Jesus, the Christians demonstrated that Jewish concerns about cleanliness had become irrelevant. The parting of the waters in Genesis, like the separation of day from night and sea from land, suggested to Jewish commentators that making distinctions and separating entities was a critical part of God's creative activities. They argued that Jews should embrace such a process in their own lives. Although involving difficulty and even sadness, distinguishing what was permitted and what was forbidden, what was pure and impure was a way of being like their creator God.[14] The reverse was true for Christians. In the waters of baptismal ritual, their commentators saw a new creation in which what had been separate was now brought together.

Similarly, by celebrating the Eucharist, Christians attacked the Jewish belief that consuming blood would defile a person. Again, the Christian ritual turned taboos upside down: what had been prohibited was now necessary for salvation. Jesus himself had told them to drink the cup of his blood for the forgiveness of their sins. In celebrating their rituals, these Christians did something akin to burning American flags before a large group of patriotic Americans while simultaneously implying that they were the "true" Americans. On a symbolic level, the Christians' seemingly innocent rituals were aggressive acts that declared war on the venerable symbolic universe that Judaism proclaimed in writing and ritual. It is no wonder that Jewish religious leaders were incensed by such actions and responded aggressively to such perceived attacks.

In case there was any doubt, the first gospel to be written emphasized Christians' antagonism toward the Jewish ritual system. In Mark, Jesus relativized the Sabbath (2:25–28), overruled Moses (10:4–12), and castigated the religious elite for either misunderstanding rituals or using them to exploit people. As Theissen points out, the Jesus of Mark began to reach out to Gentiles and break that most significant barrier between sacred and profane. In a bit of overkill, the gospel claimed that the curtain in the temple marking the holiest of holies was torn in half, probably a sign that the temple, the heart of the Jewish ritual system that separated out those who were unclean, would soon be destroyed. But that's not all. Mark began with baptism and ended with Jesus establishing the Eucharist at the Last Supper.[15] The gospel put into story form what had been acted out for a generation: the Jewish rituals were declared obsolete, replaced by others that called into being a new people of God.

The Christian rituals also offended the Romans because such practices superseded the all-important Roman rituals, including emperor worship. Christians did not sacrifice like other good citizens. In the beginning of the second century, Romans saw Christians as more of a nuisance whose superstitious behavior might disrupt good order. But before the century was over, the Romans perceived Christians as much more threatening, with rituals that seemed to emphasize the sacrifice of Christ for others.[16] In performing the rituals of baptism and Eucharist, Christians identified more and more with the suffering Jesus, who came to turn society upside down. While the Roman culture glorified wealth, Christians glorified poverty. The Roman culture overvalued the elite, whereas Christians overvalued the poor. In the testimony of Christians and pagans alike, the capacity of the Christians to risk suffering and face death was remarkable.

In the second and third centuries stories were written about some of the more inspiring Christians, such as Perpetua, who was martyred in 203 CE. She was an educated, recently married young woman whose own diary told the story of how she courageously faced torture and death, as well as the efforts of her father to change her mind. The courage exhibited by such Christians, who not only challenged the values of the dominant culture but also were willing to sacrifice their own lives in defense of their beliefs, shocked the Romans. The Christians were not just saying they were different—they acted out those differences in the rituals they developed and held sacred. Whereas early Christian writers, such as the second-century influential apologist Irenaeus, developed arguments to justify Christian behavior, as well as a new narrative to tell the Christian story, ordinary Christians, defined and nourished by their rituals, put themselves forward as a new race, separate from both Jews and Gentiles. In defining themselves as such, they risked incurring the wrath of both groups. By the second century, some so identified with the suffering Jesus that martyrdom would become an identifying mark and privileged status for this new race.

From Courage to Anxiety

The sporadic persecutions of the early second century gave way to more organized and extensive ones in the late second and third centuries. Yet the martyrs continued to come forward, and their stories continued to be disseminated. The symbolic world they championed continued to make headway against the dominant Roman culture. With Constantine's victory over Maxentius in 312 CE and the Edict of Milan promulgated the following year, the persecutions ceased, but the Christians' symbolic world faced a more insidious challenge. Having successfully conquered external threats, Christianity became preoccupied with dangers from within. Christian thinkers such as Irenaeus believed that those who swayed from orthodoxy or "right thinking" posed a dangerous threat and claimed that doctrinal errors would sully the symbolic world the Christians had created and now needed to protect.

Over time, the dramatic challenges of baptism and the Eucharist devolved into anxiety about performing ritualized behavior correctly. In celebrating the Eucharist, concern was focused on the right words to be said, the delineation of roles in the ceremony, and even the person's gender, rather than on creating a caring community of service. Given such a change, Freud was right to compare these anxiety-provoking rituals to the obsessive-compulsive behaviors of his patients. On the other hand, Christianity is no longer locked in mortal combat. The rituals no longer have the subversive quality they had in the first and second centuries, when they masked the Christians' courageous efforts to define themselves against Jews and Romans. Rituals no longer seek to break taboos or turn the culture upside down. Taboos no longer exist about blood; our culture is not so foreign, having absorbed and professed many religious values. Though facing the challenge of creating a new world is likely to cause chronic unrest, carefully following the instructions for a ritual can establish a temporary sense of comfort and peace.

How Rituals Lose Power

The temporary sense of comfort and peace that can be experienced in a Christian ritual leads to another question. How would such a feeling be distinguished from a similar one experienced in hearing a symphony or seeing a dramatic performance? There are also questions of the consequences of such good feelings. Can such experiences through ritual lead someone to see others who exist outside that experience as somehow impoverished or secondary? In this postmodern and multicultural age, how does my religious experience at church relate to the "aha!" experience of those sitting at home in their robes and slippers, reading an important article in the *New York Times*? This is a slippery slope for religious people: self-comfort can lead to self-righteousness.

Rituals may lose their power when they lose their ability to scare us. If the Canaanite elder carefully sacrificing the lamb to Baal had not been particularly worried about the rain or its influence on crops, he might have easily just gone through the motions. If the high priest had not been so concerned about remaining ritually pure, aside from some performance anxiety, he might conceivably have viewed the ritual demands as just part of his job. The same was true of the early Christians. Paul reminded them that their God was a jealous lord who had punished them with illness and even death because they had participated in the Lord's Supper in an unworthy manner (1 Cor 11:27–32). Were there no understanding that the performance of the Eucharistic meal raised expectations about moral behaviors, as well as threats of retaliation, the participants would mainly have been concerned with how much they got to eat.

Yet the greatest danger to ritual may be that the symbolic world it intends to create has lost its power. In oral history projects conducted in England over several generations, researchers observed a dramatic break between people born before roughly 1960 and those born later. When it came to religious sentiments, the latter group easily separated themselves from any religious worldview. They even marveled that at one time in their lives, these religious beliefs and feelings had actually meant something. The old symbolic world no longer made sense.[17]

The religious power that Paul preached had lost its meaning and relevance. In its place, psychological, political, and economic theories—often exploiting biblical themes for justification—fast became major sources for understanding the world and our place within it. We have a much better idea of what causes change or what prevents it from happening. Although religious stories and rituals may comfort us, we are no longer likely to see them as powerful vehicles for change.

Where Is Our Courage?

It is difficult to align ourselves with the religious imaginations of the groups who dared to develop and practice these taboo-breaking rituals. The Canaanites risked the wrath of Baal when they symbolically sacrificed him as a lamb to gain the harvest their lives depended on. The Jews made outrageous and potentially treasonous claims that through their Passover ceremony and impoverished province, they would become God's empire. The Christian Jews gloried in the shameful death of a small-town reformer. Through baptism in him, they ritually broke the barriers that separated Jew from Greek, male from female, slave from free. And in their Eucharist they drank his blood that saved them from their sins. All of those believers temporarily left the life-and-death struggles of their chaotic world and, through rituals, entered imaginary worlds where rain could be controlled, the poor would rule the world, and an executed criminal could be the son of God. Our modern religious imaginations have become limited by science's explanatory power and undercut by cynicism's corrosion. We are too invested in our present world to take the daring leaps that our religious ancestors did. The courage once associated with the breaking of taboos no longer fits a world without those taboos. Yet is there a way we may find solidarity with this courage?

A friend of mine is a pastor in a storefront church not far from a bus station. She ministers to a congregation made up of men and women who inhabit the halfway houses and rehab centers nearby. The community gathers for a ceremony in which the ritual books are not followed precisely, and the sermon is often a group effort. Yet in that sacred space, desperate men and women challenge the myths that wealth is important and success is a measure of an individual. They dare to see themselves as valuable, and even though they may never repair the wreckage of their lives, God can. Through their belief, they create a world in which all are forgiven, all are loved, and everything that has been broken can be mended. Despite the weakness and desperation in their damaged lives, they find the courage to hope again.

Most of us are strangers to a level of desperation that requires tremendous courage to merely continue living. If we ever approach such massive discouragements, we are more likely to try self-help than self-sacrifice. If we experience injustice, we are more likely to call on a lawyer than on the Lord. Although we may have some concern for the less fortunate, we spend more time developing our own fortunes as buffers against the uncertainty that comes with change, children, and old age. Given the ambiguity of our times, we are more apt to build up our own psychological and physical security systems than we are to embrace our anxiety. In such a context, we are likely to see ritual as just another vehicle for introducing security. Can ritual again turn things upside down? Is there a way for ritual to become a safe place in which we turn toward anxiety and face it in the best way we can?

The Edginess of Ritual

Theologian Graham Hughes imagines that we are living on a platform in space.[18] We don't want to get too close to the edge, so most of the time we huddle for safety in the middle of the pack. However, we are occasionally forced to move from our positions of putative safety. These are the times when we must face dramatic changes in our lives or in the lives of our loved ones: the loss of a job, the birth of a child, an illness or misfortune. These and other events have the capacity to turn our lives upside down; for a moment, we feel loss and wonder what will become of us. Hughes identifies another scenario in which people might approach the edge of the platform: when we purposely put ourselves there because we want to experience the thrill, escape from the ordinary, or simply feel alive. Religious ritual, then, can be seen as an individual effort to distance ourselves temporarily from the routines and power structures that define us. In ritual, we purposefully go to the edge of the platform and peer into the chaos.

Ritual is a safe place that allows us to move to the edge of that platform. However, we still need courage to peer intently into the unknown and confront the nothingness before us. Of course, it may not seem empty because we cannot help but project our life stories and experiences onto that space, along with the symbolic world we believe is truly out there. Any comfort from such projections is attenuated when we realize that we are talking and looking at *ourselves.* We are not really facing the void. Any solace we derive from the religious inheritance that our sacred writings and traditions contain is, to some extent, offset by new information that identifies these writings as inventions and constructions of people struggling in the cultures of their own times. This new information reminds us that any effort to understand a world beyond this one is severely constrained by our own limitations and the particular culture we inhabit. It takes a special effort to loosen ourselves from powerful structures that seek to define us and then inch ourselves closer to chaos. In ritual, we may momentarily receive some clarity concerning who we are and what we should do. The courage to look into the unknown may be salvific to the extent that for a moment, it frees us.

In this act of courage, is there some taboo we risk breaking? Is there some way in which improper participation can cause the ritual to backfire? For all our attempts to find individual meaning in a ritual, ceremonies such as the Eucharist are similar to the initiation rites that seek to develop allegiance to the traditions of a larger group. How can we continue to participate in such traditions when we can see that they have inflamed believers to harm others and become dangerously self-righteous? The new taboo we are challenged to break is the one that says that the ritual has made us special. Rituals may be a safe place in which to act as if we have classified information, unique insights, or a special connection to extraordinary power, but if we act that way outside of them, we will likely harm ourselves and those with whom we interact in such a superior manner. What is significant is not our actions within the ritual but how we act *outside* of it.

Rituals are simply an important part of the human experience. At their best, they help us celebrate our lives and communicate our deepest feelings. Although we may be hard-wired to create and use rituals, we may have some choice in the ones we develop or some discrimination in understanding the ones we traditionally observe. Although rituals may be to a great extent nonverbal, we can hold ourselves responsible for understanding their purpose and effect on ourselves and others. Something as powerful as a ritual can be misused to limit our thinking and encourage us to follow a path without considering the consequences. Although performing a ritual may take courage, challenging the rituals that claim to separate us from one another may require even greater bravery.

Chapter 10

Religion and Science in Loyal Opposition

As part of his Jewish culture, Jesus would have inherited an understanding of the universe that was something like what is pictured (see map). We can find hints of such a cosmology in his teachings that the kingdom of God was breaking into this world. Jesus and his listeners imagined God dwelling in the heavens not too far from this Earth. From what we may call their scientific perspective, God could easily break through the thin layer that separated Earth from Heaven and thereby establish kingdom on Earth. There was no scientific problem with such a belief at the time; the real issues were theological.

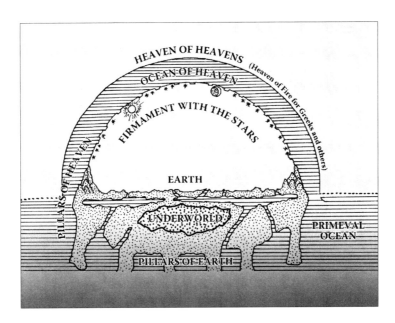

In the first place, the devil still resided in Heaven, as in the book of Job where God makes a bet with Satan at Job's expense. However, by Jesus' time things had become quite serious. Those believing they were living in the last days were convinced that the devil and his minions were now at war with the forces of God, essentially holding the kingdom hostage in Heaven. Jesus believed that his own work in casting out demons was a clear sign that the devil was being defeated and the kingdom of God was beginning to emerge on Earth. In Luke's gospel, when seventy-two disciples return from their successful mission, Jesus says that he can see the devil falling from the sky (10:18). In Mark's gospel in particular, we find Jesus doing battle with Satan. His first miracle is curing a man possessed by "an unclean spirit." Before it leaves the unfortunate man, this spirit in effect announces both Jesus' identity and his mission: he is the holy one of God who has come to destroy all the evil forces (Mark 1:23–27). A little later in the gospel, some opponents of Jesus accuse him of being possessed: "He has Beelzebul, and by the ruler of demons he drives out demons." In addition to the saying famously quoted by Abraham Lincoln that a house divided it against itself cannot stand, Jesus warned his opponents that they committed an unforgivable sin of blasphemy: they attributed to the devil what is actually the work of God (Mark 3:20–27). Jesus seems to gain strength in this war against Satan, reaching a point when someone who is not a follower simply uses the name of Jesus to drive out demons (Mark 9:38–40). Yet the struggle against Satan does not lead Jesus to a complete victory. The risen Jesus commissioned the apostles to preach the gospel to the entire world. Those who believed in Jesus Christ displayed great powers, the first of which was the ability to drive out demons (Mark 16:15–18).

The second theological difficulty was God's destructive holiness. In the Jewish tradition, a distance between God and humans needed to be maintained. Before entering the holy of holies, a high priest would have to achieve the utmost level of ritual purity, lest his contact with God become sacrilegious. For example, Jewish custom dictated that he needed to stay awake the night before to prevent seminal ejaculation, which would render him impure. That tradition addressed purity only at the ritual level; God would destroy on contact those who were actual sinners. This terrible chasm between divine holiness on the one hand and human sinfulness and impurity on the other was one reason the last days would be so horrific. The phrase "lead us not into temptation" in the Lord's Prayer probably references the testing associated with the last days. However, Jesus' role as the Messiah presented a new solution to this theological problem. Believers would be so united with him that they would be protected from God's justifiable wrath. In Jesus, God would bring about self-recognition: a glorified Christ guaranteed that all of creation, not just humans, could be united with the creator. The boundary that separated God from Earth could safely be removed, and the powerful world of Heaven would flood the imperfect one humans inhabited. No wonder Jesus' followers believed he would soon return to Earth and inaugurate the kingdom.

Although we may not be as captivated by the alternate universe created by biblical writers, religion seems to demand some kind of alternative reality—a world with the power to influence this one. However, our difficulty is not theological but scientific. A modern scientific worldview destroys the ancient cosmology and severely challenges the theology that was built upon it. We inhabit a small planet circling a modest star, on the edges of a galaxy of stars that is only one of a hundred billion other galaxies. Carl Sagan maintained that Western religions had yet to confront this new information about the enormous scale of the universe.[1] Certainly, we need a more constructive understanding of how God could enter into this world and transform it and of how God is connected to creation, given the theory of the Big Bang, estimated to have occurred twelve to fourteen billion years ago, and the formation of our solar system some five billion years ago. Although theologians may try to develop explanations that speak to scientific discoveries, their attempts only take us further away from the Bible's cosmology and the God described therein.

I have previously argued that the scientific worldview is not enough. It lacks meaning, as exemplified in the story of Viktor Frankl, a sense of community, as seen in the story of Barak Obama, and, as described in the next chapter, a dynamic belief as demonstrated in the story of Mikhail Gorbachev. Also, we seem to need a way to access the power of those "nonscientific" values, for example, through story and ritual. For all of its problems with science, the alternative religious universe creates a moral challenge to the more familiar and tangible scientific world. It asks us to look beyond the familiar and ask ourselves who we are and what we should be about. How do we relate to our fellow humans and the environment we share? Most important, is this alternate universe the home of a divine power that sustains us now and will be more fully revealed after we die? Although the cosmology has changed from the time of Jesus, these theological concerns were the same for his Jewish ancestors and Christian descendents. The difference is that today the voice of science is terribly powerful and rightfully so. Only by appreciating the value of both science and religion can the possibility of real dialogue be imagined.

Science and Religion: Four Positions

Superiority of Religion

In the ongoing relationship between religion and science, the role of God or the gods needed to be attended to. In the Christian religion in particular, the inerrancy of the

Bible, seen as inspired directly by God, was the trump card that was played, for example, when a scientist like Galileo offered evidence that contradicted existing religious beliefs. Tragically, Christianity's many errors in this long debate have not chastened some literal-minded believers who still maintain that the Bible knows more than science. Some anxious believers look for holes or gaps in evolution that they can claim as evidence of God's creative work. Theirs is a "god of the gaps," whose frail existence is called into question every time a gap is explained scientifically. Finally, there are arrogant believers who maintain that religion possesses a higher truth or value than science does. Science is asked to humble itself before the power of God and those who speak for God. Most forms of creationism are popular versions of this belief in the superiority of religion over science.

A more nuanced view of religious superiority can be found in the work of a theologian like John F. Haught, who denies the ability of scientists to create their own alternative, value-laden universe. He argues that such constructions betray faulty logic, and he describes their resulting belief systems as examples of scientism. He argues instead that "religions and theologies may, for all we know, have the capacity to pick up signals, however obscurely, of a dramatic profundity in life that science cannot reach."[2] He seems to suggest that the rituals, writings, traditions, and practices offer a particular capacity for enhancing one's life that is simply not available to the scientist.

Neutrality

Stephen Jay Gould offered a more neutral position in addressing what he sees as an unnecessary conflict between science and religion. He argues that each discipline takes a dramatically different position in its view of the world—rock of ages versus ages of rocks, for example. His argument relies on common sense and anecdotes, at one point positing that half of the scientists seem to be religious, whereas the other half are not. Remarkably, Gould's neutrality surfaced in his critical and devastating review of a book by one of those anxious believers, Phillip E. Johnson, who clumsily tried to find fault with evolution as a way to salvage a biblical god. Gould wrote, "The book, in short, is full of errors, badly argued, based on false criteria, and abysmally written."[3] Still, he advocates separate-but-equal respect for science and religion as a means of avoiding conflict, because "science treats factual reality, while religion struggles with human morality."[4] However, he may have reduced the potential for conflict by simplifying religion to morality and then taking a condescending attitude towards its more complicated aspects, for example, dogma and ritual. Such condescension was evident in a forum described in the *New York Times*. The writer covered a convention in which prominent scientists not only challenged religion but also argued that religion can impede the forward movement of science. Science must become almost evangelical and offer an alternative vision that will replace such a harmful ideology.[5] Neutrality in the debate between science and religion, though an attractive position, appears to be an unreliable starting point.

The Superiority of Science

Richard Dawkins attacks Gould for the latter's bending over backward to value religion.[6] In fact, Dawkins questions the legitimacy of the entire theological enterprise. He contends that questions of meaning, for example, can be just as well answered by scientists as by theologians. He abandons any semblance of neutrality toward religion, seeing it as dangerous, if not a source of superstition. Certainly, religion has been dangerous to science in the past—the silencing of Galileo when his conclusions flew in the face of the church's positions is not the only case in point. Sagan suggested that when followers of St. Cyril murdered the famous female scientist Hypatia in Alexandria in 415 CE, they were destroying someone they perceived to be the main representative of a scientific worldview opposed to Christianity. He believes that their actions marked the beginning of a long period during which the advance of science was halted in the Western world.[7] It is understandable that with the freedom to pursue their craft and disseminate their discoveries, some scientists railed against the religious structure that had so long oppressed their compatriots in ages past. Dawkins's blistering attack on religion is not easy for believers to hear, but dismissing it out of hand would overlook the built up animosity toward religion shared by many scientists. On the other hand, extrapolating from a scientific worldview and producing a philosophy of life might well be called scientism, an approach that claims superiority over religious interpretations of reality.

The Dialectic View

A fourth position regarding the intersection of science and religion supports an interactive, dialectical engagement and dialogue. Such a relationship begins with an appreciation of another view that may be quite antagonistic to our own. When theologian Anne Foerst received permission to teach a course on God and computers at MIT, she was challenged by scientists there who believed that the course was inappropriate for the university. They maintained—some without reading her syllabus—that such a discussion contradicted the objectivity and rationality that are MIT's hallmarks. However, over the three years that Foerst conducted the seminar, which involved scientists talking about spirituality, a noticeable shift occurred: religion was not automatically suspect, and spirituality became acceptable. She was able to communicate to scientists something of her own belief system by speaking to them in a way they could appreciate.[8]

We can extrapolate from Foerst's experience and see elements necessary for a dialectical relationship between

religion and science. She describes a situation in which opposing sides passionately held their respective positions: this
was not mere relativism. Through her efforts, the participating parties developed a respect for the other side. Finally
there was an appropriate forum for dialogue and discussion,
a trusting environment in which opposing parties could offer their own personal reflections. In the following pages, I
assume those elements as I outline how the clash between
science and religion can become a dialogue.

When Science Challenges Religion

Over the past few years, scientists have reached well-re-
searched conclusions that challenge the historicity of the
Bible's stories. First, the stories in the Hebrew bible cannot
be supported either by archaeological evidence or by evidence in the writings of other Near Eastern cultures, such as
Persian or Egyptian. Second, scientists generally agree that
the development and writing of biblical history occurred
sometime after the establishment of the Jewish province
of Yehud in the Persian Empire in the sixth century BCE.
Although the stories themselves claim to cover events that
go back hundreds if not thousands of years, they must be
understood in the context in which they were written. That
context included a power struggle over who would control
the province. Would it be the returnees from Babylon, or
those who had remained and had not been exiled? The returnees were likely the descendents of those who had been
forcibly exiled by the Babylonians beginning in the sixth
century and culminating with the destruction of Jerusalem
in 586 BCE. When the Persians conquered the Babylonians
some 30 years later, only a minority of the exiled families
returned. However, a few of those who had remained had
become prominent and resented the newcomers. Other significant questions were also important in this context. How
would the impoverished citizens of this backwater province
survive? How could the province gain some independence

while remaining part of a large empire? Could they organize themselves without a king?

In a similar fashion as with the Hebrew Bible, the major documents of the Christian Scriptures, the gospels, were also written in a particular context. Although these stories went back a few years in this case, they were written after the destruction of Jerusalem and its temple in 70 CE. Likewise, an understanding of this background leads to several questions analogous to the ones faced by the Jews in the sixth century BCE: How would this small sectarian group survive? How could it bring together Jewish and Gentile believers? How would it relate to its parent religion of Judaism? Finally, the more profound question relates to Jesus' identity. If, as in the case of the Jewish writings, concerns of the present context were retrojected into the past, how historically accurate is the portrait of Jesus in these gospels? One depiction that recent scholarship has abandoned is that of Jesus founding a new religion during his lifetime. Not only did the reforming prophet Jesus stay within his Jewish religion, his followers and family also identified themselves as members of the Jewish faith.

In short, science and critical biblical scholarship have seriously changed Jewish and Christian stories of origin, and evolution has denied the plausibility of some earlier paradise inhabited by a first man and woman. The more scientifically likely scenario is that life evolved over millions of years, with various communities of humanlike animals developing and then becoming extinct, until the emergence of the human species as we know it. The Exodus from Egypt cannot be supported by archaeological proof. Instead, the evidence strongly suggests that Israelites were indigenous to the Palestinian area. The stories of Genesis and Exodus were not edited or created at least until the sixth or fifth centuries BCE. Jesus was a prophet who, like other prophets, came to renew his faith in a time of perceived crisis. He did not establish a new religion. Science confronts the Jewish and Christian religions with data that strip their foundational stories of their historical underpinnings and thereby restores them to their original status as myths.

How Religion Might Reply

I never became religious by believing something happened a long time ago. I became religious because something truly significant happened to me in my lifetime. I experienced a call to serve others that involved leaving home and entering a high school seminary at age fourteen. As I construct my life story, this was my exodus. It was not that I was oppressed at home; it just was not a good fit. Of course, seminary and priesthood had their own oppressive qualities, and ultimately I did not fit there, either. Yet on this path I learned about fellowship, caring, and discipline. I also learned in this most hierarchical of institutions that a script would not be handed to me. I had to discover my own role and push its boundaries, in collaboration with others. That strategy of self-discovery continues as I live out my roles of husband, father, professional, and, yes, Christian.

Likewise, my attraction to Jesus was not based on the belief that he founded a religion. I was drawn to him because of a religious experience. My takeaway from that experience was that I could do something important, even though I did not know what that something was, let alone how I could do it. At times when I look deep within myself as I struggle to understand something or respond to a particular problem, I have moments of insight that both comfort and challenge. Because I am aware that others have similar experiences, I am motivated to engage such people in a conversation that both refines my own views and integrates them with those of others. In other words, I need a religious community whose members model altruistic behavior, work for social justice, and find motivation in story and ritual.

Religion's Counterpoint

I imagine that religion should preface any challenge to science by first confessing that it has often harmed the forward movement of science by censoring or threatening to censor scientists' legitimate work. Christianity's insistence on the dominance of its own truth claims has led to its having a reactionary stance in which scientific assertions are evaluated based on their potential conflict with traditional dogma. Especially problematic for Christianity has been its steadfastly literal interpretation of Genesis, which thereby demands that science not contradict the belief that God created the first humans. Religion has significantly contributed to whatever enmity exists between science and religion.

After making such a confession, religion might be in a better position to challenge science to reexamine its aggressive posture toward religion. The issue is not just that science may disparage religion as little more than superstition;[9] it may also fail to see that science has made some absolute truth claims for itself—and therefore starts looking like a religion with its own community, values, and belief systems. We can imagine a new Trinity, with science as the creative source, technology as its revelation to the world, and capitalism as an underlying power that continues its unchecked spread. The often quoted scientific historian Thomas Kuhn describes scientists as belonging to a community that holds particular beliefs.[10] Such a community would initially react defensively toward new ideas, but then change its beliefs as new information is introduced. How churchlike. The greatest heresy put forth by science is that science itself is neutral and thereby above the influence of values. On the contrary, science is heavily influenced by capitalism, which demands constant and increasing productivity, often without appreciating the consequences of such a demand for growth. Science can also be affected by politics, which can bring about the choice of one project over another, as well as by a government that will fund one approach over another. The tremendous push for progress can easily push to the sidelines the hard work of appreciating where those advances take us.

Science's Comeback

I would hope that science could acknowledge that there is some truth to the challenge that it edges over into the field of religion. For many scientists, interest in a specific field echoes what others might describe as a spiritual experience. Sagan might be a good example of someone who demonstrates a passion for knowledge as well as an enthusiasm for deepening our understanding of the universe and our place in it. In his writings and the TV series *Cosmos,* he shared that enthusiasm as he laid before us the wonders of the universe and scientists' capacity to understand it.

Undergirding Sagan's enthusiasm and vision was the epic story of evolution. He dramatically demonstrated how evolution made sense not only of billions of stars and galaxies but also for the development of life on this planet. He proposed a kind of godless faith that begins with a deep appreciation that we are the products of a multibillion-year process that would never be replicated. "Every one of us is, in the cosmic perspective, precious. If a human disagrees with you, let him live. In 100 billion galaxies, you will not find another."[11] Sagan's faith lent itself to a particular work ethic that deems science responsible for engaging in human problems. Learning from evolution that extinction is the rule and survival the exception, he was deeply concerned that the human species would destroy itself. His version of the apocalypse was nuclear war.

Although Sagan was in awe of the many earlier scientists whose discoveries increased our knowledge base, he was also committed to building on those ideas. In this way, science is dramatically different from a tradition-bound entity normally described as religion. Although their approaches and techniques vary widely, religion and science are probably irreparably separated because the former invests heavily in the past, whereas the latter looks primarily to the future for meaning. Christianity especially is dependent on a body of tradition and Scripture that is viewed as timeless and inerrant. Religious authorities are also invested in maintaining the belief system that their particular denomination espouses. Sagan incisively claims that science has an opposing belief system. "First: there are no sacred truths; all assumptions must be critically examined; arguments from authority are worthless. Second: whatever is inconsistent with the facts must be discarded or revised. We must understand the Cosmos as it is and not confuse how it is with how we wish it to be."[12] The dramatic differences between science and religion can easily lead to an antagonism that makes dialogue between them extremely difficult. Yet if dialogue is to happen, science also must consider the prejudices it brings to the table, prejudices that were all too apparent for example when Anne Foerst began her course at MIT.

Can Anything Be Salvaged from the Religion/Science Debate?

If dialogue involves reevaluating Christianity's treasured beliefs and leaving the door open for the possibility of error therein, Christians would be at a serious disadvantage. First of all, religion views itself as possessing special privileges bestowed by God. However, claiming a higher ground only makes religion more vulnerable. It is more likely to protect its own status and reputation than it is to admit error or confess to causing harm. Its impulse for self-protection and its need to safeguard truth claims encumber it with baggage that limits its effectiveness in serious discourse with science. To return to the example of Anne Foerst, religion first needs to engage science on a more phenomenological level, for example, in seeing religion and spirituality as intrinsically part of the human condition.

The second difficulty comes from the power of the scientific position. The likely one-sidedness of such a debate would leave a religious person overwhelmed by facts and chastened by the historical evidence of religion's mistreatment of science. Knowledge can take the mystery out of life, introducing a zero-sum game in which the more we know, the less we believe. Some would gravitate to the position Dawkins advocated in his book *The God Delusion*, namely, religion is viewed as superstition. In its benign form, it exists to comfort presumably weak people. At its worst, it is a kind of madness that engenders intolerance, irrationality, and violence. In an additional affront, science has also undercut the historicity that supports many religious beliefs. Religion may be tempted to make a strategic retreat because science is just too powerful, and thereby imply that science and religion inhabit different places in the world; any effort to establish a dialectical relationship is impossible. Because most of us live in a world highly influenced by science, abandoning the dialogue puts religion at a disadvantage.

Can Religion Modify Its Truth Claims?

Catholic theologian Luke Timothy Johnson[13] and Lutheran theologian Anne Foerst[14] have opened up another path for religion to pursue as it seeks to engage a world that is both postmodern (Johnson) and scientific (Foerst). They each introduce the idea of appreciating religion as a myth. For Johnson, "myth is language seeking to express the truth about the world and humans that lies beyond what we can test and prove."[15] For Foerst, it is a story that gives one's life meaning. That story can change over time, as well as attract others who wish to share in it.

For these writers, myth is powerful yet subjective. By itself it cannot claim superiority over other myths that likewise give meaning and promote community. This idea is very basic to human life: "To be human is to myth. Humans are mything machines."[16] From another angle, myths exist when they are lived out. For Joseph Campbell, whose work about myths, especially his interviews with Bill Moyers, has influenced many, the hero not only faces a challenge but returns to his community to enliven it with his discoveries. In this more active sense, a myth is something we construct from our lives' raw data and experiences; we then maintain it through a variety of rituals, beliefs, and behaviors, all of which are celebrated in some community context. Not to take part in a myth is like learning opera just by reading the lyrics without any knowledge of the music.[17] True participation in a myth requires entering into a trial-and-error process that leads to right behavior, as well as to some sense of identity. We are defined by the myths we celebrate.

If living a myth means initiating an ongoing process, then the truth claims of a particular myth must be seen as partial and temporary. If a myth claims for itself some overarching or superior truth, it runs the risk of becoming destructive to its own followers and others. The American myth of spreading democracy through force is met by a fundamentalist Islamic myth that resists to the death such a truth claim. In such cases, true believers are trapped by the intensity of their myth and fail to see that it is a construct that attempts to establish meaning and identity. Their circumstances can also lead to an addictive-like fervor that makes self-reflection extremely difficult. With so much invested in the meaning and identity functions of a particular myth, people need tremendous courage to battle something so psychologically powerful. They are challenged to work through the cognitive dissonance that new information brings on, rather than believe even more fervently in the contested myth.

On the other hand, an appreciation of the destructiveness of myth can lead to two insights. The first is that we all participate in at least one meaning- and identity-fostering myth. We may devote ourselves to a larger cause or be more focused on our own individual career and life experiences. We may celebrate a connection to a past ethnic or familial history. We could also become invested in some future accomplishment or dream. More likely, we balance several mythical ventures, though none can claim our total loyalty. The second insight is that we cannot claim the superiority of one myth in the world, just as we cannot claim supremacy for ourselves. Instead, we are challenged to learn from the myths that we can discover in ourselves and in others.

Investigating mythical power and limits can lead religion to a different view of its own truth claims. Christianity, for example, can do no better than to reflect on its own origins. In the first and second centuries, small communities, often built around particular households, created a myth centered on Jesus, called Christ. Within the communities, the members challenged each other to live a life worthy of God.[18] They struggled to understand and articulate the meaning of Jesus' death and resurrection. Although they communicated by letter and attempted some commonality via traveling preachers, the communities often went their separate ways as they struggled with different understandings and attempted to address differing problems. Though fragmentation was predictable, and many small groups did not survive, a new religion not only evolved from those groups but also defined itself as still connected to Jesus and his earliest followers. Through this "mythmaking enterprise,"[19] Christians were able to keep alive a Jesus Christ who was the center of their cult and the inspiration for their behavior. A deeper appreciation of these earlier societies might help Christian religions appreciate both the strength and the limitations of their mythical structure.

Science's Own Myth

If religion is able to accept its identity as a mythical enterprise, it may set an example for the field of science, which also stumbles into mythmaking. In his review of Daniel Dennett's book *Breaking the Spell,* literary editor Leon Wieseltier argues that the author has moved away from empirical research and constructed a belief system that the reviewer calls an example of scientism, the belief that science can explain all human conditions and expressions, mental as well as physical. Wieseltier goes on to say that such a position is a superstition and "one of the dominant superstitions of our day."[20] Thomas Kuhn has documented the role of the scientific community both in maintaining the advances of science and in blocking major changes, which he calls paradigm shifts. By emphasizing the role and limits of a particular historical era, he indicates that scientists will always be blindsided by their unconscious acceptance of their community's beliefs.[21] Sagan's scientifically inspired faith would likely have its own blind spots. Biologist and nonbeliever Stuart Kauffman argues that science's own reductionistic methodology prevents it from appreciating the creative power that appears to exist in the universe and that reason itself is not a sufficient guide to live our lives forward. Instead, we need faith to appreciate our role as co-creators in a universe that is beyond our understanding.[22] Richard Walsh, professor of religion at Methodist University in North Carolina, encourages a similar position when he states that we inevitably live with myth. When someone claims to possess an all-encompassing truth, an ultimate meaning superior to all others, that person is also articulating a myth.

The myth of science, held consciously or unconsciously, is the claim that it is the one true path to progress and the one true source of knowledge. Such a claim is not so much about science, "but is instead an ideology of belief, power, and social control."[23] Such scientists exemplify how dangerous it is to believe totally in one's own myth. When science becomes an ideology, it closes at itself off from other forms of knowing. It effectively denies, as scientist Francis Collins writes, that "the spiritual worldview provides another way

of finding truth."[24] Scientists who insist that their methodology privileges them some understanding of ultimate truth
model irrationality and prejudice by believing too much in
their own myth.

Appreciating Myth as a By-Product
of the Religion/Science Debate

The aim of dialogue is to appreciate another's position, as
well as to acknowledge any limitations in one's own stand.
However, I believe that a significant goal in the religion/
science debate could be the valuing of myth as part of everyone's frame of reference. The unconscious processes that
mediate stimuli[25] and shape our beliefs[26] are always at work.
In either the scientific or the theological realm, certainty is
an illusion. Likewise, any hope that we can be as self-reflec-
tive as to become overly aware of these processes is fruitless.
We face our own limitations because our way of knowing
is intrinsically restricted; understanding the world and ourselves will always be an interpretive process. The discipline
of interpretation, hermeneutics, is simply a means of coping
with the gaps that will always be there. The danger lies in
believing too firmly in the myths we use to fill the gaps. On
the other hand, myth is to be treasured because it can allow
someone to stay committed to a person, an idea, or a group
that is likewise limited. Again, a myth helps us cope with as
well as to adapt to life's challenges. The challenge is to appreciate that someone else's myth may have served similar
functions and therefore calls for respect.

To respect a myth's role as such is to begin a process of
empathizing with anyone who holds that myth, whether it
is a friend, an enemy, or just oneself. In social psychology
experiments, gender, social class, and ethnicity greatly influence the amount of attention one person pays to another.
However, we can temper those prejudices. For example,
with our friends, we make a concerted effort to tolerate

their mythical worldviews for the sake of our relationships with them. In the process, we sometimes gain an appreciation of the others' worldviews and incorporate some or many of those perspectives into our own myth.

This is not just some intellectual enterprise. We make the effort to relate emotionally to one another for reasons of health as well. Our bodies are so dependent on community "that they rely on interaction for their well-being."[27] Yet this desire for community is narrow in the human species. Our inherited tribal mentality and our psychological predispositions hamper our capacity for relationships.[28] These limitations are especially apparent in the way we relate to someone outside our group. We respond in a self-protective stance that makes it extremely difficult to take in information or take an empathic stance toward that person's worldview.

An Evolution-Inspired Myth

The myth that Jesus preached was in sync with the science of his time: God's kingdom was not too far above and the underworld not too far below. In our own time, the scientifically based theory of evolution has emerged as both foundation and inspiration for a more contemporary theological understanding. This position, sometimes called process theology, emphasizes the future direction of evolution and sees in that forward movement the work of God. Additionally, findings from various branches of science are taken as support for the development of a new mythical worldview. Scientist and believer Kenneth Miller expresses it this way:

> We know from astronomy that the universe had a
> beginning, from physics that the future is both open
> and unpredictable, from geology and paleontology
> that the whole of life has been a process of change
> and transformation. From biology we know that our

tissues are not impenetrable reservoirs of vital magic, but a stunning matrix of complex wonders, ultimately explicable in terms of biochemistry and molecular biology.... In many respects, evolution is the key to understanding our relationship with God.[29]

That new understanding of our relationship with God begins with an appreciation of "the restlessness and ambiguity of an unfinished universe"[30] of which we are a part. A natural consequence of such an understanding is that it redefines our role in the universe. We are not masters but co-creators: "our lives make no sense apart from the planet and cosmos we inhabit."[31] Although an evolutionary theology is future-oriented and often reflects on the work of Jesuit geologist and theologian Teilhard de Chardin, it also has at present an environmental focus, a profound ecological perspective that emphasizes our responsibility to preserve and protect our common environment. Complementing this action-oriented, outward movement is a more reflective, inward-directed appreciation of our growing consciousness that, again reflecting the work of de Chardin, is a hallmark of evolution. For example, theologian John Haught argues that with humans the universe has awakened to consciousness, and evolution has now become conscious of itself.[32] On a practical level, then, this new myth argues for a marriage of increased consciousness and improved ethical behavior toward all of creation. From a more theoretical perspective, our expanding consciousness participates in the divine consciousness. Rather than describe God as person, process theology might well describe the Godhead as consciousness.

My point is not to summarize the ideas of process theology so much as to emphasize that it builds on present-day science as a foundation for its mythical view. Some theologians have tried to incorporate a scientific view onto preexisting Christian or other religious worldviews, but such a commingling presents problems. For example, how would one translate the rituals and narratives in the Christian tradition with stories of a personal God directly intervening in history into a scientific narrative in which God is embedded in the evolutionary history of the universe? Although process theology provides significant rationale for ecological concerns and the development of a global community, it may prove difficult to use such an approach as the basis to form a local community. Rather than attempt to flee from one myth to another, the safer path may be to appreciate the presence of multiple myths in our lives. While recognizing that myths are necessary, inescapable, and highly influential, we can make an effort to distance ourselves from them, recognize the consequences of believing in them, and then modify them, as well as make room for other views. Yet how do we evaluate a myth?

How to Evaluate a Myth

Sociologist and Catholic priest Andrew Greeley has been regularly surveying church behavior and attitudes at the National Opinion Research Center since the late 1960s. In the late 1980s, using an instrument called the General Social Survey, he included questions that identified respondents' religious imaginations and then correlated their views of God with their moral behavior in five specific topic areas: capital punishment, feminism, civil liberties, and two scales regarding racial attitudes. He found that those who imagined God as mother, spouse, lover, and friend (as opposed to a more distant father, master, judge, or king) were "more likely to oppose capital punishment, to support civil liberties, to advocate government help for blacks, to reject the notion that blacks ought not to push their way in white neighborhoods, and to support feminist attitudes on the women's labor force and political participation."[33] Greeley also noted that people with a higher level of education were also positively associated with these five tendencies.

Arguably, people arrived at a similar position through two paths: one the path of reason, and the other, the path of myth.

Greeley's work suggests not only that a myth can be evaluated in terms of the behaviors it supports but also that care must be taken to understand fully what the myth is all about. He makes the case that our idea of God is equivocal, and much depends on what someone means when he or she uses the term. At this point, we face a serious dilemma when it comes to judging a myth by reviewing behaviors associated with it. Behaviors are consistent with the myths. Someone believing in a more emotionally distant, judge-like god presumably would be supportive of capital punishment, for example. It becomes extremely difficult for someone to step out their myth and find a more objective way of evaluating their behavior, and it is unlikely that there is some supermyth that judges the accuracy and utility of all other myths. In addition, a myth's power is reinforced by the community that holds it and has been defined by it. As mentioned earlier, Kuhn has pointed out that a scientific community exerts tremendous power in shaping the belief systems of the scientists that participate in that community. These observations strongly suggest that it is extremely difficult to assess one's own myth and relatively useless to criticize someone else's.

The advantage of tolerating the myths of others is that it provides an opportunity for people to work together who come from different perspectives. Nowhere is such collaboration more needed and perhaps more obvious than in facing the ongoing struggle of climate change. Although science can articulate the data that can ground religious action, scientists can also appreciate the importance of framing the challenge in religious terms, which was done as early as 1991.[34] The appeal of the scientists is not without scientific rationale. Religious writer David Wolpe is one of many who note the overwhelming evidence of religions' benefit to society. "More studies than the reader would have patience for demonstrate that religion is indeed not only very good for the people who practice it, but for society as a whole."[35] The challenge of climate change dramatically brings to the fore the interdependence of science and religion. To use the categories offered by evolutionary biologist David Sloan Wilson, the factual realism of science does not easily lend itself to the more adaptive function found in the practical realism of religion.[36] However, I do not believe that such collaboration can take place unless we both celebrate the myths that have been so meaningful to us and feel free to recognize their limitations.

If the Myth Fits…

My life experience has been relatively consistent with the Christian myth. As a youngster, I felt called to a life of service. In the seminary, I met and grew up with men who are still my friends. I benefited greatly from my mentors, who shared their love of academics and encouraged my growth. I was encouraged by the renewal movement that the Second Vatican Council introduced, as well as challenged to define my own particular contribution to that movement. This effort led me gradually to the social sciences and ultimately to psychology. In short, I can look back and see my journey from childhood to the present as consistent with the Christian myth I continue to celebrate. At the same time, I recognize that others, even those in the seminary, did not have similar experiences. They encountered alienation, not friendship; disparagement, not support; and in some cases, abuse and not love. For these reasons, coupled with other experiences, the Christian myth does not fit these people anymore.

Almost paradoxically, the fact that the Christian myth no longer resonates with certain people whom I respect has helped me appreciate that I have constructed other mythical worldviews that overlap or are in tension with others. Most obviously, there is that more complicated and conflicted community I inhabit as a clinical psychologist, which is in turn part of the larger myth of the social scientist. In this capacity, I am challenged to anesthetize my mythical constructs to value the mythical worlds in which my patients live. No matter how crippling and dangerous their perceptions appear to me, I must find a way to respect those views before we can find the strength they contain. In this effort, I hope to avoid pushing for a forced conversion to my myth and instead help them find the power in their own. I am aided in this quest by my understanding that the social sciences, especially in my particular subspecialty of clinical psychology, do not offer one overriding or consistent mythical paradigm. Although psychotherapy can be helpful, psychologists Haim Omer and Nahi Alon conclude from their survey of the literature that "no approach can claim decided superiority over others."[37]

Conversely, my exposure to both rejected and conflicted myths has encouraged me to find lasting value in the ongoing process of mythmaking. The products of this basic human endeavor cannot, strictly speaking, be judged true or false. However, the method can be similar to dialectical thinking, which postulates that a person can learn from opposing viewpoints while maintaining core values. It can also echo psychological outlines of the stages of human development that trace humanity's evolution from necessary self-centeredness to an expansive sense that we participate in a global community. Mythmaking may offer strengths that can be rediscovered as we struggle with the cognitive dissonance that new information introduces. If mythmaking can be seen as a human process, it can allow us to feel optimistic about finding meaning in a postmodern world, as well as hope for a meaningful dialogue between those two antagonists, science and religion, who could challenge each other about the limitations in their respective myths.

Sagan believed that the human enterprise was a "two-pronged investigation into the nature of the world and the nature of ourselves."[38] His belief echoes St. Augustine's prayer that he know both God and himself. These twin tasks of focusing on self and other are irrevocably intertwined. We will always be vulnerable to the myths and distortions that cloud our perspective as we peer into nature and God. Will there be, as Sagan warned, a "battle to the death of inadequate myths,"[39] or will appreciating our limitedness coax us to value other people's and communities' views? By cooperating in this larger battle for survival, science and religion can find a common cause. On the other hand, by competing in a quest for self-understanding, both can appreciate the limitations inherent in their respective mythical worldviews.

Chapter 11

Mikhail Gorbachev and the Collision of Faith and Fact

Then Jesus said, "I came into this world for judgment, so that those who do not see might see and those who do see might become blind."
—John 9:39

I cannot conceive of a genuine scientist without that profound faith. The situation may be expressed by an image: Science without religion is lame. Religion without science is blind.
—Albert Einstein, *Ideas and Opinions*

He studied the history of his people and gradually came to the position that his country was going in the wrong direction. He condemned violence and revolution, and instead argued for the beginning of a new chapter in world history in which people would become truly free. He challenged his fellow believers and saw his opponents as blocking the course of history. Ultimately he was deceived and humiliated, but he did not lose hope. He believed that his enemy's victory would introduce a transition stage and a truly new and peaceful world order would emerge. He also sought ways to continue his vision after he left the stage.

Mikhail Gorbachev headed the Soviet Union from 1985 to 1991, and at the time was the world's most important communist. Sidestepping the issue of his importance in world history, however, let us instead focus on his nonreligious but nevertheless faith-driven transformation.

Someone said that only Catholics and communists were true believers because each group took error so seriously. I think both groups also share a belief in the renewability of their systems. Pope John XXIII called for the Second Vatican Council, and Gorbachev similarly initiated changes he described as *perestroika*, major political and economic reform, and *glasnost*, open communication about those reforms. The church reexamined its own religious understandings and traditions in the face of changes in the world; Gorbachev started with those dramatic world changes and moved to challenge his deep-seated beliefs because he had developed a new understanding of history, a new way of looking at things. Much like a therapist, he argued that this new perspective or insight demanded dramatic changes in his country.

In the preceding chapters, I have argued that new information can provide the opportunity for individuals and communities to grow and evolve. I have also used the model of psychotherapy as a way to partially explain the power of religion in psychological terms. With Gorbachev, we examine someone who could be described as a change agent or therapist, not for an individual patient but for a nation and ultimately the world. In this chapter, I present him as an example of someone whose life journey can be described in terms more humanistic than religious. As I have with the other two examples, Viktor Frankl and Barack Obama, I describe his life and message from a psychological perspective as a way of organizing a process of change that might be described as spiritual but not religious. For Gorbachev, the process of change can be framed using the psychological theory of cognitive dissonance.

Cognitive Dissonance

In 1954, a few social psychologists infiltrated a religious group whose members claimed that they had been in contact with aliens who would rescue them in flying saucers just before the world ended on December 21 of that year. The psychologists were betting not only that the world would not end but also that when it did not some participants would behave in a predictable yet counterintuitive manner. Although their follow-up was not extensive, the experimenters charted three trajectories for those believers who experienced an undeniable collision between their faith and the nonevent of December 21. As we might expect, some abandoned their belief when confronted with contradictory evidence. Others, as the psychologists predicted, held on to their belief even more tenaciously while attempting to rewrite it in a way that made sense of their mistaken view. And there was a third option: at least one member salvaged something from the old belief system and began to create his own religious perspective.[1]

These social psychologists called their theory *cognitive dissonance*. The idea spawned a variety of experiments in which people were thrust into a conflict between a particular belief and a behavior or information that defied the belief. In these experiments, many resolved the dissonance by following a presumed authority figure. In one infamous experiment, an experimenter in a white lab coat directed volunteers to a room in which a man sat connected by electrodes to a machine in another room that was designed to give shocks. (The man was a confederate of the experimenter and the machine did nothing.) Each volunteer was then asked to sit by the machine and press levers that would administer a shock to the man in the other room whenever he made a mistake on a memory exam. They were told the experiment aimed to test out a hypothesis about learning and punishment. The white-coated experimenter then encouraged the volunteers to continue increasing the intensity of the shocks as the man made more and more mistakes on the exam. Although most volunteers were uncomfortable as the experiment continued, and they could hear the improvised distress sounds from the next room, many continued to participate in the experiment—even past the point that the presumed shocks would have been fatal and no sounds could be heard from the next room. Trust in the supposed "authority" figure overruled the subjects' better knowledge and human instincts. From those beginnings, cognitive dissonance has developed into a more general term and has been applied to situations where beliefs get in the way of more adaptive behavior. Even certain foreign policies have been identified as victims of cognitive dissonance—namely, when new information does not change particular political convictions, thereby resulting in extensive failures and tragedies.[2]

We can now return to the story of Mikhail Gorbachev. He can be described as someone who, when faced with new information that challenged his deep-seated beliefs, worked through the conflict to arrive at a new perspective that led him to prescribe a new course of action. His struggle is a dramatic example of the difficulties and challenges involved in confronting a belief that although not religious in the strictest sense of the term, still carries with it the intense allegiance normally ascribed to such beliefs. In March 1985, when Gorbachev was elected general secretary of the Communist Party, he had already reached a point in his journey that he was beginning to question the traditional beliefs of Soviet Communism. With the support of others he began a series of reforms and attempts at transparency that would evolve over the next few years. He also realized that although many would support his initial efforts, his changes would be contested by others. As he moved along the trajectory that he envisioned, he not only risked failure but also his own personal safety. Much was at stake as he attempted to discuss and negotiate the massive changes he outlined. It would be a kind of therapy, but on a massive scale. He was asking people to tolerate the discomfort of change, as well as to be patient with a new way of perceiving and acting. Although he survived the attempted coup against him in 1991, he lost much of his power and prestige. With the breakup of the USSR later that year, he resigned his position.

Reconstructing Gorbachev's Journey

The observable successes and failures of Gorbachev's efforts are material for another story. Here I focus on a more internal process, namely, his successful struggle with cognitive dissonance. Although not religious in a traditional sense, Gorbachev was a believer who belonged to a community of similar believers; his beliefs motivated and shaped his behavior for years; some of his beliefs were interpretations of history that could be challenged by new information.

In his autobiography, *On My Country and the World,* Gorbachev describes a multi-stage movement away from communism and toward a new arrangement based on individual liberty. As he took in new information that challenged his communist beliefs, he attempted to move himself and his country to evolve into a new system that would marry traditional socialist principles with a deep appreciation of individual freedom. Though he may have failed to introduce a truly democratic regime, his own evolution in thinking and acting is remarkable. Gorbachev's dramatic transition can be described as a four-step process, indicating a way to use cognitive dissonance as an opportunity for growth.

The Four Stages of Modifying Beliefs

1. Appreciate the Belief

Communism was an all-embracing belief system that demanded orthodoxy and repudiated error. Gorbachev grew up in this system, preached its virtues, and benefited from its opportunities. He had risen to the most powerful position in his country and was a believing communist. He deeply appreciated the sacrifices of others who had labored to bring to fruition the dream of a worker's paradise that would spread with missionary zeal to other countries.[3] Rather than reject the belief, he struggled to find within it the core values that could be applied to his new situation.

Gorbachev's insistence on staying with the values of a given belief system is something a therapist does in the first stages of treatment with a patient. It doesn't help to simply tell depressed people to cheer up or to challenge people with low self-esteem to think more highly of themselves. A therapist has to begin where people *are*. For instance, a kindly physician encouraged a mother with a disabled child to accept her child's deficiencies. This mother realized quickly where the conversation was going, and she stopped the physician in his tracks with this comment: "Don't take away my denial." Her pained outburst is a reminder that people cannot readily give up their dreams and survival strategies.

This first stage not only honors the belief system but also implicitly recognizes the critical role of beliefs in general. Some beliefs may even feel hard-wired because they are so connected to life experiences in which we found meaning or transformation in our lives. I found such meaning in a religious experience when I was a boy. I remember being an eleven-year-old in a darkened church and experiencing a powerful connection with Jesus, who was both reassuring and calling me to follow him. I treasure that memory because the experience was so formative in my personal development. In my own practice as a psychologist, I have often joined patients in honoring the powerful belief systems that once proved so helpful to them in circumstances that were nearly overwhelming. For a therapist to benefit a patient, and for a patient to take the next step toward healing, both must truly appreciate the patient's existing belief system and its values.

2. Recognize the Cognitive Dissonance

When we are convinced that our tightly held belief will retain some of its values, we can open ourselves up to new information that contradicts it. Gorbachev believed in both the wisdom of the working class and the revelatory power of history itself. Dissonance occurred in 1989 when people in the communist nations of Eastern Europe had the freedom to vote for a different political system, thereby expressing their belief that the older system was harmful and incapable of producing the society idealized in the revolution. They saw the system and the beliefs that supported it as repressive, and they voted for a system that would guarantee more individual freedoms.[4] Gorbachev did not discount the actions of people who voted against the system he represented by denying the importance of their votes or by rationalizing that they were mistaken. Instead, he accepted their critique—despite the substantial discomfort it caused him. In his readings on socialism and his conversation with like-minded reformers, he was able to experience this cognitive dissonance as an indication of the beginning of a new historical epoch.

In psychotherapy, progress may be especially difficult when patients believe that the therapist may not respect their stories and the maladaptive or even harmful self-image associated with them. One anxious patient of mine, when facing a potential conflict in her life, would imagine the worst possible outcome and just how she might manage. Rather than challenge such an extreme planning process, I accepted it as a survival strategy and supported her need for it. Knowing that she would always rely on the worst-case-scenario approach as a backup, she felt freer to develop other anxiety-management techniques. In this instance, appreciating the cognitive dissonance did not lead to the disappearance of the old belief, but rather helped her integrate it into other techniques that came with new information. Like my patient, as well as with Gorbachev, affecting change required something else.

3. Take Responsibility for Change

Gorbachev took on cognitive dissonance by using tools at his command. His philosophical background was based on an interpretation of history, so he reexamined the flow of historical events and reinterpreted them using what he described as a scientific method. He met with like-minded reformists within the communist system to explore creative solutions. He therefore stayed with the dissonance, neither rejecting the evidence nor totally abandoning his own belief system. He developed new concepts, glasnost and perestroika, that he hoped would provide a rationale and direction for change. While searching for some middle ground, he did not lose his original idealism, which focused on greater freedom.[5] In short, he took responsibility for thinking and acting in a way that was consistent with his new awareness, despite the significant obstacles to, if not the impossibility of, being successful.

Psychotherapy sometimes involves a great test of wills: the patient wants the therapist to tell him what to do, and the therapist wants the patient to take responsibility for change. In some instances, a therapist avoiding a patient's direct questions seems like a comedy sketch. "Why do you keep answering my questions with questions?" mutters the patient. "What's wrong with questions?" the therapist replies. I remind myself and my patients that it is *their* life and *they* get to choose what to do, as well as discover what happens when they do it. Those moments of discovery are precisely what liberate a patient from dysphoria-producing beliefs and behaviors, as well as introduce a perception of reality that offers direction and hope for the future.

4. Develop a More Global Solution

Gorbachev asserted that individuals should not be bogged down by local or transitional problems, and should instead strive for a global perspective. He sought a solution by developing a larger picture that would make sense not only for the problems he faced but also for the problems of the human race in general. The change he was envisioning could have an impact on civilization as a whole, and he built his solution based on his trust that in the long run, individuals would choose solutions that maximized personal freedom for themselves and others.[6] Gorbachev saw government's role as fostering a movement toward global emancipation, and he condemned governments that sought to repress it. He hoped for a synthesis between new information and old beliefs about history's march toward human freedom.

The individual freedom that can be achieved through psychotherapy is perhaps more a by-product of the process. Therapists do not push for growth so much as seek to minimize the problems that interfere with such growth. In other words, the therapist does not have a blueprint for human growth but assumes that patients can develop one for themselves. By the same token, individual psychotherapy has a communal dimension if it is at all successful. First, patients are less angry and blaming toward others because they no longer assign themselves a victim role. Likewise, someone who has been depressed and withdrawn becomes more outgoing and social, seeking and valuing relationships with others. Freed from having to manage significant anxiety, a patient may become more grateful and wish to help others. Children and adolescents who have worked through significant family problems are more likely to act differently when they raise their own families.

But therapy doesn't mean that all dreams will come true. "I never promised you a rose garden," says the fictionalized therapist to her patient in the novel of the same name. Likewise, Gorbachev's appeal to address global problems in his time—including the environmental crisis, the uneven distribution of wealth, the pursuit of profit at any cost, and the continuation of weapons development and purchase—is still some distance from the tipping point. His restructuring efforts in the Soviet Union led to a loss of popularity and his replacement as party chief and head of state. The process of cognitive dissonance leads not to some steady state of achievement but to an ongoing faith in one's insights as a vehicle for continued growth, as well as a foundation for one's existence in the world—that sense of meaning and value that lies at the heart of religion itself. Indeed, Gorbachev held that only by returning to traditional spiritual and moral values could people ultimately face and resolve the world's gravest problems.

Change as an Evolutionary Demand

Within his communist ideology, Gorbachev saw history as an ultimate reality that could be studied, a process from which people could gain understanding. However, he interpreted history from an evolutionary perspective, the goal of which was human freedom. As he stated in his report to the Communist Party conference in June 1988, "To oppose freedom of choice is to set oneself in opposition to the objective course of history."[7] This analysis led Gorbachev to the belief that authoritarian regimes are doomed because their use of force means that they not only distrust their own citizens but that they will likely confront and not cooperate with more democratic nations. He concluded that the world's issues could be resolved only if democratic nations entered freely into a common problem-solving process. Although he believed that the world was in a transitional stage and authoritarian regimes would still exist, he hoped for a better outcome as the evolutionary-based need for democracy became even more apparent.

Gorbachev experienced cognitive dissonance when he identified error within his belief systems. Yet he embraced the discomfort he experienced and moved past his own insecurities and into a more transformed relationship with others, evidencing what theologian James Fowler describes as "universalizing faith." In this highest level of spiritual development, according to Fowler, a person moves away from the anxious and defensive view of a creature and begins to view humankind from the vantage point of a loving creator.[8]

I argue that Gorbachev's struggles to pursue more adaptive beliefs in a time of crisis are relevant to all believers. Despite all its difficulties, the journey through cognitive dissonance to a new synthesis can be motivated by a deep-seated appreciation of the need to change so as to grow. The more comfortable our lives are, of course, the more difficulty and anxiety we experience when contemplating such movement. However, like Gorbachev, we can be motivated and supported by those whose words and actions challenge our comfortable belief systems, whether they are political, religious, or otherwise. We can choose to study the thoughtful critiques and inspiring actions of those who express discontent and evaluate for ourselves the need for change in our own as well as our collective evolution. We can take responsibility for discernment and critical thinking, rather than give over those responsibilities to authority figures.

We may even be comforted by indications of religious change in the United States. Evangelicals like Jim Wallis argue that individual piety be tied to global concerns.[9] Sociologist Robert Wuthnow describes the restructuring of American religion since World War II, and identifies it as a dynamic process in which religion's internal resources are used in response to dramatic cultural changes.[10] The 2008 Pew report describes the religious scene in the United States as quite fluid with large numbers of people moving between denominations or describing themselves as non-affiliated.[11] We are increasingly searchers. Struggling with change and its consequences, we look for guidance and stability, meaning and community. Although we may not have the resources or opportunities to be heroes, we are increasingly aware of the boundaries that divide us and the need to find more universal solutions to global problems.

One example of religious evolution stemming from crisis is provided by the history of the Catholic nuns in the United States. As described earlier, and documented in the book *Double Crossed*,[12] many nuns left their religious orders when they felt their independence was constrained by the hierarchy. Recently, some orders of nuns have begun to demonstrate what religion can be in the twenty-first century. In various communities across the country, sisters have initiated projects that connect ecology and sustainability, spirituality and social justice. Both creatively and counter-culturally, they are demonstrating a way to respond to the new awareness of life's challenges both as individuals and as a global community. Although they start from Catholic traditions, their spirituality is inclusive and their practices environmentally sensitive. Their work suggests that a resolution of cognitive dissonance can occur in certain communities that stress individual responsibility rather than overvalue authority.

The Challenge to
Change Our Thinking

Writing in 2000, Gorbachev argued for a "radical turn-around in our thinking, one that is global, historically long-lasting, and humanist in the fullest and truest sense of the word."[13] When Jesus preached to his fellow Jews, he used a word that we commonly translate as "repent," but which can be otherwise translated as, "You have to change your thinking," an ongoing process.[14] What psychotherapy adds to this seemingly random mix of atheism and religion is the argument that such change is psychologically demanding but possible. Loyalty struggles, anxiety, and the psychological stress of moving into uncharted territory present fierce obstacles to anyone attempting such change. Additionally, the acceleration of global problems and the increasingly undemocratic use of political power challenge the value of any individual effort. Nevertheless, a way is open to slowly change one's thinking through a process that promises more individual freedom and the hope of more collective emancipation. The motivation for such an effort begins with the knowledge that belief systems themselves are inadequate if they cannot make use of and integrate new information that promises to be a way of life now and in the future. While the examples of Gorbachev and others show that dramatic change can still occur, their life stories demonstrate that it is not easy.

If undergoing cognitive dissonance means experiencing uncomfortable feelings and disturbing thoughts, moving through cognitive dissonance can resemble psychotherapy. In a safe and predictable environment, for example, a person in a long-term relationship can begin to face the conflicts he or she has suppressed or compartmentalized in an effort to live out a romantic ideal. If the relationship continues once these realizations surface, it may change significantly for both partners. Sometimes a partner who undergoes psychotherapy becomes so aware of the difference between reality and those romantic ideals that the relationship cannot survive. The patient slowly begins to absorb information that challenges a long-held belief in a common destiny and can start to accept the need to begin anew. If the process is slow, the pain is distributed over time and can be managed more easily. In other situations, the information comes in a surge that leaves the person feeling overwhelmed and desperate. In this situation, successful psychotherapy involves recovering individual identity and some optimism that the person can continue to progress without the other partner's physical presence. Memories and attendant feelings remain, but the sadness over lost opportunities and dreams needs to be attenuated by future hope and promise. Both believers and patients undergo a mourning process in which they search for past experiences or actions that can provide continuity as they develop their identity into the future. In both of these processes, friends and family members become significant in both distracting and encouraging the mourner. In many instances, the future is embraced more tentatively because the past is remembered so fondly.

Toward a New Synthesis

Embracing cognitive dissonance places us in limbo between old certitudes and new information, but with the knowledge that replacement certitudes are neither likely nor obvious. Irving Greenberg articulated a way of managing such tension when he wrote about how Jews managed to sustain their faith after the Holocaust. He wrote that their knowledge of what happened could at times overwhelm the Jewish faith in a merciful God and render them hopeless. He sees faith as ebbing and flowing between hope and despair—no longer a constant certitude but an unpredictable experience, what he calls "moment faith."[15] The distinguishing mark of faith is not that it consistently remains but that it consistently *reappears*. The difference between the believer and the cynic is a matter not of certitude but of frequency. Even doubters have their moments of faith.

Just as our faith may be temporary, our solutions may be partial. Gorbachev's efforts at political and economic reform in the Soviet Union led to mixed results. Although certain freedoms were introduced in the USSR and Eastern Europe, some former Soviet countries, including to some extent Russia, have reintroduced authoritarian regimes. Here again is a parallel with psychotherapy. For most therapy patients, past traumas and deep-seated conflicts do not go away entirely. The individuals make compromises and adjustments and are able to limit their more harmful impulses, realizing that the search for perfection is itself destructive. They begin to see that the more they are invested in an ideology that provides absolute answers, the more they are likely to be blind to the need to change and evolve.

Any individual will have good reason to either embrace or avoid religion. I have proposed that an investment in religion can lead to an experience of cognitive dissonance. However, in the process of managing that dissonance, an individual invests in an evolutionary struggle now made more acute by global challenges that threaten our world and possibly our continued evolution as a species. Therefore, a hallmark of such a process is the development of a person who is guided by beliefs and values and truly respects others' beliefs and values in turn. To return to the analogy of psychotherapy, the goal of that enterprise is not the resolution of conflict but the introduction of freedom. Our choice is to either take hold of that freedom or let someone else make decisions for us.

How do we work through the conflict between our deep-seated religious yearnings and the information, much of it scientific, which challenges such feelings? Any attempt to compartmentalize faith and fact into non-overlapping domains misses the opportunity to synthesize such competing forces into a process that, to reintroduce Einstein's phrase, is neither lame nor blind. But it would be quite difficult to participate in such a process. We would have to learn to listen to positions we oppose and accept that our own beliefs may have serious flaws. We would have to work at expressing and defending our ideas, risking that what we cherish may become criticized. We would have to negotiate and compromise. We would experience discomfort as we moved away from what was comfortable, hoping to discover some as-yet-unknown perception in which we saw things differently and therefore acted differently. It would be a kind of therapy and a way of understanding religion.

Ancient Judaism and primitive Christianity can be understood in part as responses to cognitive dissonance. Religious Jews believed God had promised always to be with them, and never to let the sacred dwelling in Jerusalem, the temple, be destroyed. When Jerusalem was conquered and the temple destroyed in 586 BCE, the disconnect between the promise and the reality caused a crisis of faith. Likewise, some 600 years later, when their beloved leader was killed in a most shameful fashion, Jesus' Jewish followers faced a similar crisis. Where was their God? I have argued that we face a similar crisis as science challenges some of our basic ideas about religion, especially about Judaism and Christianity.

Yet crises and conflict can be opportunities for individual growth and group evolution. Gorbachev could hold in tension the pull to science and the need for spiritual values; the importance of belief and the necessity for change. Yet neither change nor evolution is an even or easy process. Only in hindsight can we discover whether opportunities were missed or real progress occurred. Although the desire for power and security may be hard-wired in us, the individual journey to authenticity and the personal contribution to the common good may require something like faith, an inspiring belief in something beyond ourselves. That faith may include a search for meaning or an experience of community. It may be inspired by an awareness that our survival as a species depends on the development of a more democratic and just world. Such faith may only emerge when bedrock values are challenged by new perspectives, a powerful conflict that ultimately contributes to a deeper understanding of that basic commandment to love oneself and one's neighbor.

Conclusion

Accordingly, human moral action can be measured
by the extent to which it advances or detracts from
the precarious but creative cosmic impulse toward
community.
    —John Haught, *God after Darwin*

Almost 2,500 years ago, the philosopher Plato
gave us two definitions of myth in a dialogue
entitled *Phaedrus*. The book describes a lazy afternoon discussion between the philosopher Socrates and his would-
be pupil, Phaedrus. The student points to an area near a
hillside and asks if Socrates believes the story about it being
the spot where a struggle between mythical creatures took
place. Phaedrus describes the story as a fairy tale and suggests that sophisticated people find rational explanations for
such stories: a myth is simply an archaic way of trying to
explain events that science can explain better.

Phaedrus gives us a common understanding of myth,
one that scholars Elizabeth Barber and Paul Barber explore
in their 2004 book *When They Severed Earth from Sky: How
the Human Mind Shapes Myth*. The authors assert that in
a prescientific age, people postulated supernatural explanations for natural occurrences, for example earthquakes and
volcanic eruptions. The ground shook; therefore, some su-
perhuman entity was stomping around the Earth. With the
advent of science, the myths lost credibility and significance.

Socrates, however, offered another explanation of myth.
He stated simply that when he thought of those legends, he
asked himself how much he was still like Typho, a Greek
god associated with uncontrolled rage and chaos, and a god
he had chosen to follow. Socrates pointed out that the archaic stories were still important to him. He looked beyond the historical, scientific issues and moved into another

world that provided powerful, personal meaning and commitment for him.

The centuries-old dialogue between Phaedrus and Socrates is relevant in our own times. The most sacred texts of the Jewish Scriptures, the first five books known as the Torah, have been robbed of their historical bases. Many of the stories about Jesus and his early followers—who, incidentally, would also have revered the Torah—are likewise dramatically called into question by modern scientific approaches. How do we respond to the present-day, earth-shattering conflict between faith and fact? Do we follow Phaedrus and adopt a scientific attitude, perhaps even complimenting ourselves on our more sophisticated outlook? Or do we follow Socrates and find in the same stories elements that provide value and direction?

In his book *A Secular Age,* Templeton Prize-winning philosopher Charles Taylor suggests that the cultural changes of the past few centuries have created an age of authenticity. We are all pushed to look within ourselves to discover who we really are and how we should live in this world. Yet this individual search creates serious obstacles to finding an overarching meaning that connects us to others. Taylor believes that such pressure has introduced "a new age of religious searching."[1]

Although our lives are saturated with scientific explanations, as well as the products of science and technology, scientific explanation cannot speak to the religious search, just as Phaedrus could not appreciate Socrates's self-disclosing insight. However, one branch of science—psychology—can provide tools and methodology for us to embark on a Socratic search for religious meaning. One could argue that the conflict we experience is similar, perhaps isomorphic, to the one Jews faced in 586 BCE after the destruction of Jerusalem, or to what Jesus's followers went through after his crucifixion in 30 CE.

Our challenge is to create an authentic religious path that can survive and thrive in our secular age. The culture of authenticity rightly supports our individual efforts to discover and define the values that will guide us. At the same time, we can appreciate the need for commonalities, such as narrative, ritual, and community that offer reference points and resources in our search. Additionally, we benefit from others' support and feedback, not only to clarify our own views but also to avoid turning individual truth into universal dogma. The challenge for such an individual journey lies in its connection to the larger context: does it contribute to or contaminate the evolutionary thrust toward a global community?

Finally, one's individual religious search need not fear science, although science continues to confront traditional religious views with new information. Like Phaedrus and Socrates, science and religion work on different levels, although the two collide in their respective searches for truth.

In our own times, our challenge is to learn to appreciate myth as a valid vehicle for religious thought. Socrates was apparently not discouraged by the term "myth." Catholic sociologist Andrew Greeley also embraced it in his 1971 book *The Jesus Myth* and suggested that people who are uncomfortable with the concept should just get used to it. Catholic theologian Luke Timothy Johnson argued that the early creeds are symbolic statements that open up a mythical world for us, one that must coexist with other constructed worldviews.[2] Wasn't this what Albert Schweitzer was suggesting when he wrote that Christians are invited to meet Jesus at the lakeside, where he asks them to follow him and promises that they will come to know him in their own experiences?[3]

Few of us may have the kind of intense and life-changing religious experience Schweitzer discusses. We are more likely to encounter modest conflicts between what we believe and what we know. It is in those instances of cognitive dissonance that psychology may be helpful. First, psychology validates the importance of religious behavior for the development of good mental health. There is no question that individuals who live out their faith, not just adhere to a set of doctrines, are happier and less likely to be pulled into addictive behavior, a counterfeit form of spirituality that seeks transcendence in a drug. Second, the gradual development of psychological growth has religious overtones, in the sense that we slowly move beyond less adaptive and more idiosyncratic worldviews to a more expansive, if not transcendent, perspective. These more altruistic and community-centered perspectives are precisely what are necessary if our species is to survive. Finally, psychology encourages us to embrace tendencies toward meaning making, ritual behavior, and community participation that are part of our natural makeup. Although we may experience such tendencies as awkwardly childish, something we must outgrow to be an adult, we suppress these impulses at our own peril. If we do not embrace them directly, these same tendencies may well return in a maladaptive or less creative form.

Ultimately, psychology is not religion, but it can persuade us to move to the threshold of faith by validating the importance of the religious and religious-like experiences we have encountered. If we step over that threshold, we progress beyond psychology, in some ways, to a faith-based view of reality. We enter a realm in which we are challenged to believe not just something beyond ourselves, but something so mysterious that our limitations as humans prevent us from describing it. However, psychology's echo may still be with us in our faith journey. By validating the significance of the individual search, as well as providing some practical tools for it, psychological theories and the model of psychotherapy can be helpful companions on a person's spiritual journey.

Notes

Introduction

1. Gottwald, "Origins of Ancient Israel," 195.
2. Barstad, *Hebrew Bible,* 17.
3. Wade, *The Faith Instinct,* 16.
4. Armstrong, *Short History of Myth.*
5. Fowler, *Stages of Faith,* 4.
6. Eagleton, *Reason, Faith, and Revolution.*
7. See Van Hagen, "New Identity."
8. See Van Hagen, "Canaanite Ritual."

Chapter 1: Beginning the Journey

1. One scholar maintains that some of the most influential biblical stories, including the first chapter of Genesis, were written at Bethel. See Guillaume, *Land and Calendar.*
2. Jobling, *1 Samuel,* 18.
3. Thompson, *Patriarchal Narratives,* 327.
4. Grabbe, *Judaic Religion,* 215.
5. Akenson, *Surpassing Wonder,* 43.
6. Bilefsky, "Frustrated with West."
7. Grabbe, *Judaic Religion,* 30–36.
8. Levinson, *Legal Revision,* 89.
9. Levinson, 19.
10. LaCocque and Ricoeur, *Thinking Biblically,* xiii.
11. Blenkinsopp, *Prophecy and Canon.*
12. Blenkinsopp, "Servants of the Lord."
13. Bautch, *Glory and Power.*
14. Petterson, *Behold Your King.*
15. Hultgard, "Persian Apocalypticism."
16. Davies, *Daniel,* 113.
17. Hecht, *Doubt: A History,* 47.
18. Hunt, *Missing Priests,* 190.
19. Horsley, *Scribes, Visionaries, and the Politics,* 28.
20. Van Dyke and Elias, "Expressions of Forgiveness."

Chapter 2: The Story of Joshua and His Warrior God

1. Pryor, "Moral Reading," 30.
2. Pryor, 41 n. 49.
3. Finkelstein and Silberman, *The Bible Unearthed.*
4. Grabbe, "Comfortable Theory," 182.

5. Finkelstein and Silberman, *The Bible Unearthed*, 90.
6. Finkelstein and Silberman, 118.
7. Garbini, *History and Ideology*, 127–32.
8. Wade, *The Faith Instinct*.
9. Nickelsberg, *Book of 1 Enoch*, 5.
10. Galloway, *Cellist of Sarajevo*, 223.
11. Wright and Dixon, *Dissent: Voices of Conscience*.
12. Kauffman, *Reinventing the Sacred*.
13. Levinson, *Legal Revision*.
14. Thompson, *Mythic Past*, 31.

Chapter 3: Viktor Frankl and the Search for Meaning

1. Frankl, *Man's Search for Meaning*, 121.
2. Frankl, 136.
3. Frankl, 170.
4. Vaillant, *Spiritual Evolution*, 206.
5. Dever, *Biblical Writers*, 290.
6. Frankl, *Man's Search for Meaning*, 133.
7. Graber, *Viktor Frankl's Logotherapy*, 73.
8. Frankl, *Ultimate Meaning*, 125.
9. Frankl, *Man's Search for Meaning*, 141.
10. Finkelstein and Silberman, *David and Solomon*.
11. Whitelam, "Imagining Jerusalem," 284.
12. Barna, "Religious Beliefs."
13. Frankl, *Ultimate Meaning*, 135.

Chapter 4: The Jesus of History and the Christ of Faith

1. Hick, *Metaphor of God Incarnate*.
2. Crossan, *The Birth of Christianity*, 27.
3. Brown, *Beginnings of the Church*.
4. Meier, *Marginal Jew*, 2:1045.
5. Meier, 309.
6. Brown, *New Testament Scholarship*.
7. Fitzmyer, *One Who Is to Come*.
8. Jenkins, *Lost History*.
9. Pelikan, *Jesus through the Centuries*.
10. Fox, *Jesus in America*.
11. Prothero, *American Jesus*.
12. Arnal, *The Symbolic Jesus*, 76.
13. Meier, *Marginal Jew*, 2:646–1038.
14. Brown, *Beginnings of the Church*.
15. Steinfels, *A People Adrift*, 241.
16. Klawans, "Moral and Ritual Purity."
17. Dunn, *Partings of the Ways*, 114.

18. Hedrick, *When Faith Meets Reason.*
19. L.T. Johnson, *The Creed,* 324.
20. Pagels, *Beyond Belief,* 184–85.
21. Fowler, *Stages of Faith.*
22. Basseches, *Dialectical Thinking,* 3.
23. Basseches, 29.
24. Basseches, 304.
25. Basseches and Mascolo, *Psychotherapy.*
26. Linehan, *Cognitive-Behavioral Treatment.*
27. Briggs, *Double Crossed.*
28. Johnson, *The Creed,* 321.
29. Jost, "End of Ideology."
30. Jost, 657.
31. Brown, *Beginnings of the Church,*
32. Meier, *Marginal Jew,* 3:646.
33. Schweitzer, *Historical Jesus,* 403.
34. Appiah, *Experiments in Ethics.*

Chapter 5: The Miraculous Conception of the First-century Christian Community

1. Meier, *Marginal Jew,* 3:163.
 2. Meier, 4:647–58.
 3. Brown, *New Testament,* 232.
 4. Brown, *Beginnings of the Church.*
 5. Brown, *Churches Left Behind,* 147.
 6. Kee, *People of God.*
 7. Crossan, *The Birth of Christianity.*
 8. Freeman, *New History,* 42.
 9. Meier, *Marginal Jew,* 1:3.
10. Brown, *Beginnings of the Church,*
11. Spence, *Parting of the Ways,* 8.
12. Meier, *Marginal Jew,* 3:221–45.
13. Brown, *Beginnings of the Church.*
14. Brown, *Beloved Disciple,* 167.
15. Goodacre, *Goulder and the Gospels.*
16. Griffith-Jones, *Four Witnesses,* 212–36.
17. Brown, *Churches Left Behind,* 123.
18. Meeks, *Christian Morality,* 151.
19. Brown, *Churches Left Behind,* 33.
20. Harmon-Jones and Mills, *Cognitive Dissonance,* 107.
21. Almond, *The Healing Community,* xxix–xxxii.
22. Almond, 25–32.
23. Greenspan and Shanker, *The First Idea.*
24. Greenspan and Shanker, 255.
25. Sagan, *Cosmos,* 283.

Chapter 6: The Development of Second-century Christianity

1. Moll, *The Arch-Heretic Marcion*, 134.
2. Borg and Crossan, *The First Paul*.
3. Pervo, "Dating Acts."
4. Tyson, "The Date of Acts."
5. Brown, *Beginnings of the Church*.
6. Spence, *Parting of the Ways*, 351.
7. Brewin, *Post-Traumatic Stress Disorder*, 67.
8. Margolis and Marx, *History of the Jewish People*, 206.
9. Speller, *Following Hadrian*, 201.
10. Dungan, *Synoptic Problem*, 57–58.
11. Pagels, *Beyond Belief*.
12. Pervo, *The Making of Paul*, 235.
13. Meeks, *Christian Morality*, 210.
14. Stark, *The Rise of Christianity*, 7.
15. The group in Qumran also designated twelve individuals, who may have had a similar symbolic function, as part of their ruling group. See Vermes, *Dead Sea Scrolls*, 30.
16. Brown, *Beginnings of the Church*.
17. Sullivan, *From Apostles to Bishops*, 14–15.
18. Haring, "Distrust That Wounds;" and Selling, "*Veritatis Splendor*."
19. Bernstein and Politi, *His Holiness*, 25.
20. Bernstein and Politi, 83.

Chapter 7: Barack Obama and the Journey to Community

1. Lugo et al., "U.S. Religious Landscape Survey."
2. L. T. Johnson, *Religious Experience*.
3. Cohen, Gruber, and Keltner, "Comparing Spiritual Transformations."
4. Obama, *Dreams from My Father*, 294.
5. Fowler, *Stages of Faith*, 208–9.
6. Obama, *The Audacity of Hope*, 66.
7. Wuthnow, *Christianity*, 101.
8. Obama, *Dreams from My Father*, 286.

Chapter 8: The Biblical Narrative

1. Meier, *Marginal Jew*, vol. 2.
2. Hays, *Faith of Jesus Christ*.
3. Witherington III, *Paul's Narrative Thought World*, 163.
4. Hays, *Faith of Jesus Christ*, 283.
5. L. T. Johnson, *Letter of James*, 250.
6. Klein, "Narrative Construction," 69–70.
7. Omer and Alon, *Constructing Therapeutic Narratives*, 151.
8. White and Epston, *Narrative Means*, 86.

9. White and Epston, 13.
10. Dawsey, *Lukan Voice*, 86.
11. White and Epston, *Narrative Means*, 13.
12. Barna, "Religious Beliefs."
13. Witherington, *Paul's Narrative Thought World*, 339.
14. Ricoeur, *Time and Narrative*, 1:81.
15. Hays, *Faith of Jesus Christ*, 225.
16. Omer and Alon, *Constructing Therapeutic Narratives*, 223.
17. Omer and Alon, 176.
18. Boyer, *Religion Explained*, 204.
19. Witherington, *Paul's Narrative Thought World*, 352–55.
20. Brown and Meier, *Antioch and Rome*, 124–27.
21. Fiorenza, *Politics of Interpretation*, 73.
22. Bruner, *Making Stories*, 84.
23. Ricoeur, *Time and Narrative*, 3:259.
24. Wuthnow, *Christianity*, 103.
25. Cox, "Market as God."

Chapter 9: Rituals

1. Minuchin, *Families and Family Therapy*.
2. Imber-Black and Roberts, *Rituals for Our Times*, 53–54.
3. Boyer, *Religion Explained*, 119.
4. Boyer, 239.
5. Boyer, 246.
6. Aronson, "Dissonance," 106.
7. Aronson, 107.
8. Prosic, *Passover until 70* CE.
9. Carter, *Emergence of Yehud*, 321.
10. Theissen, *Earliest Churches*, 163.
11. Theissen, 133–36.
12. Meeks, *Urban Christians*, 154.
13. Theissen, *Earliest Churches*, 132–33.
14. Lieber and Harlow, *Etz Hayim*, 5.
15. Theissen, *Earliest Churches*, 171–75.
16. Perkins, *The Suffering Self*.
17. Van Rooden, "Power and Piety," 516–17.
18. Hughes, *Worship as Meaning*.

Chapter 10: Religion and Science

1. Sagan, *Scientific Experience*, 27.
2. Haught, *Making Sense of Evolution*, 131.
3. Gould, "Self-Appointed Judge."
4. Gould
5. G. Johnson, "Free-for-All."
6. Dawkins, *The God Delusion*.

7. Sagan, *Cosmos,* 279.
8. Foerst, *God in the Machine.*
9. Miller, *Finding Darwin's God,* 19.
10. Kuhn, *Structure of Scientific Revolutions,* 3rd ed.
11. Sagan, *Cosmos,* 283.
12. Sagan, 279.
13. L.T. Johnson, *The Creed.*
14. Johnson
15. Johnson, 54
16. Walsh, *Mapping Myths,* 140.
17. Armstrong, *Short History of Myth,* 35.
18. Meeks, *Christian Morality,* 151.
19. Mack, *Who Wrote the New Testament?* 73.
20. Wieseltier, "The God Genome."
21. Kuhn, *Structure of Scientific Revolutions,* 4.
22. Kauffman, *Reinventing the Sacred.*
23. Miller, *Finding Darwin's God,* 186.
24. Collins, *Language of God,* 229.
25. Kuhn, *Structure of Scientific Revolutions,* 195.
26. Jost, "End of Ideology"
27. Foerst, *God in the Machine,* 122.
28. Foerst, 176–77.
29. Miller, *Finding Darwin's God,* 291.
30. Haught, *God After Darwin,* 45.
31. O'Murchu, *Quantum Theology,* 192.
32. Haught, *Deeper Than Darwin,* 155.
33. Greeley, *Catholic Myth,* 42.
34. Kearns, "Cooking the Truth."
35. Wolpe, *Why Faith Matters,* 177.
36. Wilson, *Darwin's Cathedral.*
37. Omer and Alon, *Constructing Therapeutic Narratives,* 229.
38. Sagan, *Scientific Experience,* 213.
39. Sagan, 217.

Chapter 11: Mikhail Gorbachev and the Collision of Faith and Fact

1. Festinger, Reicken, and Schachter, *When Prophecy Fails.*
2. Perr, "Cognitive Dissonance."
3. Gorbachev, *On My Country,* 23.
4. Gorbachev,206.
5. Gorbachev,59–60.
6. Gorbachev, 238.
7. Gorbachev, 190.
8. Fowler, *Becoming Adult, Becoming Christian,* 55–56.
9. Wallis, *God's Politics.*

10. Wuthnow, *After the Baby Boomers.*
11. Lugo et al., "U.S. Religious Landscape Survey."
12. Briggs, *Double Crossed.*
13. Gorbachev, *On My Country*, 243.
14. Brown, *Beginnings of the Church.*
15. Greenberg, "Judaism, Christianity and Partnership," 13.

Conclusion

1. Taylor, *A Secular Age*, 535.
2. Johnson, *The Creed.*
3. Schweitzer, *Historical Jesus*, 403.

Bibliography

Akenson, Donald Harman. *Saint Saul: A Skeleton Key to the Historical Jesus*. New York: Oxford University Press, 2000.

———. *Surpassing Wonder: The Invention of the Bible and the Talmuds*. Chicago: University of Chicago Press, 2001.

Alim, Tanya N. et al. "Trauma, Resilience, and Recovery in a High-Risk African American Population." *American Journal of Psychiatry* 165, 12 (2008): 1566–75.

Almond, Richard. *The Healing Community; or, Dynamics of the Therapeutic Milieu*. New York: Jason Aronson, 1974.

Appiah, Kwame Anthony. *Experiments in Ethics*. Cambridge: Harvard University Press, 2008.

Armstrong, Karen. *A Short History of Myth*. New York: Canongate, 2005.

Arnal, William. *The Symbolic Jesus: Historical Scholarship, Judaism, and the Construction of Contemporary Identity*. Oakville: Equinox Publishing, 2005.

Aronson, Elliott. "Dissonance, Hypocrisy, and the Self-Concept." Pp. 103–26 in *Cognitive Dissonance: Progress on a Pivotal Theory in Social Psychology*. Edited by Eddie Harmon-Jones and Judson Mills. Washington, DC: American Psychological Association, 1999.

The Barna Group. "Religious Beliefs Vary Widely by Denomination." *Barna Update,* June 25, 2001, http://www.barna.org/barna-update/article/5-barna-update/53-religious-beliefs-vary-widely-by-denomination.

Barstad, Hans M. *History and the Hebrew Bible: Studies in Ancient Israelite and Ancient Near Eastern Historiography*. Tubingen: Mohr Siebeck, 2008.

Basseches, Michael. *Dialectical Thinking and Adult Development*. Norwood: Ablex Publishing, 1984.

Basseches, Michael and Michael F. Mascolo. *Psychotherapy as a Developmental Process*. New York: Brunner-Routledge, 2010.

256

Bautch, Richard J. *Glory and Power, Ritual and Relationship: The Sinai Covenant in the Postexilic Period.* New York: T&T Clark, 2009.

Bernstein, Carl and Marco Politi. *His Holiness: John Paul II and the History of Our Time.* New York: Doubleday, 1996.

Bilefsky, Dan. "Frustrated with West, Turks Revel in Empire Lost." *New York Times,* Dec 4, 2009.

Blenkinsopp, Joseph. *Prophecy and Canon: A Contribution to the Study of Jewish Origins.* Notre Dame: University of Notre Dame Press, 1977.

_____."The 'Servants of the Lord' in Third Isaiah: Profile of a Pietistic Group in the Persian Epoch." In *The Place Is Too Small for Us: The Israelite Prophets in Recent Scholarship,* 392–412. Edited by Robert. P. Gordon. Winona Lake, IN: Eisenbrauns, 1995.

Borg, Marcus J. and John Dominic Crossan. *The First Paul: Reclaiming the Radical Visionary behind the Church's Conservative Icon.* New York: HarperCollins, 2009.

Boyer, Pascal. *Religion Explained: The Evolutionary Origins of Religious Thought.* New York: Basic Books, 2001.

Brewin, Chris R. *Posttraumatic Stress Disorder: Malady or Myth?* New Haven, CT: Yale University Press, 2003.

Briggs, Kenneth A. *Double Crossed: Uncovering the Catholic Church's Betrayal of American Nuns.* New York: Doubleday, 2006.

Brown, Raymond E. *The Beginnings of the Church.* Wales: Welcome Recordings, 1998. Audiocassette.

_____.*The Churches the Apostles Left Behind.* New York: Paulist Press, 1984.

_____.*The Community of the Beloved Disciple: The Life, Loves and Hates of an Individual Church in New Testament Times.* New York: Paulist Press, 1979.

_____.*An Introduction to the New Testament.* New York: Doubleday, 1997

_____.*New Testament Scholarship as We End One Century and Open Another.* Wales: Welcome Recordings, 1997. Audiocassette.

Brown, Raymond E. and John P. Meier. *Antioch and Rome: New Testament Cradles of Catholic Christianity.* New York: Paulist Press, 1982.

Bruner, Jerome. *Making Stories: Law, Literature, Life.* New York: Farrar, Straus and Giroux, 2002.

Carter, Charles E. *The Emergence of Yehud in the Persian Period: A Social and Demographic Study.* London: Sheffield Academic Press, 1999.

Cohen, Adam B., June Gruber, and Dacher Keltner. "Comparing Spiritual Transformations and Experiences of Profound Beauty." *Psychology of Religion and Spirituality* 2, 3 (August 2010): 127–35.

Collins, Francis C. *The Language of God: A Scientist Presents Evidence for Belief.* New York: Free Press, 2006.

Cox, Harvey. "The Market as God." *Atlantic Monthly* 283, 3 (March 1999): 18–23.

Crossan, John Dominic. *The Birth of Christianity.* New York: HarperCollins, 1998

Davies, P. R. *Daniel.* Sheffield: JSOT Press, 1985.

Dawkins, Richard. *The God Delusion.* New York: Houghton Mifflin, 2006.

Dawsey, James W. *The Lukan Voice: Confusion and Irony in the Gospel of Luke.* Macon, GA: Mercer University Press, 1986.

Dever, William G. *What Did the Biblical Writers Know and When Did They Know It?* Grand Rapids, MI: Eerdmanns, 2001.

Dungan, David Laird. *A History of the Synoptic Problem.* New York: Doubleday, 1999.

Dunn, James D.G. *The Partings of the Ways between Christianity and Judaism and Their Significance for the Character of Christianity.* Philadelphia: Trinity Press International, 1991.

Eagleton, Terry. *Reason, Faith, and Revolution.* New Haven: Yale University Press, 2009.

Esler, Philip F. *The First Christians in Their Social Worlds: Social-Scientific Approaches to New Testament Interpretation.* New York: Routledge, 1994.

Festinger, Leon, Henry W. Reicken, and Stanley Schachter. *When Prophecy Fails.* New York: Harper, 1956.

Finkelstein, Israel. "Archaeology and Text in the Third Millennium: A View from the Center." Pp. 323–42 in *Congress Volume Basel 2001*. Edited by A. Lemarie. Boston: Brill, 2002.

Finkelstein, Israel andNeil Asher Silberman. *The Bible Unearthed*. New York: Free Press, 2001.

_____. *David and Solomon: In Search of the Bible's Sacred Kings and the Roots of the Western Tradition*. New York: Free Press, 2006.

Fitzmyer, Joseph A. *The One Who Is to Come*. Grand Rapids: Eerdmans, 2007.

Foerst, Anne. *God in the Machine: What Robots Teach Us about Humanity and God*. New York: Penguin Group, 2004.

Fowler, James W. *Becoming Adult, Becoming Christian*. San Francisco: Jossey-Bass, 2000.

_____. *Stages of Faith: The Psychology of Human Development and the Quest for Meaning*. New York: Harper Collins, 1981.

Fox, Richard Wightman. *Jesus in America: Personal Savior, Cultural Hero, National Obsession*. New York: HarperCollins, 2004.

Frankl, Viktor E. *Man's Search for Meaning*. New York: Simon & Schuster, 1946.

_____. *Man's Search for Ultimate Meaning*. New York: Basic Books, 2000.

Freeman, Charles. *A New History of Early Christianity*. New Haven, CT: Yale University Press, 2009.

Galloway, Steven. *The Cellist of Sarajevo*. New York: Riverhead Books, 2008.

Garbini, Giovanni. *History and Ideology in Ancient Israel*. New York: Crossroad, 1988.

Goodacre, Mark S. *Goulder and the Gospels: An Examination of a New Paradigm*. Sheffield: Sheffield Academic Press, 1996.

Gorbachev, Mikhail. *On My Country and the World*. New York: Columbia University Press, 2000.

Gottwald, Norman K. "Rethinking the Origins of Ancient Israel." Pp.190–201 in *Imagining Biblical Worlds*. Edited by David M. Gunn and Paula M. McNutt. Sheffield: Sheffield Academic Press, 2002.

Gould, Stephen Jay. "Impeaching a Self-Appointed Judge." *Scientific American* 267, 1 (1992): 118–21.

Grabbe, Lester L. "The Comfortable Theory: Maximal Conservatism and Neofundamentalism Revisited." Pp. 174–93 in *Sense and Sensitivity: Essays on Reading the Bible in Memory of Robert Carroll.* Edited by Philip R. Davies and Alistair G. Hunter. New York: Sheffield Academic Press, 2002.

_____. *Judaic Religion in the Second Temple Period.* London: Routledge, 2000.

Graber, Ann V. *Viktor Frankl's Logotherapy.* Lima, OH: Wyndham Hall Press, 2004.

Greeley, Andrew M. *The Catholic Myth: The Behavior and Beliefs of American Catholics.* New York: Scribner's, 1990.

Greenberg, Irving. "Judaism, Christianity and Partnership after the 20th Century." Pp. 25–36 in *Christianity in Jewish Terms.* Edited by Tikva Frymer-Kensky et al. Boulder: Westview Press, 2004.

Greenspan, Stanley I. and Stuart D. Shanker. *The First Idea: How Symbols, Language, and Intelligence Evolved from Our Primate Ancestors to Modern Humans.* Cambridge: Da Capo Press, 2004.

Griffith-Jones, Robin. *The Four Witnesses.* San Francisco: Harper, 2000.

Guillaume, Philippe. *Land and Calendar: The Priestly Document from Genesis 1 to Joshua 18.* New York: T&T Clark, 2009.

Haring, Bernard. "A Distrust That Wounds." Pp. 9–13 in *Considering Veritatis Splendor.* Edited by John Wilkins. Cleveland: Pilgrim Press, 1994.

Harmon-Jones, Eddie. "Toward an Understanding of the Motivation Underlying Dissonance Effects." In *Cognitive Dissonance: Progress on a Pivotal Theory in Social Psychology.* Edited by Eddie Harmon-Jones and Judson Mills. Washington, DC: American Psychological Association, 1999.

Haught, John F. *Deeper Than Darwin: The Prospect for Religion in the Age of Evolution.* Boulder: Westview Press, 2003.

_____. *God After Darwin: A Theology of Evolution*. Boulder: Westview Press, 2000.

_____. *Making Sense of Evolution: Darwin, God, and the Drama of Life*. Louisville: Westminster John Knox Press, 2010.

Hays, Richard B. *The Faith of Jesus Christ: The Narrative Substructure of Galatians 3:1–4:11*. Grand Rapids, MI: Eerdmans, 2002.

Hecht, Jennifer M. *Doubt, A History*. San Francisco: Harper, 2003.

Hedrick, Charles W., ed. *When Faith Meets Reason: Religion Scholars Reflect on Their Spiritual Journeys*. Santa Rosa: Polebridge Press,2008.

_____. *When History and Faith Collide: Studying Jesus*. Peabody, MA: Hendrickson Publishers, 1999.

Hick, John. *The Metaphor of God Incarnate: Christology in a Pluralistic Age*. 2nd ed. Louisville: Westminster John Knox Press, 2005.

Horsley, Richard A. *Scribes, Visionaries, and the Politics of Second Temple Judea*. Louisville: Westminster John Knox Press, 2007.

Hughes, Graham. *Worship as Meaning: A Liturgical Theology for Late Modernity*. New York: Cambridge University Press, 2003.

Hultgard, Anders. "Persian Apocalypticism." Pp. 39–83 in *The Encyclopedia of Apocalypticism*. Edited by Bernard McGinn, John Joseph Collins, and Stephen J. Stein. Vol. 1, *The Origins of Apocalypticism in Judaism and Christianity*, edited by John J. Collins. New York: Continuum, 1998.

Hunt, Alice. *Missing Priests: The Zadokites in Tradition and History*. New York: T&T Clark, 2006.

Imber-Black, Evan and Janine Roberts. *Rituals for Our Times*. New York: HarperCollins, 1992.

Jenkins, Philip. *The Lost History of Christianity: The Thousand-Year Golden Age of the Church in the Middle East, Africa, and Asia—and How It Died*. New York: HarperOne, 2009.

Jobling, David W. *1 Samuel*. Collegeville: Liturgical Press, 1998.

Johnson, George. "A Free-for-All on Science and Religion." *New York Times*, November 21, 2006.

Johnson, Luke Timothy. *The Creed: What Christians Believe and Why It Matters*. New York: Doubleday, 2003.

_____. *The Letter of James*. New York: Anchor Bible, Doubleday, 1995.

_____. *Religious Experience in Earliest Christianity*. Minneapolis: Fortress Press, 1998.

Jost, John T. "The End of the End of Ideology," *American Psychologist*, 61, 7 (2006): 651–70.

Karr, Mary. Lit: A Memoir. New York: HarperCollins, 2009.

Kauffman, Stuart A. *Reinventing the Sacred*. New York: Basic Books, 2008.

Kearns, Laurel. "Cooking the Truth: Faith, Science, the Market, and Global Warming." Pp. 97–124 in *Echospirit: Religions and Philosophies for the Earth*. Edited by Laurel Kearns and Catherine Keller. New York: Fordham University Press, 2007.

Klawans, Jonathan. "Moral and Ritual Purity." Pp. 266–84 in *The Historical Jesus in Context*. Edited by Amy-Jill Levine, Dale C. Allison Jr., and John Dominic Crossan. Princeton: Princeton University Press, 2006.

Klein, Kitty. "Narrative Construction, Cognitive Processing, and Health." Pp. 56–84 in *Narrative Therapy and the Cognitive Sciences*. Edited by David Herman. Stanford: CSLI Publications, 2003.

Kuhn, Thomas S. *The Structure of Scientific Revolutions*, 3rd ed. Chicago: University of Chicago Press, 1996.

LaCocque, Andre and Paul Ricoeur. *Thinking Biblically*. Chicago: University of Chicago Press, 1998.

Levinson, Bernard M. *Legal Revision and Religious Renewal in Ancient Israel*. Cambridge: Cambridge University Press, 2008.

Lieber, David L. and Jules Harlow, eds. *Etz Hayim: Torah and Commentary*. New York: Rabbinical Assembly, 2001.

Linehan, Marsha M. *Cognitive-Behavioral Treatment of Borderline Personality Disorder*. New York: Guilford Press, 1993.

Lugo, Luis, et al., "U.S. Religious Landscape Survey." The Pew Forum on Religion and Life. Accessed February 28, 2008, http://religions.pewforum.org.

Mack, Burton L. *Who Wrote the New Testament?: The Making of the Christian Myth.* San Francisco: Harper, 1995.

Margolis, Max L. and Alexander Marx. *A History of the Jewish People.* New York: Scribner's, 1969.

Meeks, Wayne A. *The Origins of Christian Morality.* New Haven, CT: Yale University Press, 1993.

Meier, John P. *A Marginal Jew: Rethinking the Historical Jesus.* 4 Vols. New York: Doubleday, 2009.

Miller, Kenneth R. *Finding Darwin's God: A Scientist's Search for Common Ground Between God and Evolution.* New York: HarperCollins, 1999.

Minuchin, Salvador. *Families and Family Therapy.* Cambridge, MA: Harvard University Press, 1974.

Moll, Sebastian. *The Arch-Heretic Marcion.* Tübingen: Mohr Siebeck, 2010.

Nickelsberg, George W. E. *1 Enoch 1: A Commentary on the Book of 1 Enoch, Chapters 1–36; 81–108.* Minneapolis: Fortress Press, 2001.

Obama, Barak. *The Audacity of Hope.* New York: Three Rivers Press, 2006.

_____. *Dreams from My Father.* New York: Three Rivers Press, 1995.

Omer, Haim and Nahi Alon. *Constructing Therapeutic Narratives.* Northvale, NJ: Jason Aronson Publishers, 1997.

O'Murchu, Diarmuid. *Quantum Theology: Spiritual Implications of the New Physics.* New York: Crossroad Publishing, 2004.

Pagels, Elaine. *Beyond Belief: The Secret Gospel of Thomas.* New York: Random House, 2003.

Pelikan, Jaroslav. *Jesus through the Centuries: His Place in the History of Culture.* New York: Harper and Row, 1985.

Perkins, Judith. *The Suffering Self: Pain and Narrative Representation in the Early Christian Era.* New York: Routledge, 1995.

Perr, Jon. "Cognitive Dissonance, Terrorism and 9/11." *Perrspectives.* Last updated March 30, 2004. http://www.perrspectives.com/blog/archives/000081.htm.

Pervo, Richard I. "Dating Acts." *Forum* 5, 1 (2002): 53–72.

_____. *The Making of Paul: Constructions of the Apostle in Early Christianity.* Minneapolis: Fortress Press, 2010.

Petterson, Anthony R. *Behold Your King: The Hope for the House of David in the Book of Zechariah.* New York: T&T Clark, 2009.

Prior, Michael. "A Moral Reading of the Bible in Jerusalem." Pp. 16–45 in *Jerusalem in Ancient History and Tradition.* Edited by Thomas L. Thompson. London: T & T Clark, 2003.

Prosic, Tamara. *The Development and Symbolism of Passover until 70 CE.* London: Continuum, 2005.

Prothero, Stephen. *American Jesus: How the Son of God Became a National Icon.* New York: Farrar, Straus and Giroux, 2003.

Ricoeur, Paul. *Time and Narrative.* Vol. 3. Chicago: University of Chicago Press, 1988.

Sagan, Carl. *Cosmos.* New York: Ballantine Books, 1980.

_____. *The Varieties of Scientific Experience: A Personal View of the Search for God.* New York: Penguin Press, 2006.

Schüssler Fiorenza, Elisabeth. *Jesus and the Politics of Interpretation.* New York: Continuum, 2000.

Schweitzer, Albert. *The Quest of the Historical Jesus.* Baltimore: Johns Hopkins University Press, 1998.

Selling, Joseph A. "The Context and the Arguments of *Veritatis Splendor.*" Pp. 11–70 in *The Splendor of Accuracy.* Edited by Jans, Jan and Selling, Joseph A. Grand. Rapids, MI: Eerdmans, 1994.

Speller, Elizabeth. *Following Hadrian.* New York: Oxford University Press, 2003.

Spence, Stephen. *The Parting of the Ways: The Roman Church as a Case Study.* Leuven: Peeters, 2004.

Stark, Rodney. *The Rise of Christianity.* San Francisco: Harper, 1997.

Steinfels, Peter. *A People Adrift: The Crisis of the Roman Catholic Church in America.* New York: Simon and Schuster, 2004.

Sullivan, Francis A. *From Apostles to Bishops.* New York: Newman Press, 2001.

Taylor, Charles. *A Secular Age.* Cambridge, MA: Belknap Press, 2007.

Theissen, Gerd. *The Religion of the Earliest Churches: Creating a Symbolic World*. Minneapolis: Fortress Press, 1999.

Thompson, Thomas L. *The Historicity of the Patriarchal Narratives*. New York: Walter de Gruyter, 1974.

_____. *The Mythic Past: Biblical Archaeology and the Myth of Israel*. New York: Basic Books, 1999.

Tyson, Joseph B. "The Date of Acts: A Reconsideration." *Forum* 5, 1 (2002): 33–51.

Vaillant, George E. *Spiritual Evolution*. New York: Broadway Books, 2008.

Van Dyke, Cydney J., and Maurice J. Elias. "How Expressions of Forgiveness, Purpose, and Religiosity Relate to Emotional Intelligence and Self-Concept in Urban Fifth-Grade Students." *American Journal of Orthopsychiatry* 78, 4 (October 2008): 481–93.

Van Hagen, John. "From Canaanite Ritual to Jewish Passover and Christian Eucharist." *The Fourth R* 22, 1 (2009): 15–19

_____. "From Paralyzing Trauma to New Identity." *The Fourth R* 19, 1 (2008): 19–21.

Van Rooden, Peter. "Power and Piety in Contemporary Church History and Social Science." Pp. 513–32 in *Religious Identity and the Problem of Historical Foundation*. Edited by Judith Frishman, Willemien Otten, and Gerard Rouwhorst. Leiden: Brill Academic, 2004.

Vermes, Geza. *The Complete Dead Sea Scrolls in English*. New York: Penguin Books, 1997.

Wade, Nicholas. *The Faith Instinct*. New York: Penguin Press, 2009.

Wallis, Jim. *God's Politics: Why the Right Gets It Wrong and the Left Doesn't Get It*. New York: HarperCollins, 2005.

Walsh, Richard G. *Mapping Myths of Biblical Interpretation*. Sheffield: Sheffield Academic Press, 2001.

White, Michael and David Epston. *Narrative Means to Therapeutic Ends*. New York: Norton, 1990.

Whitelam, Keith W. "Imagining Jerusalem." Pp. 272–89 in *Jerusalem in Ancient History and Tradition*. Edited by Thomas L. Thompson. London: T & T Clark, 2003.

Wieseltier, Leon. "The God Genome," review of *Breaking the Spell: Religion as a Natural Phenomenon,* by Daniel C. Dennett. *New York Times,* February 19, 2006, Sunday Book Review: 11–12.

Wilson, David Sloan. *Darwin's Cathedral: Evolution, Religion and the Nature of Society.* Chicago: University of Chicago Press, 2002.

Witherington III, Ben. *Paul's Narrative Thought World: The Tapestry of Tragedy and Triumph.* Louisville: Westminster/ John Knox Press, 1994.

Wolpe, David. *Why Faith Matters.* New York: HarperCollins, 2008.

Wright, Ann and Susan Dixon. *Dissent: Voices of Conscience.* Kihei, Hawaii: Koa Books, 2008.

Wuthnow, Robert. *After the Baby Boomers: How Twenty- and Thirty-Somethings are Shaping the Future of American Religion.* Princeton: Princeton University Press, 2007.

_____. *Christianity in the 21st Century.* New York: Oxford University Press, 1993.

Index

About the Author

John Van Hagen is a licensed psychologist with more than thirty years experience in a variety of clinical, training and teaching positions. Now retired from private practice, he continues to work as a psychological consultant and to offer workshops. A native San Franciscan and former Catholic priest, Van Hagen left the ministry, married and earned a Ph.D. in clinical psychology at Adelphi University. The work of the Jesus Seminar inspired him to study the effect of biblical scholarship on the beliefs of religious individuals. Over the past ten years he has written articles and led workshops on the potential impact and influence of scientific information on one's journey of faith. He and his wife Phyllis have two adult sons and three grandchildren.

CPSIA information can be obtained at www.ICGtesting.com
Printed in the USA
BVOW020743140212

282793BV00005B/3/P